Faith in Democracy

Faith in Democracy

Framing a Politics of Deep Diversity

Jonathan Chaplin

scm press

© Jonathan Chaplin 2021

Published in 2021 by SCM Press
Editorial office
3rd Floor, Invicta House,
108–114 Golden Lane,
London EC1Y 0TG, UK
www.scmpress.co.uk

SCM Press is an imprint of Hymns Ancient & Modern Ltd
(a registered charity)

Hymns Ancient & Modern® is a registered trademark of
Hymns Ancient & Modern Ltd
13A Hellesdon Park Road, Norwich,
Norfolk NR6 5DR, UK

British Library Cataloguing in Publication data

A catalogue record for this book is available
from the British Library

978-0-334-06023-9

Typeset by Regent Typesetting
Printed and bound by
CPI Group (UK) Ltd

Contents

About Theos

Theos is the UK's leading religion and society think tank. It exists to bring a thoughtful, non-tribal Christian perspective to the public square and stimulate better conversations about the role of faith and belief in society through research, events, and media commentary.

Theos hosts conversations, debates and lectures on religion, politics and society, and provides commentary and analysis on current affairs and popular culture.

At the core of Theos' work is an extensive programme of research exploring the big issues impacting UK society, from the ethics of debt to the phenomenon of religiously-inspired violence, from the increasing religiosity of our capital city to faith–based social action and multi-culturalism.

Find out more at www.theosthinktank.co.uk

Acknowledgements

I am grateful to Theos, one of the leading practitioners of 'faith in democracy' in the UK, for their congenial partnership in this project (which is not to say they endorse everything in this book). The following colleagues commented on all or parts of the manuscript: Paul Bickley, Jonathan Boston, Andrew Bradstock, Julian Rivers, Nick Spencer and Nicholas Townsend. The usual disclaimer applies, but their critical insights have, I think, made the book much better and I am indebted to them. Barnabas Elbourn helped get my legal case citations in order but, again, any remaining errors are my own. Chapter 3 draws on material first published in Thomas Schirrmacher and Jonathan Chaplin, 'European Religious Freedom and the EU', in Jonathan Chaplin and Gary Wilton, eds, *God and the EU: Faith in the European Project* (Abingdon: Routledge, 2016), pp. 151–74. Chapters 4 and 5 draw extensively on *Talking God: The Legitimacy of Religious Public Reasoning* (London: Theos, 2008). I am grateful to the publishers for permission to use this material here.

During the final months of writing, Aldo our two-year-old grandson was hurtling around our house while his parents, our son Paul and his American wife Laura, lived with us, awaiting new accommodation. His presence slightly delayed its completion, but kept me focused on what it was all about. The virtues of 'democratic pluralism' are, at this point in his life, a work in progress. My hope is that he will grow up to be not only a person of faith but – as possessor of both British and American passports – one who finds reasons for, perhaps even contributes to, 'faith in democracy'. The book was completed days before the November 2020 US presidential election. I dedicate the book to Aldo – and to the future of his generation.

Introduction
Faith and Democracy – Defining the Questions Before We Shout Out the Answers[1]

In the contest between the principles of modern democracy and doctrines of faith, democracy and the rule of secular law must always win. Janet Daley[2]

The question is sometimes raised, whether Catholicism is compatible with American democracy. The question is invalid as well as impertinent … It must … be turned round to read, whether American democracy is compatible with Catholicism. John Courtney Murray[3]

It would be hard to find two more starkly opposed judgements than these about the place of religious faith in a modern liberal democracy. The first was delivered in 2008 by Janet Daley in the *Daily Telegraph* in response to Archbishop Rowan Williams' proposal that aspects of Islamic law might be accommodated within the English legal system – a prospect that unleashed a firestorm of tabloid outrage that has left permanent scorch-marks on British public discourse about faith.[4] The second, published over half a century ago, was penned by Jesuit philosopher John Courtney Murray in *We Hold These Truths: Catholic Reflections on the American Proposition*, a book written to overcome deep suspicions still existing between Roman Catholics and political liberals in the USA. It was on account of such suspicions that presidential candidate John F. Kennedy felt bound to insist in 1960 that he believed in an America 'where no religious body seeks to impose its will directly or indirectly upon the general populace or the public acts of its officials'.[5]

No one needs reminding that the relationship between religion and democracy in many liberal democracies today remains fraught with profound anxieties. This is true also in Britain, the principal focus of this book. Even setting aside fears about violent Islamist extremism, persisting concerns about the apparent threat of Islam as such to British democracy surfaced again in *The Casey Review* on integration in 2016, which warned that some religious devotees are 'keen to take religion backwards and away from 21st Century British values and laws on ... gender equality and sexual orientation, creating segregation and pulling communities apart'.[6] While the role of religion in the Brexit trauma is not yet easy to specify, the acrimonious divisions Brexit has unleashed pose acute additional challenges to the capacity of British democracy to reckon with deep diversity.[7]

In the USA, even before the headlong evangelical embrace of Donald Trump,[8] alarms about religious 'imposition' were reignited by the latest wave of the 'religious right', from which emerged in 2015 'Project Blitz', a carefully orchestrated campaign to encourage the sponsorship of 'Christian' bills in state legislatures across the USA. The project has been described as reflecting 'a Christian supremacist agenda, the idea that God intended and mandates Christians to lead and control the United States for the religious vision that they hold and the policy implications that flow from it'.[9]

The current debate is often framed in a way that is unhelpfully polarizing. Many religious believers profess themselves appalled by the bald assertion that democracy must always win against religion, just as many secular-minded people react viscerally to the claim that democracy must be subordinated to the demands of religion. Each assertion seems to offend against a deep and seemingly non-negotiable conviction held by the other side. The declaration that democratic principles must *always* defeat religious doctrines whenever they clash strikes many religious believers as a dangerously arrogant vaunting of human political power over divine authority – one that could, at best, leave 'theology on mute' in public life, or, at worst, legitimize the kind of systematic suppression of religion witnessed in the 'people's republic' of China. Equally, the suggestion that the legitimacy of democracy might depend on its compatibility with religious doctrine sounds to many secular observers like a reactionary throwback to an age of religious supremacy – potentially unleashing just the sort of 'theocratic' adventurism apparently at work in Project Blitz.

This book places itself squarely in the force-field opening up between these contending assertions. It takes the risk of simultaneously addressing two normally distinct audiences. It does so in the hope of kick-starting some productive exchanges between advocates who seem to talk at – or past – each other more than they converse with each other. It is intended, first, for secular-minded citizens who may be troubled by the marked upsurge of public religion in liberal democracies like the UK and anxious that newly assertive public religions might undermine what they take to be the unique achievements of a 'secular democracy'. The second audience is religious citizens concerned about how their faith might properly inform and guide their participation in democracy, and who may be perturbed by a revived 'exclusivist secularism' seemingly bent on keeping them on the margins, or, at least, insisting on their religious anonymity in public life.[10] A book on 'faith in democracy' might, however, be tempted to rush straight into an examination of how religious groups can legitimately insert themselves into our existing democratic order, taking for granted the basic legitimacy and design of the system. But confusions about the proper role of faith in democracy, already rife, will only proliferate if there is insufficient clarity about what is actually meant by 'democracy', how it might be evaluated from the standpoint of a religious faith, and whether, and how, religiously motivated interventions subvert or enhance it.

The book is not aimed in the first instance at scholars, although I hope it will be of interest and use to them.[11] It is aimed primarily at reflective practitioners who hold democracy in their hands – political office-holders and activists, campaigners, faith leaders, journalists and many other professionals engaged in public life – and no less at students and young people on whose commitment to a healthy form of democracy the future of all our political communities depends.

Its aims are twofold: the first is clarificatory, the second programmatic. The clarificatory aim is to shed light on what is really at issue in the case of *Daley v Murray*. Are religion and democracy essentially at odds with each other, engaged in a zero-sum game in which advance for one must mean retreat for the other? Given that they inevitably interact, how can we negotiate the rising tensions appearing between 'the obligations of citizenship and the demands of faith'?[12] Are such tensions always destructive, or might they at least sometimes be constructive for democracy? Are certain kinds of religion – or certain strands within one or other religion – more conducive, or obstructive, to democracy than others? What might we make of claims, made mostly but not always by Christians, that Christianity has been a necessary historical condition for the emergence of Western democracy, without which democracy's long-term future is in jeopardy? And whatever we make of those substantive questions, can we construct a principled modus vivendi to 'frame' the relationship between religion and democracy, one that might cause a workable peace to break out, or even nurture a shared vision of the common good?[13]

What follows proceeds from the assumption that religion and democracy cannot be assigned to separate compartments of human life but necessarily impact upon each other, and that such interaction, while inescapably risky, can often be productive for both. It will also argue that these risks and opportunities arise in the relationship between democracy and non-religious ultimate visions of the human good – 'secular faiths'. In this book, what is typically thought of as 'religion' will be viewed as one species of 'faith', a category including a range of non-religious world views that are not held purely on the basis of 'reason' alone but rest on some prior, pre-rational commitments. I realize the term 'secular faith' will be resisted by some; I explain what I mean by it in Chapter 3.

The book also acknowledges that what counts as a 'productive' exchange between religion and democracy is itself deeply contested. While religion and democracy will often be mutually supportive, a truly productive relationship, it is argued here, will inevitably involve recurrent tensions between 'religious' claims and 'democratic' claims, sometimes of a dramatic and disturbing nature – as the US civil rights movement made clear when it deployed religious claims of momentous political potency to expose the racism in the 'voice of the people' in the American South. At least that will be so, insofar as adherents to those religions which, like Christianity, have 'public theologies', seek to live consistently with their principles and not treat their faith as a matter of purely private concern.

Such authentic living out will (often) also ultimately be good for any kind of democracy worth defending, even if it makes for a rough ride along the way. To pit 'religion' and 'democracy' straightforwardly against each other would thus be both simple-minded and dangerous. But religious stances – just like stances motivated by any deep and wide set of moral or spiritual convictions – will sometimes collide with what some hold to be core tenets of 'democracy'. This is evident from the responses of various political establishments to faith-based activists as diverse as Mahatma Gandhi, Elizabeth Cady Stanton (a nineteenth-century American Christian feminist), Mohamed Morsi (Muslim Brotherhood candidate for President of Egypt, elected in 2012, deposed in 2013) and Edward Miall (Nonconformist founder of the Liberation Society in 1844, which campaigned for the disestablishment of the Church of England).

While the outcomes of such public contests cannot always be safely managed, and some will indeed be damaging to one or both sides (the case of Egypt is not encouraging), I argue that we would be in a far worse plight if we tried to construct a system in which they could *never* occur. We would be on the road to a totalitarian state – even if under a 'democratic' guise. Yet the terms of public engagement between 'religion' (or other ultimate visions) and 'democracy' cannot be determined by a mere power play between contending interests. They must where possible be 'framed' – meaning both facilitated and limited – by clear and widely endorsed political principles. This book is an attempt at such a 'framing'.

In pursuing its clarificatory aim, I will be pleased if people on opposing sides end up not only understanding each other better but also agreeing on more than they currently do. But I have no illusions about how deep the differences can be over the place of religion in democracy, nor about how taxing it may be to resolve them. Yet if it is true that (as John Courtney Murray also observed) disagreement is itself an achievement – because it implies the attainment of mutual understanding – then my first goal is simply to achieve a better disagreement between the various protagonists in the debate.

The second aim of the book is programmatic: to defend a particular model of energetic and constructive faith-based engagement in contemporary democratic politics – to propose the seemingly paradoxical idea of 'Christian democratic pluralism'. This is a vision, inspired by Christian faith, for a democracy that does justice to all faiths. 'Pluralism' refers not to a faith or an ideology but to a condition in which plural faiths are treated even-handedly by the democratic state. Christian democratic pluralism is obviously not something to be 'imposed' upon a largely non-Christian society. Rather it is 'proposed' as one contribution to a new democratic settlement, which could only emerge and win sustainable agreement out of a dialogue that involved multiple voices and in which no one would get all they wanted. I will show how being committed to democracy, whatever one's faith, confers many benefits but also means being prepared to live with loss. I argue that the search for a just settlement of the place of faith in democracy, and the necessary compromises it entails, are themselves theologically mandated (in Christianity, at least).

On such a model, the democratic system will remain as open as possible to constructive contributions from a wide range of moral, philosophical and religious convictions, even while remaining firmly committed to a baseline of core constitutional principles without which it will risk permanent instability and injustice (democracy must thus *sometimes* win against *some* 'doctrines of faith'). The model defends space for maximal representation of a plurality of faith-based political visions, especially those held by the democratically marginalized – the 'politically poor'. It will encourage an open deliberative forum, allowing for boisterous, noisy and often fractious political debate. This will sometimes make for 'slow democracy'. Yet it can also sometimes make the attainment of a broad political consensus on important matters of public policy more likely – certainly more likely than either a 'theocratic' or an 'exclusivist secularist' system would.

Defenders of such a forum will not champion diversity for its own sake, as if just any kind of 'difference' or any source of contestation were intrinsically valuable. The book utilizes insights of the school known as 'agonistic' political thought (from the Greek word *agon*, meaning 'struggle').[14] It resists the lure of an easy consensus that risks silencing dissenting minorities. But it repudiates the idea that we should luxuriate in conflict itself or suspect that behind every manifestation of 'consensus' is the veiled fist of hegemonic power. Democratic pluralists need not hold that the mere manifestation of a view, however abhorrent, somehow helps preserve the long-term health of democracy by keeping its adherents 'inside the tent'. The presence in the UK of the English Defence League or Hizb ut-Tahrir (a radical Islamist organization opposed to democracy) are not forms of diversity to be celebrated as part of a 'rich texture of public life'. Rather, the open, diverse democracy I will commend will be animated, and simultaneously constrained, by a *shared search for justice and the common good*. Plural voices will be facilitated and encouraged insofar as they can make out a plausible case that they are intentionally engaged in such a search, and discouraged to the extent that they cannot. Political engagement should not be seen as merely expressive, as if the point were only to put one's tribal convictions on public display and then walk away satisfied.[15]

Rather, such engagement must be constructive and policy-focused: its goal must be to work towards the establishment of just laws conducive to the common good. That expectation, I suggest, 'comes with the territory' of participation in the polity. It is not a counsel of perfection, nor does it assume unattainable levels of public altruism. Participation in such a project inevitably involves not only vigorous argumentation and mobilization but also a firm commitment to deliberation, negotiation, expertise, civic respect, the striking of workable agreements and the renunciation of all hegemonic ambitions – religious or secular. Moreover, principled democratic pluralists do not regard such political virtues as merely strategic – as tools in a long game in which a position of political dominance might in time be seized once their own supporters can muster an electoral majority; or, 'blitz-like', can put a determined minority to work to exploit the system for partisan ends.

I noted that allowing a more open democratic forum could make for a 'rough ride'. This is because the goals of such a forum can only be realized if at least some among the plural voices heard are prepared to engage in rigorously critical, dissenting and sometimes destabilizing interventions – to project radical ('prophetic') visions of justice and the common good into the democratic arena. Some of those will inevitably be religious, or otherwise faith-based. Some such interventions will be destructive of that very democratic forum and will need to be firmly resisted, sometimes by law. Not all of them, even those thoroughly committed to democracy, will look pretty – at least through the (sometimes distorting) lens of whatever happens to be the prevailing political consensus. Consider the patronizing scorn heaped a century ago upon the suffragettes, now widely hailed as transformative agents of political justice.

Obviously, the terms 'justice' and 'common good' will need to be carefully specified for them to serve as meaningful guides to how democracy should operate and what the goals of public policy should be. I begin that task in Chapter 1. Any proposal regarding the goals democracy should pursue will, of course, be the focus of continuing debate and disagreement in democratic forums. This presents a serious challenge for any political system, but especially a democratic one in which principles of public governance are not handed down from on high (whether from hereditary rulers, religious leaders, bureaucratic mandarins or, more recently, senior judges) but – on a good day – forged out of open, reasoned contestation; or, at least, out of a fair tussle between rival democratic interests.

This contest operates at two levels. One is the level of familiar 'ideological' political debate. Does 'justice' mean a shrinking state and a deregulated capitalist economy, as a libertarian vision mandates? Does it call for an ever-expanding regime of equality rights engaged in a 'long march through the institutions', as many secular liberal egalitarians hold? Does 'the common good' demand extensive state intervention in response to the ecological crisis, as a Green conception insists? Does it imply commitment to, or retreat from, transnational political authorities, such as the European Union, that constrain the exercise of national sovereignty?

What makes the contest even more demanding is the deeper level: 'justice' and 'the common good' have implications for the core constitutional principles on which the regime as a whole rests. In any democracy, such principles are themselves subject to contestation (not every month or year but over time), so that there can never be a final or closed settlement of the foundations of the system. That may seem disturbingly open-ended. It is, however, a prospect for which we must be profoundly grateful and over which we must be continually vigilant. For it allows the possibility that grievous political injustices – such as the exclusion of women, or propertyless citizens, or people of colour, from the franchise; or Jews and Roman Catholics from political office; or gay, lesbian and transgender citizens from legal protection against discrimination – can eventually be overcome. This book offers an outline of such an 'open, plural democracy' and an explicitly faith-based justification for one: a sketch of 'Christian democratic pluralism'.

I should make clear that to defend 'Christian democratic pluralism' is not to endorse 'religious pluralism' in one important sense of that term: the confident assertion that all religions are, in some sense, equally valid destinations to 'the divine'. Although I find this view problematic (from what vantage point could we know it is true?), I strongly affirm the importance of interfaith respect, dialogue, learning and partnership. But such a doctrine is not necessary for the kind of political, democratic pluralism I defend here. In my theology of democratic pluralism, defending public space for the expression of religious plurality does not mandate the 'affirmation' or 'celebration' of a plurality of faiths, or any particular faiths, either by individual citizens or by the state. I will argue in any case that, while most state acts cannot be morally neutral,[16] the state should remain religiously impartial, not claiming for itself the authority to take an official view on matters of faith, whether religious or secular.

The book discusses a number of issues typically addressed under the heading of 'multiculturalism'.[17] Evidently, faith is inescapably bound up with questions of ethnicity, race and culture.[18] For example, one cannot understand the contested politics of Islam in the UK without appreciating that two-thirds of British Muslims originate from traditional South Asian cultures marked by powerful kinship loyalties and hierarchical gender roles from which many younger Muslims are trying to break free.[19] For many believers and for the social scientists who study them, it is often difficult to disentangle these different strands of personal or communal identity. Sociologists speak, for example, of 'ethno-religious communities' (a term that arguably also applies to sections of the English Christian community, or, indeed, the English secularist community). Theorists of multiculturalism have observed that, since the 1960s, issues arising from religious difference have increasingly been moving to the centre of debates about multiculturalism.[20] This book, however, limits itself strictly to questions where faith, rather than culture, ethnicity or race, is to the fore of debates about deep diversity.

While the book will not meet all the objections it will undoubtedly evoke from various sides, it does seek to navigate a distinctive pathway between two increasingly influential alternative positions: on the one hand, a newly assertive 'exclusivist secularism', and, on the other, a 'Christian nation' response to this assertiveness. Advocates of exclusivist secularism hold that the only way to secure a neutral state – one that is fair to all citizens and protects their rights equally – is for the state to be 'secular'. This means not only a state with no special privileges for religion but also the thoroughgoing secularization of democratic debate and decision-making. Advocates of a 'Christian nation' position argue the opposite: that the state requires an *official* public acknowledgement of Christianity. Liberal democracy, they argue, itself grew organically out of distinctive elements of Christian (or 'Judeo-Christian') culture and its future sustenance depends on contemporary culture being replenished by these sources. There are valid insights in both positions, but I argue that, in important respects, each misconstrues the proper place of faith in democracy.

While the book addresses both secular and religious audiences, it makes no pretence of neutrality. Throughout, it draws on insights from Christian political thought and seeks to demonstrate their relevance for contemporary democracy. It proceeds from the assumption that the sooner we all put behind us the illusion that public debate can be governed by a detached 'objectivity' – a 'view from nowhere' – the more likely we are to edge towards mutual understanding; or, at least, towards better disagreement. My hope is that by offering an openly Christian model of democratic pluralism I will encourage those of other faiths to make explicit the deeper groundings of their own accounts of democracy. This might generate a rich, multi-sided exchange in which a more durable political consensus on the place of faith in British democracy could begin to swing into view.

The process is, of course, already under way, as seen, for example, in the fruits of several dialogues and projects over the last decade or so: *Faith in the Nation: Religion, Identity and the Public Realm in Britain Today*, published by the Institute for Public Policy Research (2008);[21] *British Secularism and Religion: Islam, Society and the State* (2011), sponsored by the Islamic Foundation and the Markfield Institute for Higher Education;[22] *The Faith Collection* on the role of faith in public life, published by Demos (2013);[23] *Living with Difference; Community, Diversity and the Common Good* (2015), the report of the Commission on Religion and Belief in British Public Life convened by the Woolf Institute, Cambridge,[24] and the House of Lords debate occasioned by it in 2014;[25] *A Secularist Response to the Commission on Religion and Public Life*, published by the University of Warwick (2016);[26] *Cohesive Societies: Faith and Belief*, published by the British Academy and the Faith and Belief Forum (2020). I hope this book casts further light on the proper role of, potential for, pitfalls of, and genuine threats from, faith-based democratic activity – and, indeed, on 'democracy' itself, now rendered even more vulnerable than it already was in the UK through the profound and lasting damages of the Brexit process. We are in urgent need of better public dialogues about how to attain a more sustainable 'framing' of the relationship between faith and democracy in the UK, and we will need a wide array of constructive partners at the table if such dialogues are to succeed.

Notes

1 After Julia Stronks, 'Christians, Public Policy and Same-Sex Marriage: Framing the Questions Before We Shout Out the Answers', *Christian Scholar's Review* 26.4 (1997), 540–62.

2 'Removing the State from Dr Rowan Williams', *The Sunday Telegraph* (11 February 2008).

3 *We Hold These Truths: Catholic Reflections on the American Proposition* (Kansas City, MO: Sheed & Ward, 1960), ix–x.

4 The proposal came in a lecture now included in Robin Griffith-Jones, ed., *Islam and English Law: Rights, Responsibilities and the Place of Shari'a* (Cambridge: Cambridge University Press, 2013). See also Samia Bano, 'In Pursuit of Religious and Legal Diversity: A Response to the Archbishop of Canterbury and the "Sharia Debate" in Britain', *Ecclesiastical Law Journal* 10.3 (2008), 283–309; Jonathan Chaplin, 'Legal Monism and Religious Pluralism: Rowan Williams on Religion, Law and Loyalty', *International Journal of Public Theology* 2.4 (2009), 1–24.

5 Remarks to the Greater Houston Ministerial Association, 12 September 1960. See www.nationalreview.com/2010/09/jfks-religion-speech-fred-schwarz/ (accessed 1/12/20).

6 Dame Louise Casey, *The Casey Review: A Review into Opportunity and Integration* (London: DCLG, 2016), 128.

7 See John Curtice, N. Hudson and Ian Montague, eds, *Political Consequences of Brexit: Has Brexit Damaged Our Politics?*, British Social Attitudes: The 37th Report (London: The National Centre for Social Research, 2020). On Anglican divisions over Brexit, see Jonathan Chaplin and Andrew Bradstock, eds, *The Future of Brexit Britain: Anglican Reflections on National Identity and European Solidarity* (London: SPCK, 2020).

8 John Fea, *Believe Me: The Evangelical Road to Donald Trump* (Grand Rapids, MI: Eerdmans, 2018).

9 David Taylor, 'Project Blitz: The Legislative Assault by Christian Nationalists to Reshape America', *The Guardian* (4 June 2016), www.theguardian.com/world/2018/jun/04/project-blitz-the-legislative-assault-by-christian-nationalists-to-reshape-america (accessed 1/12/20).

10 'Exclusivist secularism' is close to what Rowan Williams calls 'programmatic secularism', which he distinguishes from 'procedural secularism', an open democratic forum in which no one faith dominates. *Faith in the Public Square* (London: Bloomsbury, 2012), chapter 2.

11 For scholarly accounts convergent with my own, see Hans-Martien ten Napel, *Constitutionalism, Democracy and Religious Freedom* (Abingdon: Routledge, 2017); Luke Bretherton, *Resurrecting Democracy: Faith, Citizenship, and the Politics of a Common Life* (Cambridge: Cambridge University Press, 2015).

12 Nancy L. Rosenblum, ed., *Obligations of Citizenship and Demands of Faith: Religious Accommodation in Pluralist Democracies* (Princeton, NJ: Princeton University Press, 2000).

13 A recent report on attitudes to diversity (Julian Hargreaves et al., *How We Get Along: The Diversity Study of England and Wales 2020* (Cambridge: Woolf Institute, 2020)) presents mixed findings on that score: 'far from being divided and highly polarised, there is an emerging national consensus that diversity is good for our country, but that the pace of change has been too fast … [But] while racism and

xenophobia by individuals may be in decline, negative attitudes towards diversity based on religion, especially Islam, are still widely held' (5). Further, 43 per cent of people agree that 'religious diversity in Britain has increased too quickly in the past 10 years', while 19 per cent disagree (8).

14 Chantal Mouffe, *The Democratic Paradox* (London: Verso, 2000), chapter 4.

15 See James Mumford, *Vexed: Ethics Beyond Political Tribes* (London: Bloomsbury Continuum, 2020).

16 Which side of the road cars drive on is morally neutral, but having a law that decides the issue is not.

17 See Jonathan Chaplin, *Multiculturalism: A Christian Retrieval* (London: Theos, 2011); Matthew Kaemingk, *Christian Hospitality and Muslim Immigration in an Age of Fear* (Grand Rapids, MI: Eerdmans, 2018).

18 The Labour Party's 2019 election document, *Race and Faith Manifesto* (London: Labour Party, 2019), is useful but is much more about race and ethnicity than about faith.

19 Philip Lewis and Sadek Hamid, *British Muslims: New Directions in Islamic Thought, Creativity and Activism* (Edinburgh: Edinburgh University Press, 2018), 19; Philip Lewis, *Young, British and Muslim* (London: Continuum, 2007).

20 Ralph Grillo, 'British and Others: From "Race" to "Faith"', in Steven Vertovec and Susanne Wessendorff, eds, *The Multiculturalism Backlash: European Discourses, Policies and Practices* (Abingdon: Routledge, 2010), 50–71.

21 Edited by Zaki Cooper and Guy Lodge (London: IPPR, 2008).

22 Edited by Yahya Birt, Dilwar Hussain and Ataullah Siddiqui (Markfield: Kube Publishing, 2011).

23 Edited by Jonathan Birdwell with Stephen Timms MP (London: Demos, 2013).

24 See Jonathan Chaplin, '"Living with Difference": Time for a Constructive Christian Engagement', *KLICE Comment* (January 2016).

25 See https://hansard.parliament.uk/Lords/2014-11-27/debates/14112775000 396/ReligionAndBeliefBritishPublicLife.

26 Available from https://warwick.ac.uk/fac/soc/pais/people/kettell/a-secularist-response/a-secularist-response.pdf. For a response, see Jonathan Chaplin, 'The Right Kind of Secular State', *KLICE Comment* (January 2016).

PART I

Democracy: As If Faith Mattered

I

Defining and Defending Democracy

Introduction

In its 2019 annual *Audit of Political Engagement* in the UK, the Hansard
Society asked if Britain 'needs a strong ruler *willing to break the rules*'.
Fifty-four per cent of respondents said yes; only 23 per cent said no.[1] No
doubt there was a powerful contextual factor behind this alarming result
– the widespread perception that parliament had 'undemocratically' prevented government from 'getting Brexit done'.[2] A plurality of the voting
public then promptly elected a leader who not only 'got Brexit done'
but also showed a willingness to break a few rules along the way – even
deliberately to break the law. The survey result is an unsettling outcome
for the contemporary inheritors of a nation regarded as a birthplace of
democracy. Can we really act 'democratically' while ditching some of
the rules of democracy itself? Clarity about both the importance and the
nature of democracy is today clearly at a premium.

The first part of this book presents a robust reaffirmation, but also an
alternative reading, of democracy. It retrieves insights from the Christian
political tradition to defend a particular account of democracy (one in
which rulers not only keep the rules but promote the common good).
While this tradition has, to say the least, not proposed that democracy is
the only political form consistent with Christianity, today it preponder-
antly favours – as Kenneth Grasso aptly puts it – 'a preferential option for
constitutional democracy'.[3] Christians have their own distinctive reasons
for endorsing constitutional democracy. In this and the next chapter I
will argue for a conception of constitutional democracy that flows out
of these reasons, even as it converges on many matters of principle and
practice with secular accounts.

Developing this conception will require both a critique of a popular
liberal understanding of democracy and an elaboration of a critical – and
self-critical – conception of 'Christian democracy'.[4] I will propose that
Christians should bring such a conception to the democratic table and
be willing to declare it as such when occasion requires. At that table, of
course, they will find themselves in dialogue with those whose conception

of democracy is informed by other religious faiths, or 'faiths' such as secular liberalism, nationalism, libertarianism, postmodernism, radical feminism, Marxism, radical ecology, and more. They too are invited to 'show their workings', when necessary. Perhaps the majority around the table, however, will purport to eschew all such fundamental perspectives and espouse a purely 'pragmatic' approach to politics. That claim, too, must be aired and critically tested in democratic debate.

My aim is not to reassure the secular-minded that Christians (or other religious citizens) can be 'good democrats', moderate and amenable types who will put the chairs out, not rock the boat, and will 'get with the programme'.[5] They must decide after reading the book whether they feel reassured or whether reassurance is what they sought or are even entitled to. As I indicated in the Introduction, a readiness to disturb settled liberal democratic pieties is to be expected from some religious citizens who wish to live faithful public lives according to their particular, and sometimes counter-cultural, lights. But the same is true for any citizen, whatever their fundamental commitments. All democratic citizens must be prepared to be dissenters – disturbers of the democratic peace. To adapt the words of an ancient Hebrew prophet, the good citizen is not the one who says '"peace, peace", when there is no peace at all' (Jer. 6.14). Democracy must be readied for what American legal thinker Stephen Carter calls 'the dissent of the governed'.[6] Accordingly, one of the goals of my alternative account is to address the question whether, as theologian Stanley Hauerwas puts it, contemporary Western liberal democracy 'polices' religious believers into conformity to practices in tension with their faith, suppressing their proper dissenting instincts.[7] I will show how they can avoid such complicity by grasping the deeper purpose behind democracy and allowing this to inspire and guide their democratic activity.

Nor is the aim to reassure religious believers that participation in the democratic system as it exists today is entirely unproblematic, or, worse, that the question at stake is only what they can get out of it and how. Skipping the task of defining and assessing democracy would risk playing into a form of faith-based politics in which democratic activity is merely instrumental to the aspirations of faith. Arguing for a theological affirmation of democracy should never be a cover for special pleading – to get that coveted 'seat at the table', or, worse, just to pocket some of the spoils that fall from it. Nor is it to parade one's own position merely as another manifestation of a sectional identity politics. Rather, whatever particular goals are being pursued, a controlling aim should be to bolster the public structures of democracy itself, for the sake of the common good – in which, of course, they also have a stake. As the same ancient Hebrew prophet exhorted the Jews who found themselves stuck in Babylon for

4

the long haul: 'seek the welfare of the city where I have sent you into exile, and pray to the LORD on its behalf, for in its welfare you will find your welfare' (Jer. 29.7).

The first section begins by explaining why a faith-based account of democracy might be useful at all. The second defines the sense in which the term 'democracy' will be used in the book and lays initial foundations for a theologically informed account of constitutional democracy.

Why a faith-based approach to democracy?

Three considerations suggest why an account of democracy informed by religious faith might be of public interest and not only an in-house concern of the religious.

Reckoning with the 'return of religion'

The first consideration is the need to learn democratic lessons from the 'return of religion' to the global public square over the last 40 years.[8] The focus of this book is Britain, but this remarkable and unsettling worldwide phenomenon should counsel British citizens, both religious and secular, to increase their literacy about the relationship between faith and democracy. Political scientists have long been documenting the phenomenon of the 'global resurgence of religion'.[9] We have witnessed what one observer called the 'unexpected outcome' that while the world has become more modernized it has also become 'more democratic *and more religious*'. This has debunked the long-standing assumption that 'democracy's progress is naturally accompanied not merely by the advance of secularism but by the waning of religion'.[10] As secular political theorist Mark Lilla observes: 'Intellectual complacency, nursed by implicit faith in the inevitability of secularization, has blinded us to the persistence of political theology and its manifest power to shape human life at any moment.'[11]

Observers are also beginning to register not only the (amply documented) extent to which religious actors in some contexts impede or subvert processes of democratization but also the potential for them to play constructive roles. For example, Christian-inspired actors and movements have proved to be influential, and on occasion decisive, in resistance to anti-democratic regimes in as diverse contexts as Spain, Latin America (Brazil, Nicaragua, Chile, El Salvador), Africa (Zimbabwe, South Africa, Kenya), Asia (Philippines, South Korea and, today, Hong Kong) and Eastern Europe (Poland, Lithuania, East Germany, Hungary).[12] Some

Christians have, of course, also been enlisted in support of authoritarian regimes: Spain under Franco and South Africa under apartheid leap out as obvious cases from the previous list. Some Christians who saw the Sandinista revolution in Nicaragua as a 'just insurrection' struggled to take distance from it after it had lapsed into undemocratic tendencies. But their errors have been widely criticized by many of their contemporary co-religionists. For many Christian pro-democracy actors, a commitment to democratization is not incidental to their faith but is understood as a religiously inspired duty.[13] They are exemplifying today what Graham Maddox concluded of earlier religious impulses behind democracy: 'For the democrat whose will has been fortified in the spiritual domain the need to pursue justice through political means comes as a divine imperative.'[14]

Two leading scholars summarize the finding of a large-scale research project, somewhat anti-climactically perhaps, in the claim that 'religion is neither inherently pro-democracy nor inherently anti-democracy'.[15] Defenders of religion might have hoped for a more resounding endorsement of religion's democratic potency, but this finding at least rebuts the long-standing perception that religion is essentially reactionary and authoritarian. Contrary to remaining perceptions, there is no necessary causal link between the two. Given conducive conditions, these scholars report, religion can turn out to be a significant inspiration for faith-based democratizing movements. This book hopes to offer one intellectual resource for such movements, at home and abroad.

Embracing faith-based mutual learning

The second reason why a faith-based account of democracy is of general interest is the democratic possibilities offered by faith-based mutual learning. Christian philosopher Nicholas Wolterstorff puts the point straightforwardly:

> In a participatory democracy such as ours, it's important that we each be open with and open to our fellow citizens concerning the deep sources of how we think about political issues. If there are distinctly Jewish [or Muslim or secular utilitarian] ways of thinking about those issues ... I want to hear about those. Not only does respect for my fellow citizens require that I invite them to tell me how they think about these issues and that I listen attentively to what they say; by their speaking and by my listening I get a sense of what they care most deeply about, and thereby some sense of what a politics that is fair to all would be like. And there is always the possibility of learning from them.[16]

I hope to show that a theologically informed account can shed light on the nature of democracy, even when its religious basis is bewildering or objectionable to others. I will suggest that such an account is eminently worthy of consideration by my fellow secular citizens – in exactly the same way that a radical Green theory of democracy might offer valuable insights to a Kantian liberal who nevertheless repudiated (or was baffled by) the former's underlying cosmology; and vice versa. This doesn't assume that such accounts of democracy are ultimately detachable from their supporting foundations – 'freestanding with respect to comprehensive doctrines', as liberal political philosopher John Rawls puts it.[17] It only assumes that there is sufficient common human experience of the struggle for political justice to allow fruitful conversations to take place across those divides about the kind of democracy we might jointly aspire to. That might, perhaps, eventuate in commitments to democracy endorsed by several faith traditions, somewhat like the 'Democratic Charter' proposed by Catholic philosopher Jacques Maritain in the aftermath of war and fascism (but, I would suggest, with the faith inspirations on display).[18] Or, to use a more recent example, it might take the form of a sequel to the path-breaking declaration *A Common Word Between Us and You* issued by Muslim scholars to Christians in 2007, but one focused on politics.[19]

Given the dominant secular mindset of much political thinking today, the obstacles to learning from faith-based political thinking are daunting. Some committed secularists will doubt that religion could in any sense be an equal partner in rational political discourse. As Lilla observes, the pervasive assumption of secular modernity has been that religiously based political thinking is now irredeemably alien:

> ... we are separated from our own long theological tradition of political thought by a revolution in Western thinking that began roughly four centuries ago. We live, so to speak, on the other shore. When we observe civilizations on the opposite bank, we are puzzled, since we have only a distant memory of what it was like to think as they do ... The river separating us is narrow, yet deep. On one shore the basic political structures of society are imagined and criticized by reference to divine authority; on the other they are not. And this turns out to be a fundamental difference.[20]

But as signs of the 'post-secular' begin to creep up on us, to disallow at the outset the possibility of interfaith learning, among religions and between them and other 'faiths', would be pre-emptive. To be open to such learning does not require any 'suspension of disbelief' (so to speak). It only presupposes an initial readiness to entertain a religiously based proposal as a *potential* bearer of political wisdom. Charles Taylor has proposed that a 'secular age' is one in which a religious vision can no longer be presumed to be the default framework for public discourse but must justify itself among a plurality of visions.[21] This is true, but the point also applies to secular visions, which can no longer be seen as the default setting against which religious visions must justify themselves. Jürgen Habermas thus calls for a willingness of secularists to step outside their own secularist world view and to engage in a 'self-reflective transcending of a secularist self-understanding of Modernity'.[22] If religious believers do the same, mutual learning might ensue.

Enlisting fellow believers behind democracy

A third reason why the faith-democracy nexus is of general importance is the growing need for faith-based democrats to enlist both sceptical co-religionists and adherents of other religions in support of healthy forms of democracy. Christian endorsement of democracy remains, after all, far from universal, or, where it is accepted, far from unconditional. The readiness of an overwhelming majority of professed American evangelicals to support President Trump in spite of his brazen contempt for fundamental democratic norms discloses the fragility of that community's adherence to democracy in the face of what they experience as cultural marginalization.[23] Hungarian prime minister Victor Orbán now defends 'illiberal democracy' – involving significant incursions into civil liberties and judicial independence – as an expression of his national populist version of 'Christian Democracy'.[24] Prominent figures in the Russian Orthodox Church continue to lend their support to President Putin in spite of his ruthless authoritarian nationalism.[25] Brazilian evangelicals have offered enthusiastic support for the aggressive populism of Jair Bolsonaro.[26] Contemporary followers of Islamist radicals like Sayyid Qutb openly question democracy as an inversion of divine sovereignty and a debased product of a bankrupt, secular Western culture.[27] Prime minister Modi's governing party openly promotes an aggressive and discriminatory Hindu supremacism in India through the ideology of Hindutva.[28] Since such dangerous populisms and nationalisms find support in certain quarters in the UK – and because British diplomats, businesspeople and activists encounter them abroad – the argument needs to be conducted here as well.[29]

It will not do simply to pour contempt on such religiously inspired resistance to democracy and carry on regardless. Where adherents to such movements ground their politics explicitly in their faith, wholly secular arguments for democracy are unlikely to prove persuasive. Representatives of these movements typically present religiously based arguments (however weak and self-serving) for their political standpoints, inviting those Christian or other religious actors thrust into political dialogue with them to articulate their own religious reasons for democracy. This may prove a more effective 'conversation starter' than a resolutely secular discourse of individual autonomy or human rights.[30]

The same point applies in more promising situations where Christians find themselves in dialogue with faith-based pro-democracy advocates. For example, Christians will win more credibility with reformist Muslims seeking to identify authentically Islamic foundations for democracy if they themselves can defend democracy in Christian rather than merely secular terms. And, of course, the initiative could go the other way: Muslim democrats in Tunisia (perhaps the only success story of the 'Arab Spring') or Hindu democrats in India (there are many) might need to help Christian (or other religious) fellow citizens articulate their own religious commitments to democracy more clearly.

Already in 1995, commenting on American diplomatic failures to comprehend the significance of religion in conflict situations, Douglas Johnston noted that we 'inadequately appreciated the transformational possibilities that exist when the parties involved in a conflict can be appealed to on the basis of shared spiritual convictions or values'.[31] Secular-minded democrats should recognize the potency of religious arguments to reach parts of the global campaign for democracy they cannot reach. The same applies to British secularists (or Christians, for that matter) who are solicitous of democracy at home. They may quickly strike up comfortable alliances with groups such as British Muslims for Secular Democracy,[32] but find they have less leverage with those relying on more traditional Islamic arguments, such as the Islamic Foundation or the Muslim Public Affairs Committee.[33]

A Christian account of constitutional democracy

Sources of Christian democratic thought

To what voices might we turn in constructing a Christian account of constitutional democracy? In fact we find a surprisingly large 'host of witnesses' in the Christian tradition to that end. A large chorus appeared in the middle of the last century in response to war and totalitarianism. In 1944 Reinhold Niebuhr published *The Children of Light and the Children of Darkness: A Vindication of Democracy and a Critique of its Traditional Defenders*, the last globally influential Protestant work.[34] Three substantial Catholic offerings appeared around the same time: Jacques Maritain's *Christianity and Democracy*[35] and *Man and the State*,[36] and Yves Simon's *The Philosophy of Democratic Government*.[37] By the time these works appeared, the majority of Western Christians had, in fact, already accepted democracy, not only as a permissible but as the decidedly preferable, form of government. When official Catholicism belatedly registered its official approval of democracy at the Second Vatican Council, notably in *Gaudium et Spes* (1965),[38] the reception of democracy by Western Christianity was formally complete.

These mid-twentieth-century works were to inform a good deal of Western Christian thought about democracy for decades to come. Political theology's interest in democracy seems then to have lain dormant for nearly half a century. By the 1970s, those earlier works on democracy had been overshadowed by political theology's preoccupation with other (no less legitimate and pressing) concerns, such as liberation theology's resistance to capitalism and dictatorship in Latin America, black theology's opposition to racism and colonialism and feminist theology's critique of patriarchy. But since the 1990s, Christian reflection on democracy has been undergoing a remarkable revival.[39] The fruit of such work needs to be developed further and disseminated beyond the academy; that is part of the purpose of this book.

The purpose of the political community

If there is one conviction that unites many theologians of democracy it is that democracy is not simply about 'Who gets what, when, and how?' (as one political scientist described politics decades ago),[40] but must be understood in terms of the larger moral purpose it exists to serve.[41] In the rest of this chapter I reclaim this idea, arguing that we can only grasp the point and proper design of democracy if we first identify the central purpose of the political order in which it finds its place. Democracy is not the whole of a political order but only one of its parts. The point of the part is determined by the point of the whole. To know why democracy is important, and what kind we should strive for, we first have to grasp why political orders exist at all – why human societies repeatedly create and recreate them, often against formidable odds. Oliver O'Donovan reminds us of the scale of the challenge Western societies face on this score:

> not thirty years after the victory of democracy over totalitarianism triumphantly proclaimed with the fall of the Berlin Wall, the West

is facing the possibility of a general breakdown of its institutions ... This ... has happened because the supporting narrative that made the democratic institutions intelligible has been eroded to the point that it is no longer understood ... Democracy promised institutions and structures that could win general consent to broadly just, though not infallible, government, and for some time it fulfilled its promise. But its condition was that all participants understood the ends that those institutions served. Now reinterpreted as a populism of the common will, democracy collapses in on itself, as laws, political parties, elections and executives no longer appear as collaborative instruments of just and wise government ...[42]

He ventures, however, that Christian political theology can still 'speak to the rationale and discipline of governing institutions in words that are otherwise missing from public debate'. This book presents one such rationale.

First, an important note about terminology. O'Donovan speaks here of 'government'. In ordinary language this usually refers to *the* government; that is, 'the executive branch' – the body that actually runs things (and gets blamed when things go wrong). We also often speak of 'the state', referring collectively to the executive, the legislature and the judiciary and their various sub-units. When I use the term 'state' or 'state institutions', I will have this wider sense in mind. Often we think of 'the state' as something outside us, even alien to us. We think of it as standing over against 'the people' and we see it as doing things to us or for us (things we might like or hate). But a key concern of this book is to show how 'the people' is indispensable to the work of politics. So I will also use a term naming a still wider entity, 'the political community'. By 'political community' I mean *state and people* united into a single community organized to pursue a particular purpose. Our sense of being partners with 'the state' in a common project is, admittedly, often thin at best. I will argue that a state is healthy to the degree that it actively embraces the moral energies and convictions of the people, and thus strives to actually *become* a 'political community', rather than a remote and abstract bureaucracy that merely 'manages' the people. The people is not merely the object of governance but a partner in governance.

'The people' is the entire body of individual citizens, those enjoying full membership of the political community (sometimes referred to as the 'citizenry'). Democracy is the arrangement ensuring that the people is entitled both to choose (occasionally) who will hold elective offices of state and able to exercise influence (continuously) on the state as it discharges its purpose. The people should be recognized as a constitutive, active agent within the political community, alongside (or sometimes in opposition to) the institutions of state.[43]

The name that I will give to the characteristic purpose of the political community – its *raison d'être* – is the pursuit of 'public justice': the provision of an array of just laws and policies governing the public spaces of society. The desire for society-wide justice, and outrage at egregious structural injustice, seem universal. Human societies display a recurring need for an institution able to administer justice across its whole terrain – to promote the equitable distribution of resources, to defend against threats to order, to protect basic rights, to resolve conflicts fairly, to create public infrastructure that make human life stable and commodious. When these are lacking, societies are anarchic, chaotic and oppressive – and, eventually, the people often rise up and demand an order that can remedy the injustices invariably unleashed by such disorder.

The term 'public justice' tries to capture this aspiration. It partly overlaps with the more familiar idea of 'the common good', and I explain the meaning of and relation between these terms below. 'Public justice' refers not to any *particular tasks* the political community might happen to pursue, such as keeping sewers – or banks – clean, important though they are. Those tasks change greatly over time, and new circumstances demand new tasks – as climate change and the COVID-19 pandemic dramatically remind us. Public justice refers instead to the enduring institutional vocation of the political community – the unique contribution it must make to the flourishing of human society.

But what kind of idea is it? The term is not an empirical *description* of what political communities actually do; we know that many often act unjustly and seek private enrichment over the public good. It is rather a proposal as to what they *should* do, *given the specific human needs and possibilities they must serve*. We might say that public justice is the constitutive *telos* of the political community. It is constitutive in the sense that citizens do not autonomously conjure it up themselves but rather 'find' it. They encounter it in the demands of social life itself, especially in common struggles for justice – struggles against the kinds of domination, exploitation or humiliation that require a more powerful custodian and greater resources than they can muster individually. What is more, people mostly desire that such a custodian pursues its purposes *legitimately*. They want their political institutions to possess not just might, but right – not only the power to create just order, but the authority to do so. An illegitimate political community, even one with a lot of power, will be hamstrung in its efforts to achieve justice (or much else).

The idea that political institutions have any kind of *normative* (or 'moral') purpose is contested. Self-styled 'realists' – or just ordinary cynics

– assert that political institutions are basically explained by a drive for survival, expansion or power. Normative or 'ideal' principles merely hover above them, mostly ineffectually. Norms like justice may serve to shore up myths of legitimacy but don't do any real work in shaping what states do. 'Deconstructionists' go further and assert that conceptions like 'justice' are deceptive illusions, deployed by those with power only as a cloak for political land-grabs. At bottom, they are discursive instruments of domination.[44] Most secular liberals who defend liberal democracy reject these radically sceptical views. On this point, at least, I stand with liberals. I think normative visions make a difference, and, at times, change history.

The idea that the normative purpose of the political community is *inherent within it*, rather than imported from without, is also contested. To suggest that the purpose – *telos* – of an institution is inherent within it is sometimes called a teleological way of thinking. It is not a uniquely Christian or religious approach. Its first formidable advocate in the Western tradition was Aristotle. But teleological thinking was taken up and transformed in the political thought of the thirteenth-century Catholic thinker Thomas Aquinas, who used it to express the idea that the whole world was shot through with moral purposes rooted in divine creation. Human flourishing would be advanced insofar as humans, and their institutions, aligned themselves with these purposes by 'working with the grain of human nature' (rightly understood). The idea has been the staple of Thomistic political thought ever since, as well as of a good deal of Protestant thought influenced by Thomism. On such a view, political community, and political authority, are 'natural' in the sense of arising from the recurring inclinations of social human nature. God is seen as active in the generation of political authority, not primarily through sudden, revelatory interventions but through the act of creating human beings with inbuilt tendencies towards political community, and then sustaining those tendencies against the corrupting effects of 'the fall'.

This 'politics-as-natural' view can be contrasted with another widely influential position, the 'politics-as-remedial' view. This position holds that political authority has been instituted by God through specific providential interventions as a merciful remedy for the anarchic tendencies unleashed by the fall – human rebellion against the Creator. Political authority is an 'order of providence', a work of divine damage limitation. The remedial view has exercised long and deep influence in the Christian tradition. Versions of it were held by, for example, Augustine and Luther. Its strengths are two: first, its realism about the need for the coercive protection of the innocent, who would otherwise be prey to the violent; and second, its cautionary stance towards the 'arrogance of power': the political community must know its place and not be lured by utopian ambitions regarding the transformation of the souls of citizens (requiring an intrusive 'soul craft') or the wholesale refashioning of society (which invariably ends in disaster).

But the idea of political authority as a mere 'remedy' against sin cannot adequately capture many tasks that have been widely and rightly recognized as necessary to the realization of even a minimum level of justice in society. Consider, for example, opportunities for basic human flourishing such as travel (requiring, for example, the construction of roads) or education (requiring, for example, support for providers of schools or the granting of charters to universities). The absence of such opportunities is not the result of human fallenness; rather the establishment of these goods are historical tasks that humans must recognize over time and then organize (where they can). Shared public resources like these must be provided by those equipped to do so, and political authorities are among the prime candidates to do so. *Not to do so* when the possibility exists would indeed be a failure, even a 'sin of neglect'. Without transport infrastructure, human life would be significantly diminished and many people would suffer from isolation and restricted opportunities for flourishing. Without organized structures of education, those for whom voluntary provision would be unavailable would lack vital opportunities for development and service. They would suffer injustices that could be pre-empted or at least mitigated by the action of political authorities.

Political community, then, is 'natural' to human societies in the sense that a people's common yearning for justice across society almost invariably requires a public agency capable of and authorized to promote it. Such an agency expresses an incessant aspiration arising from the conditions of human social life. This is 'the political community'. In it, the people should serve as an active contributor to the process of discerning public justice and thus be accorded democratic avenues to do so.

Modern liberalism and the purpose of the political community

Later it will become clear that my model of democracy converges on many matters of institutional detail with contemporary secular liberal accounts. But it differs on a fundamental matter with one popular liberal account and it is important to see how.[45] The theory I have in mind is what O'Donovan refers to in the passage above as a 'populism of the common will'. It can be summed up thus: the purpose of the political community is not *given* to us but *constructed* by us: it is sovereignly determined by the pooled wills of those who freely associate in order to establish it. This is often called a voluntarist view (from the Latin term *voluntas* = will). It is not only that the people retain the power to elect and hold to account the officers of a particular government – the rascals currently in power, who can be turfed out when the people's patience expires; I will defend that view. Rather, the people possess a more foundational authority, an awesome 'constituent power' – the right to create political community and political authority *ex nihilo*. Free individuals, imagined in an ideal, normless 'state of nature', agree to conjure up the right to exercise political authority where none exists and then to decide what purposes it will pursue.[46]

This view implies that the political community lacks any inherent, constitutive purposes *of its own*, which the people ought to recognize or align themselves with or to which they might defer. So if the people collectively will that the political community should be charged with protecting our rights, then that, and that alone, it is authorized to do. But by the same logic, if the people were to choose to designate that purpose as guaranteeing order, upholding tradition, or maximizing economic growth, then that would be its mandate. For, many will ask, who else could decide it?

There is, however, confusion on the point. Suppose people were asked if a democratic majority is entitled to exclude a disfavoured religious or ethnic minority from full citizenship – as the British state did with Catholics and Nonconformists until 1829, or the Israeli state does today with Palestinians and the state of Myanmar does with Rohingyas? They would hastily deny it. But that denial would amount to an implicit recognition that collective will meets its limit in an objective moral demand; in this case, universal anti-discrimination rights. Radical voluntarism is difficult to live by consistently.

There have been substantial challenges to this voluntarist view since its emergence in the late seventeenth century. The most influential was that propounded by traditionalist conservatism, which asserted that it is *tradition*, not popular will, that tells us what the purpose of the political community is. That purpose might be construed as the protection of historical property entitlements, the preservation of customary social order, the maintenance of national character or defence against enemies. On this view, 'tradition' is entitled to instruct us about the purpose of the political community because it is the repository of the accumulated, tested wisdom of centuries. To this, the present generation must defer; it cannot simply be set aside by johnny-come-lately popular assemblies wielding their rights, reason or will. This view has few defenders today, even in religious circles, and I spend little time on it. Indeed, such traditional*ism* is antithetical to Christian thought, even though some Christians have in the past espoused it. O'Donovan, who holds a very high view of tradition, declares such a view of the supreme authority of tradition a 'heresy'.[47]

I suggest that the liberal view just outlined – the view that the normative purpose of the political community can only be determined by acts of collective sovereign will – is, strictly speaking, another Christian 'heresy'. Arguably, it is a 'faith-based' ideology rooted in the radical secular Enlightenment, in which the people place their trust in their own collective will to secure political 'salvation'.[48] Christians today, I suggest, should reject this liberal view, while remaining passionately committed to constitutional democracy. As Luke Bretherton puts it, 'while democratic politics leads to and flourishes best within a liberal constitutional order, a commitment to democracy does not necessitate a commitment to liberalism as a political philosophy.'[49] By contrast, the common starting point of the Christian traditions of political thought on which I draw is that political authority – the power to issue binding, and if necessary coercive demands – does not flow ultimately from collective human will but from the imperatives of human social nature as created by God. Humans, of course, are the agents who actually set up political institutions, but they do so in response to the social needs of human nature as given by God.

Invoking divine authority as a counterweight to authoritarianism

It is often supposed by secular liberals – and some religious thinkers – that locating the ultimate source of political authority in divine authority plays into the hands of authoritarianism. There is no lack of historical instances of that causal relationship. In early modern Europe, including England, it took the form of the novel 'divine right' theory of kingship – the view that the ruler not only was in some sense divinely appointed (that was standard fare since the early Church) but that s/he exercised virtually unlimited, or at least unchallengeable, authority as God's 'vicar' on earth.

There is, however, no necessary connection between the ascription of a divine source to political authority and authoritarianism.[50] On the contrary, Christian thought has typically asserted that God authorizes *many* institutions, each with their own proper and limited sphere of authority. Institutions like marriage, family, property and even workers' associations (as Pope Leo XIII proposed in 1891) have also been construed as 'divinely established'.[51] As with the political community, this does not mean that such institutions are brought into being by some mysterious divine fiat (still less one mediated via a clerical or prophetic human authority). Rather, the claim is, again, that these institutions arise out of the inherent inclinations of created social human nature. God is at work in creating and sustaining the possibility of institutional conditions for a flourishing society, in the face of the effects of 'the fall'. These inclinations are in some sense experienced by all human beings, so that anyone could, in principle, come to recognize and understand them, whatever their faith position. They do not presuppose any esoteric religious knowledge, but they do demand careful discernment of the imperatives of human social order (which, of course, will be much contested).

The claim that God, via created human nature, is the ultimate origin of many human institutions does not imply that society is populated by a series of mini-theocracies. It implies the opposite: that all institutions – including the political community – are limited in relation to each other. The authority assigned to each is restricted to the specific human purpose it pursues, and no one institution may usurp the authority to pursue, or even supervise the pursuit of, all such purposes. Marriage realizes companionship and reproduction; families offer emotional and moral nurture; universities pursue truth and knowledge; trades unions embody worker solidarity; and so forth. To each is attached an ensemble of constitutive expectations, enjoyments, rights and duties, pursuant to the institution's specific purpose.[52] The authority of each must in the first instance be deferred to by other institutions, including by the political community. Social authority in the purposes of God is constitutively plural not singular – distributed not concentrated. No single human institution can arrogate to itself comprehensive authority over society or suppose that it is the sole fount of authority from which all other kinds derive. Construing political authority in this way thus tends not towards authoritarianism or theocracy but to a model of mutually self-limiting institutional diversity.[53]

I have argued that the existence of political communities answers to enduring human needs and possibilities – however irksome or even oppressive we may find their particular demands at the best of times. The political order is not fundamentally 'alien' to human beings. When we align ourselves with properly functioning political communities, we embrace one of the essential conditions for human flourishing. If we cast a corrupt state aside, we shall have to construct another in short order. As Jacques Maritain put it, 'Man is not for the State. The State is for man.'[54]

I stress that by 'properly functioning' political communities I mean political communities insofar as they pursue their normative purpose. The ones we actually live in, of course, frequently veer recklessly away from this purpose or flagrantly violate it: by waging unjust war against their enemies, by terrorizing their own populations, or by maximizing economic growth above maintaining a sustainable environment. This is the powerful element of truth in the 'realist' theories noted above.

Even conservative thinker Edmund Burke pointed out in the eighteenth century that the East India Company should never have been accorded the authority of a state because it was something structurally different – a commercial enterprise, and a dangerously rapacious one at that. It was evidently not fitted to the promotion of the public good but had become 'a state in the disguise of a merchant'.[55]

Thus, to 'align ourselves' with the *normative purpose* of the political community will inescapably involve criticizing our *actual* political communities. In the case of egregious injustices, this could involve disobeying or resisting them, or, at the extreme, removing their sitting office-holders or even constituting a new regime. The characteristic normative purpose of the political community itself *requires* citizens who are willing to disturb, and if necessary subvert, the ones they actually live under, in order to move them closer to their true purpose.[56] What exactly is that purpose?

'Public justice' as the purpose of the political community

Let me now explain more fully my characterization of the normative purpose of the political community as the promotion of 'public justice'. This is an important term of art in the book; it is my attempt to capture the political community's *raison d'être*. Christian thinkers have, over the centuries, defined the purpose of the political community in a wide variety of ways, such as securing 'peace', establishing 'public morality', defending 'true religion' or protecting the 'common weal'. But the most comprehensive and enduring descriptions in the tradition have been 'promoting the common good' (especially in Catholicism) and 'establishing justice' (especially in Protestantism). Both are rich and multilayered ideas and I draw on each. But I will suggest that neither in itself captures precisely enough what the proper purpose of the political community is, in distinction to the purposes of other institutions. On their own they are not institutionally specific enough. For that we need a different term, and I will use 'public justice' to that end. First, I explain what is valuable in the idea of 'the common good' and why we need to go beyond it.[57]

The common good

The common good was influentially defined in the Vatican II document *Gaudium et Spes* (1965) as 'the sum total of social conditions which allow people, either as groups or individuals, to reach their fulfilment more fully and more easily'.[58] This is a hugely capacious definition. The idea of 'social conditions facilitating human fulfilment' embraces an enormous range of relationships, resources, opportunities, activities, projects and services that allow individual and corporate human fulfilment.[59] Such conditions could, in principle, include anything from the transportation or education systems I alluded to earlier, to robust civic virtues, to sound banking practices, to stable families, to humane ancient customs, to clean air, to university accreditation rules, to a minimum wage, to the rule of law. Such a definition evidently does not suffice as a way of delimiting the unique contribution of the political community towards such wide-ranging goals. A political community attempting to guarantee all such things would be on the road to totalitarianism.

The definition is, however, not intended to do so alone. In Catholic social teaching, it stands as one fundamental idea that must be read alongside many others. In fact 'the common good' in its fullest meaning is not intended in the first instance as a *political* principle at all, but speaks of the shared final destiny of humankind in eternal communion with God. In Catholic thought, the journey towards that destiny is, however, seen as 'passing through' the temporal realm of human society, meaning that humans are indeed called to elevate and transform – to 'humanize' – society in the light of that beckoning vision of union with God. They are to promote the 'temporal' common good. The many detailed principles of Catholic social teaching – solidarity, subsidiarity, justice, freedom, dignity and so forth – are intended to specify what that humanizing project might look like in the here and now.

Let me elaborate on the meaning of the common good in three steps. First, the common good is not something above or over against the many 'particular goods' that people own or make use of or share in – their possessions, their life projects, their families or local communities, or the many other associations they participate in. This worry is sometimes evoked when the common good is spoken of as taking 'priority over' particular goods (as it is by Thomas Aquinas). But such priority does not mean that the common good has its own independent claims that can be ranked alongside and placed in competition with those of particular goods. Rather, the common good is the aspiration towards a *just coordination of particular goods*. To say that the common good has priority over particular goods is simply to say that the latter need to be thus coordinated in a way that benefits all. This is not a mysterious idea. Where claims to particular goods (rights, benefits, resources and so forth) tug against or undermine just coordination – as when market exchanges are stacked in favour of powerful corporate elites, for example – the imperatives of the common good will take precedence over those of particular goods.

The just coordination of particular goods occurs in every community, not only the political community. Every community, association or institution has its own specific 'common good'. Seeking the common good of the family is what parents are engaged in on a daily basis in managing the many competing demands of their families (even though the daily grind of parenting often doesn't feel like such an elevated idea). Equally, business managers and university administrators have to be adept at justly coordinating the numerous interests that clamour for their attention. This is more than 'brokering' or 'managing' conflicting interests, a stance that could permit those with the most power to prevail. It should be guided by the normative purpose of the body in question, facing down undue power when necessary.

Second, every human being shares in the responsibility for promoting the common good. They do this, in the first instance, not by taking up *political* tasks but by contributing to human flourishing in ordinary life: living virtuous individual lives, raising well-adjusted children, nurturing supportive neighbourhoods, caring for the environment, consuming for need not excess, using productive resources efficiently, practising just employment relationships, and so on. Much of this activity takes place outside the direct control of the political community. It occurs, for example, in the intimate spheres of family, friends, neighbourhoods, churches; in the network of voluntary associations and other non-government organizations often called 'civil society'; in the labyrinth of economic interactions we call 'markets'; and in the realm of civic discourse often termed 'the public sphere', where the task is to stimulate vigorous and critical public discourse about, among other things, the common good itself. Certainly, our individualistic society needs to recapture a public vision of the common good as everyone's responsibility.[60] This will mean practising what Pope John Paul II calls the virtue of 'solidarity': '*a firm and persevering determination* to commit oneself to the *common good*; that is to say to the good of all and of each individual, because we are *all* really responsible *for all*'.[61] This is an essential requirement if a 'Christian democratic' vision of politics is to make any headway.

A third feature of the common good takes us to its specifically political application. It is sometimes wrongly supposed that the political community – even 'the government' – is solely responsible for securing the common good. Careless formulations of the term have sometimes given this impression. But, as already indicated, from its beginning Christian political thought has generated a powerful anti-centralizing momentum that shapes how we interpret the common good. The essential point can be put this way: the political community is not responsible for promoting every aspect of the common good, but only those aspects *essential to the integrity of public space* in its territory. This includes a great deal but also excludes much. Pursuing the common good does not mean ascribing to the political community responsibility for securing all the goods of community.

In modern Catholic social thought, for example, this limitation has been specified in a variety of ways. For example, it is implicit in the idea that the political community cannot itself deliver human *flourishing*, but it can, through the limited medium of law, protect the human *rights* that are one of the minimum conditions for such flourishing. It has also been specified in terms of the 'principle of subsidiarity', which licenses governments to intervene in another social authority only when that authority is in danger of violating the basic rights of its members or undermining some aspect of the common good. Subsidiarity is not a principle that 'balances' the common good but is implied in the idea itself.[62] Thus, when Western governments intervened after the 2008 banking crisis to restrict the private rights of financial institutions to order their own affairs (such as by imposing liquidity caps on banks), this was an eminently justifiable curtailment of a particular good in the shared interest of a stable financial system. The responses of governments across the world to the public health threat of the COVID-19 pandemic illustrate the point even more emphatically (even if not all their actions will in hindsight be judged necessary or wise).

Public justice

'Common good' language emerges principally from the Catholic tradition. While Protestants have also invoked this language, they have been more likely to refer to the purpose of the political community as the establishment of *justice*. This has included the idea of retributive (or penal) justice but has often embraced the idea of distributive or social justice. For example, Protestant philosopher Nicholas Wolterstorff grounds his political thought fundamentally in an account of justice, leaving 'common good' language aside. He defines justice as the 'righting of wrongs', and defines 'wrongs' as violations of fundamental rights.[63] Like other Protestants, he understands justice as a capacious term including, for example, social and economic justice.

But justice and the common good are not rival principles.[64] For Protestants like Wolterstorff, the content of justice overlaps considerably with what Catholics intend by the common good. Equally, in Catholic thought, principles of justice – such as commutative and distributive justice – are seen as integral components of the common good. Many specific requirements of the common good bring with them particular justice-claims: the 'rights' of workers to a fair share of the fruits of industry; the 'duty' of a school to care for students; the 'authority' of government to protect citizens from danger; and so forth (rights, duties and authority being among the key components of justice).

This last point draws our attention to the fact that justice is a pervasive idea, showing up in numerous different social contexts. Like the common good, it is not only a political norm. Political theorist Michael Walzer, for example, distinguishes diverse 'spheres of justice' in different social settings, such as family, market or state, insisting they not be conflated.[65] We can see claims of justice arising in, for example, close interpersonal relationships, where we might speak of not 'doing justice' to a friendship; or marriage, where we might properly affirm the 'rights' of marriage partners, such as the right to expect one's partner normally to cohabit. It also applies within many associations, such as businesses or trades unions, where the rights and duties of employers and employees need clearly defining; or a university, where there are disciplinary processes to protect the rights (and sometimes enforce the duties) of students and staff.

If we could speak *only* of 'justice' in such settings we would be completely missing the larger purpose being pursued. A marriage dominated by rival rights-claims is likely to be close to collapse; a university in which academic discussion is overshadowed by assertions of the 'right not to be offended' has lost sight of what rational inquiry is. But if we *never* spoke of justice in these settings we would be leaving many parties vulnerable and at risk of mistreatment. The primary responsibility for ensuring that justice is done in each of these social spheres lies with the parties themselves: employers, for example, should be willing to pay fair wages to their employees without having to be coerced by government.

None of the above instances, however, yet tell us what the political community's unique responsibility for justice amounts to. The general concept of 'justice' alone does not inform us what this is. Earlier I suggested that the purpose of the political community is 'the establishment of just laws and policies governing the public spaces of society'. It is the idea of 'public space' that identifies the unique 'sphere of justice' of the political community. Many individuals and associations realize justice in particular and limited spheres of society. But societies need an agency whose role is to ensure that the broader terrain in which everyone operates is organized justly. The precise scope of what is 'public' cannot be defined once and for all because the structure of societies changes so much over time. But we can understand 'public' as the space *between* the many particular agents making up society (individuals, associations and so forth). Sometimes called the 'public realm', it refers to an arena of reciprocal interaction, communication or exchange among these particular agents that is open to all and not owned by anyone (not even the state). It is a space of opportunity and enrichment, but also of possible threat and injustice. *Public* justice, then, comprises that broad swathe of justice-claims that arise in this realm of open interaction. Pursuing public justice involves protecting and facilitating the free action of individuals, associations and other agents as they operate in that space.

To relate the two key notions I have been unfolding: we can say that 'public justice' names that part of the common good that falls uniquely within the remit of the political community. Its scope can embrace many things, but let me at least specify further three basic categories of action it implies. Public justice calls, first, for the protection of the fundamental rights of individuals, such as civil rights, political rights and certain social and cultural rights. It might be thought that these are our particular 'possessions', things we can enjoy 'privately'. But rights only have meaning in the context of human relationships, where individuals may experience vulnerability and so need protection. We have come to speak of the most important of these rights as 'human rights'. The term refers to essential human interests and needs (physical security, personal liberty, access to biological needs, for example) that merit very strong legal protection by political communities. Only political communities have the capacity to guarantee these. The set of rights to be secured by the state will also include rights of individuals that might be threatened by the associations in which they participate (for example, children suffering parental abuse; women being denied equal pay for equal work; breaches of natural justice in university or church courts). States can indeed legitimately intervene in such associations in order to defend such individual rights. They may do so because we deem a certain category of minimum rights to be enjoyed by people irrespective of their associational memberships and so meriting public protection. Spheres of justice are not islands of immunity.

Second, public justice requires the protection of the realm of 'civil society'. This includes defining and securing the just legal rights and autonomy of many associations. These are the associations needed by humans in order to secure their basic needs, unleash their creative potentials or permit their flourishing in many other ways: families, neighbourhoods, educational and economic organizations, cultural and religious associations, and so forth. (Chapter 7 discusses one species of associational rights.)

Third, public justice calls for the securing of the requirements of public space itself. Individuals and associations need large, stable and fair arenas of public interaction within which they can pursue their own very diverse purposes, separately or together. This can require a wide range of conditions, such as public resources (health services), institutions (courts), infrastructures (digital communications), networks of exchange (markets) and more. In these areas, political communities must often take the lead in laying down minimum conditions of justice, even when they must cooperate with and depend on the initiatives and resources of many individuals and other associations in delivering them.

Public justice is thus a potentially very broad mandate, the detailed implications of which can never be fully specified in advance. Like other basic political norms such as liberty, equality or order, its specific demands have to be forged out of the concrete circumstances of particular societies. It is also a prime example of what philosophers have called an 'essentially contested concept':[66] its meaning rests on a range of deeper convictions about human dignity, social order or morality over which there will, in conditions of deep diversity, inevitably be profound disagreement. What public justice requires will thus be a primary issue of debate in a plural society. Democracy will be animated, often noisily, by contending visions of what public justice (or some other political norm) requires, some of which will be shaped by one or other faith. A key part of the argument of this book is that public justice itself demands ample public space for the articulation of such contending visions. It is thus not only a substantive norm in its own right but also a 'hospitable' one, securing an arena in which its own meaning and validity must be up for debate. I develop that point further in Chapters 3 and 4.

Conclusion

In this chapter I have proposed that we understand 'democracy' as the channel through which the people take an active share in the pursuit of the normative purpose of the political community. Because the political community includes 'the people' as an integral component, democracy is a dynamic partnership between the institutions of state and all citizens. All must have opportunities to engage (if they wish and are able to) in the demanding, difficult, frustrating but noble common pursuit of its central purpose, often against powerful forces and interests – including 'popular' ones – that would distort or thwart it. Because the political community embraces the entire citizenry as participating members, state institutions must be prepared, indeed structurally required, to exercise co-responsibility with the people for the discernment and pursuit of public justice. They must not merely reluctantly concede the people's input but actively solicit it. This implies entitlements for citizens to participate in the choice of leaders and in the ongoing shaping of government policy. The *point* of those rights to participation is to allow each citizen to join in discerning the central mandate of the political community. Equally, citizens – jointly and severally – stand under a shared duty to contribute to that essential task. It is this shared institutional vocation, not some supposed prior individual right to self-expression or self-determination, that most deeply grounds our democratic rights.

My argument may strike some as hopelessly high-minded, far removed from the real, messy motivations of most citizens. Isn't the reality of democracy overwhelmingly a competition for personal or group advantage – a relentless clash of all-pervasive 'interests'? Or, if that is thought to be too vulgar a notion, isn't it about the more noble goal of an 'ordered pursuit of our individually chosen plans of life' – as some contemporary liberals put it? I submit that in relatively stable liberal democracies like the UK, these assumptions are empirically questionable as well as normatively impoverished. This is not only because many voters, activists and public officials actually do sometimes seek goals going beyond these narrow individual horizons, but also because the institutional framework of the political community itself serves to some degree to contain private interest and corral it into beneficial collective goals. The 'visible hand' of the political community can sometimes discipline the pursuit of narrow self-interest and steer people that bit closer to a common good. The remarkable degree of compliance with COVID-19 regulations in the months after lockdown, even in the face of profound personal loss, is one exceptional example.[67] An account of democracy that is both normatively and empirically adequate must reckon with both poles of this dynamic. It must attend to the full spectrum of potential human performances, from narrow self-interest to impressive self-sacrifice. It must resist sliding either into naive optimism or defeatist cynicism about the possibilities of justice that even our flawed democratic institutions might afford.

Democracy is one element of the political community, naming not the whole of a political system but one of its parts. A better name for the whole is 'constitutional democracy'. A just constitutional framework will establish robust and accessible structures of democratic representation and participation, but it will also specify many *other* necessary features of the system, including the proper *limits* on democracy. In a just political order, constitutional government – government under law – is more foundational than democratic government, even though the latter is often the means by which the former is attained and sustained.[68]

This chapter has laid initial foundations for a theological account of constitutional democracy. The next chapter develops them further by exploring how the Christian political tradition has birthed three distinct and mutually reinforcing arguments for a certain kind of constitutional democracy. Each construes democratic institutions as one component of a larger constitutional framework orientated to justice and the common good.

Notes

(Websites accessed 5/12/20)

1 See www.hansardsociety.org.uk/publications/reports/audit-of-political-engage ment-16. Emphasis added. The report found that people's opinion of the UK system of governing is the lowest for 15 years; people are more pessimistic about the country's problems and more willing to entertain radical solutions; feelings of political powerlessness are intensifying (3).

2 See Hansard Society, *Audit*, 18.

3 Kenneth L. Grasso, 'Beyond Liberalism: Human Dignity, the Free Society and the Second Vatican Council', in Kenneth L. Grasso et al., eds, *Catholicism, Liberalism and Communitarianism* (Lanham, MD: Rowman & Littlefield, 1995), 30.

4 This is not to be confused with the European political movement of that name, which I discuss in Chapter 8.

5 The term used by David Cameron when criticizing the Church of England's General Synod for narrowly voting against a measure on women bishops in 2012. See Jerome Taylor and Nigel Morris, '"Get with the Programme": David Cameron condemns Church of England Decision to block Women Bishops', *The Independent* (21 November 2012). My point is not to oppose women bishops but to question the legitimacy of a sitting prime minister using the platform of parliament to attack a religious body for following its own lights on a doctrinal matter.

6 Stephen Carter, *The Dissent of the Governed: A Meditation on Law, Religion, and Loyalty* (Cambridge, MA: Harvard University Press, 1998).

7 Stanley Hauerwas, 'The Democratic Policing of Christianity', in *Despatches from the Front: Theological Engagements with the Secular* (Durham, NC: Duke University Press, 1994), 91–106.

8 Mark Juergensmeyer, Dinah Griego and John Soboslai, *God in the Tumult of the Global Square: Religion in Global Civil Society* (Oakland, CA: University of California Press, 2015); Eduardo Mendieta and Jonathan VanAntwerpen, eds, *The Power of Religion in the Public Sphere* (New York: Columbia University Press, 2011); John Micklethwait and Adrian Wooldridge, *God is Back: How the Global Rise of Faith is Changing the World* (London: Penguin, 2009).

9 Scott Thomas, *The Global Resurgence of Religion and the Transformation of International Relations: The Struggle for the Soul of the Twenty-First Century* (London: Palgrave Macmillan, 2005).

10 Philip J. Costopoulos, 'Introduction', in Larry Diamond, Marc F. Plattner and Philip J. Costopoulos, eds, *World Religions and Democracy* (Baltimore, MD: Johns Hopkins University Press, 2005), ix–x. Emphasis added.

11 Mark Lilla, *The Stillborn God: Religion, Politics, and the Modern West* (New York: Alfred A. Knopf, 2007), 4.

12 On Catholic contributions, see Samuel P. Huntington, 'Religion and the

Third Wave', *National Interest* 24 (Summer 1991); George Weigel, *The Final Revolution: The Resistance Church and the Collapse of Communism* (Oxford: Oxford University Press, 1992). On Protestantism, see Robert D. Woodberry and Timothy S. Shah, 'The Pioneering Protestants', in Diamond et al., eds, *World Religions and Democracy*, 117–31.

13 See Diamond et al., eds, *World Religions and Democracy*.

14 Graham Maddox, *Religion and the Rise of Democracy* (London: Routledge, 1996), 12.

15 See Nancy T. Ammerman and Grace Davie, 'Is religion bad for Democracy?', *The Conversation* (28 June 2018), https://theconversation.com/is-religion-bad-for-democracy-97351.

16 Nicholas Wolterstorff, *The Mighty and the Almighty: An Essay in Political Theology* (Cambridge: Cambridge University Press, 2012), 8.

17 John Rawls, *Political Liberalism* (New York: Columbia University Press, 1996), 12.

18 Jacques Maritain, *Man and the State* (Chicago, IL: Chicago University Press, 1951), 108–46. The Charter would amount to a 'democratic secular faith'.

19 This is reproduced, with commentaries, in Miroslav Volf, Ghazi bin Muhammad and Melissa Yarrington, eds, *A Common Word: Muslims and Christians on Loving God and Neighbor* (Grand Rapids, MI: Eerdmans, 2010).

20 Lilla, *Stillborn God*, 4–5.

21 Charles Taylor, *A Secular Age* (Cambridge, MA: Harvard University Press, 2007).

22 Habermas, 'Religion and the Public Sphere', *European Journal of Philosophy* 14.1 (2006), 15.

23 See Peter Wehner, 'There is no Christian Case for Trump', *The Atlantic* (30 January 2020), www.theatlantic.com/ideas/archive/2020/01/there-no-christian-case-trump/605785/.

24 Shaun Walker, 'Orbán deploys Christianity with a Twist to tighten Grip in Hungary', *The Guardian* (14 July 2019), www.theguardian.com/world/2019/jul/14/viktor-orban-budapest-hungary-christianity-with-a-twist.

25 See Elizabeth Prodmorou, 'The Ambivalent Orthodox', in Diamond et al., eds, *World Religions and Democracy*, 137.

26 Dom Phillips, 'Evangelical Christians in Brazil resolve to "bring Jesus" to Carnival Revelers', *The Guardian* (26 February 2020), www.theguardian.com/world/2020/feb/26/evangelical-christians-in-brazil-resolve-to-bring-jesus-to-carnival-revelers.

27 Paul Berman, 'The Philosopher of Islamic Terror', *The New York Times Magazine* (23 March 2003); Philip Lewis and Sadek Hamid, *British Muslims: New Directions in Islamic Thought, Creativity and Activism* (Edinburgh: Edinburgh University Press, 2018), chapter 3.

28 Azeem Ibrahim, 'Modi's Slide Toward Autocracy', *FP* (13 July 2020), https://foreignpolicy.com/2020/07/13/modi-india-hindutva-hindu-nationalism-autocracy/.

29 See Judd Birdsall, Jane Lindsay and Emma Tomalin, eds, *Toward Religion-Attentive Foreign Policy: A Report on an Anglo-American Dialogue* (University of Leeds, 2015).

30 The term alludes to Richard Rorty, 'Religion as a Conversation-stopper', in Richard Rorty, *Philosophy and Social Hope* (London: Penguin, 1999), 168–74. Rorty later modified his position.

31 'Introduction: Beyond Power Politics', in Douglas Johnston and Cynthia Sampson, eds, *Religion, the Missing Dimension of Statecraft* (New York: Oxford University Press, 1994), 5.

32 See www.bmsd.org.uk/.

33 See www.islamic-foundation.org.uk/ and https://mpacuk.org/.

34 New York: Charles Scribner's Sons, 1944.

35 London: Geoffrey Bles, 1945.

36 Chicago, IL: University of Chicago Press, 1951.

37 Notre Dame, IN: University of Notre Dame Press, 1993 (1951).

38 Pope Paul VI, *Gaudium et Spes* (1965), available from www.vatican.va/archive/hist_councils/ii_vatican_council/documents/vat-ii_const_19651207_gaudium-et-spes_en.html.

39 See, for example, John De Gruchy, *Christianity and Democracy* (Cambridge: Cambridge University Press, 1995); Oliver O'Donovan, *The Ways of Judgment* (Grand Rapids, MI: Eerdmans, 2005); Franklin I. Gramwell, *Politics as a Christian Vocation: Faith and Democracy Today* (Cambridge: Cambridge University Press, 2005); Jean Bethke Elshtain, *Sovereignty: God, State, and Self* (New York: Basic Books, 2008); Eric Gregory, *Politics and the Order of Love: An Augustinian Ethic of Democratic Citizenship* (Chicago, IL: University of Chicago Press, 2008); Graham Ward, *The Politics of Discipleship: Becoming Postmaterial Citizens* (London: SCM Press, 2009); Nicholas Wolterstorff, *Understanding Liberal Democracy: Essays in Political Philosophy*, ed. Terence Cuneo (Oxford: Oxford University Press, 2012); Luke Bretherton, *Resurrecting Democracy* (Cambridge: Cambridge University Press, 2015); *Christ and the Common Life: Political Theology and the Case for Democracy* (Grand Rapids, MI: Eerdmans, 2019).

40 Harold Lasswell, *Politics: Who Gets What, When, and How* (New York: Meridian, 1958 [1936]).

41 See Nick Spencer and Jonathan Chaplin, eds, *God and Government* (London: SPCK, 2009).

42 'Review' of James K. A. Smith, *Awaiting the King: Reforming Public Theology* (Grand Rapids, MI: Baker Academic, 2017), *International Journal of Systematic Theology* 20.2 (2020), 280–1.

43 The relationship between 'the people' construed as a body of citizens and 'the nation' understood as a cultural or ethnic community raises distinct issues that I do not directly address in this book.

44 See, for example, Stanley Fish, *The Trouble with Principle* (Cambridge, MA: Harvard University Press, 1999).

45 My target here is a leading conception of democracy operative in liberal political cultures and in public discourse, rather than the sophisticated conceptions espoused by philosophical liberals.

46 This is close to a Hobbesian view. Some versions of liberalism, such as Locke's, recognize natural moral constraints holding prior to the establishment of the political community – for Locke, 'natural rights', with which people are equally endowed by God. See Jeremy Waldron, *God, Locke and Equality: Christian Foundations in Locke's Political Thought* (Cambridge: Cambridge University Press, 2002).

47 Oliver O'Donovan, 'Response to Respondents: Behold the Lamb', *Studies in Christian Ethics* 11.2 (1998), 99.

48 See David T. Koyzis, *Political Visions and Illusions: A Survey and Christian*

Critique of Contemporary Ideologies, 2nd edn (Downers Grove, IL: InterVarsity Press, 2019), chapter 5. Koyzis endorses democracy as 'structure' but rejects it as a 'creed', which he terms 'democratism'.

49 Bretherton, *Christ and the Common Life*, 463.

50 Anthony Black shows that there was no 'natural affinity between Christianity and hereditary monarchy, including its absolutist variant' and asserts that 'there was no less a potential connection between Christianity and republicanism' ('Christianity and Republicanism: From St. Cyprian to Rousseau', *American Political Science Review* 91.3 (1997), 647, 654).

51 In the encyclical letter *Rerum Novarum*, www.vatican.va/content/leo-xiii/en/encyclicals/documents/hf_l-xiii_enc_15051891_rerum-novarum.html (§§ 49–51).

52 See David T. Koyzis, *We Answer to Another: Authority, Office, and the Image of God* (Eugene, OR: Pickwick, 2014), chapters 5, 6.

53 See Jürgen Moltmann, 'Covenant or Leviathan? Political Theology for Modern Times', *Scottish Journal of Theology* 47.1 (1994), 19–41.

54 Jacques Maritain, *Man and the State* (Chicago, IL: University of Chicago Press, 1951), 13.

55 Edmund Burke, *Selected Writings and Speeches*, ed. Peter J. Stanlis (Washington, DC: Regnery Gateway, 1963), 394.

56 See Alasdair MacIntyre, 'Natural Law as Subversive: The Case of Aquinas', *Journal of Medieval and Early Modern Studies* 26.1 (1996), 61–83.

57 On the common good, see Nicholas Townsend, 'Government and social infrastructure', in Nick Spencer and Jonathan Chaplin, eds, *God and Government* (London: SPCK, 2009), 108–33.

58 *Gaudium et Spes*, www.vatican.va/archive/hist_councils/ii_vatican_council/documents/vat-ii_const_19651207_gaudium-et-spes_en.html.

59 A definition offered by Jacques Maritain is even more comprehensive. See *Man and the State*, 11–12.

60 This is a goal of the ecumenical movement 'Together for the Common Good', https://togetherforthecommongood.co.uk/. See Nicholas Sagovsky and Peter McGrail, eds, *Together for the Common Good: Towards a National Conversation* (London: SCM Press, 2015).

61 Pope John Paul II, *Sollicitudo Rei Socialis* (1987), www.vatican.va/content/john-paul-ii/en/encyclicals/documents/hf_jp-ii_enc_30121987_sollicitudo-rei-socialis.html, §38. Emphasis original. The theme is powerfully reaffirmed in Pope Francis, *Fratelli Tutti* (2020), www.vatican.va/content/francesco/en/encyclicals/documents/papa-francesco_20201003_enciclica-fratelli-tutti.html.

62 See Jonathan Chaplin, 'Subsidiarity and Social Pluralism', in Michelle Evans and Augusto Zimmerman, eds, *Global Perspectives on Subsidiarity* (Dordrecht: Springer, 2014), 65–84.

63 *Justice: Rights and Wrongs* (Princeton, NJ: Princeton University Press, 2008); *Journey Toward Justice: Personal Encounters in the Global South* (Grand Rapids, MI: Eerdmans 2013). Wolterstorff proposes an account of political authority on this basis: 'Accounting for the Political Authority of the State', in Nicholas Wolterstorff, *Understanding Liberal Democracy: Essays in Political Philosophy*, ed. Terence Cuneo (Oxford: Oxford University Press, 2012), 245–74. Philip D. Shadd builds a theory of legitimacy on a similar basis: *Understanding Legitimacy: Political Theory and Neo-Calvinist Social Thought* (Lanham, MD: Lexington, 2017).

64 See Jonathan Chaplin, '"Justice," the "Common Good," and the Scope

of State Authority: Pointers to a Protestant-Thomist Convergence', in Manfred Svensson and David VanDrunen, eds, *Aquinas Among the Protestants* (Oxford: Wiley-Blackwell, 2018), 287–306.

65 Michael Walzer, *Spheres of Justice: A Defence of Pluralism and Equality* (Oxford: Blackwell, 1983).

66 William E. Connolly, *The Terms of Political Discourse*, 2nd edn (Oxford: Martin Robertson, 1974), chapter 1.

67 I thus disagree with David Runciman that the most important thing revealed by the pandemic is that 'politics is ultimately about power and order'. David Runciman, 'Coronavirus has not suspended Politics – it has revealed the Nature of Power', *The Guardian* (27 March 2020), www.theguardian.com/commentisfree/2020/mar/27/coronavirus-politics-lockdown-hobbes.

68 Bretherton's account of 'democratic politics' in *Christ and the Common Life* focuses on democracy as a set of 'relational practices'. His account is broader than mine in that it includes aspects of 'common life' that I see as outside the political community proper, but narrower in that it does not deal at length with 'statecraft' (32–4). I try to integrate the two dimensions.

2

Recasting Constitutional Democracy

Introduction

The resounding cry of frustrated Leavers in the aftermath of the 2016 EU referendum was that 'the will of the people' must prevail. Remainers seemed not to have got the memo and were refusing to bow to the 'sovereignty' of 'the people'. The people had 'instructed' the government to 'get Brexit done' but the Remainer 'elite', especially those in parliament, were refusing to accept the legitimacy of the largest expression of popular will in modern Britain, using every procedural trick in the book to thwart it.

I put these terms in scare quotes not to mock them but to flag up that the meaning of all of them is contestable – as were key terms in the Remainer counter-narrative. What was obscured in the divisive rancour of the Brexit debates was that two distinct and legitimate elements of the British democratic system – the popular and the representative – were being pitted against each other. Leavers saw the referendum as an expression of 'popular' democracy – the direct expression of a majority of individual voters' wills (if not quite 'the mind of the nation' since the nation as a whole seemed to be in two minds). Because the government had promised to follow the will of the '17.4 million', Leavers assumed that this expression should prevail over the hesitations of a few dozen disgruntled parliamentarians living in denial. Remainers (mostly) recognized the procedural validity of the vote but looked to parliament – the nation's 'representatives' – to determine what it actually meant. The 'in-out' referendum, they insisted, hardly settled the issue of how we should actually leave the EU or the terms of our future relationship with it. They urged that, in the British constitutional tradition, it is parliament – elected by the people to do a job on their behalf – that is finally responsible for deciding on the practical shape of the 'will of the people' (as indeed it was, and remains).

Lurking beneath the debate lies a deeper one: what is 'the will of the people' anyway and what might it mean to assert its 'sovereignty'? Are contingent, shifting popular majorities the final authority on matters of justice and the common good?[1] Left unconstrained, might they not get things badly wrong or harm vulnerable minorities – as many black and minority ethnic citizens complained was occurring during the Brexit process itself? What exactly should the role of 'the people' be in shaping government policy?

My reply in this chapter is that *democracy must be tethered to the purpose of the political community.* I will affirm democracy robustly, while showing how it must be harnessed to a purpose beyond expressing mere collective will. In the previous chapter I proposed that the normative purpose of the political community is best captured in the term 'public justice' (while recognizing that others may propose different terms). I also argued that not only is the *object* of the political community's action public in character but also that the people is a public *subject*. This means that the purpose of the political community must be the people's own purpose – and vice versa. By virtue of being citizens, we are co-responsible with state institutions for the discernment and pursuit of public justice. The entitlement of the people to elect and exercise ongoing influence on their government confers upon the citizenry the possibility of exercising that demanding vocation and affords them effective institutional channels to do so. That, I argue, is the inestimable value of 'democracy' – which has little to do with 'sovereignty'. I will show that the Christian tradition, from which emerged the notorious 'divine right of kings', also yields a powerful 'divine right of citizens'. But the tradition also holds that the purposes of citizenship are not sovereignly decided by autonomous human will. A just constitutional order must support democratic rights but much else besides, including constraints on bare democratic will. The 'will of the people' must be tested against the bar of justice.

This, at any rate, is what I think emerges from a complex and often faltering trajectory of Christian political thought. As noted, the preponderance of global Christian opinion today regards democracy as, at least, not incompatible with Christian faith and, more likely, either as fully consonant with it or as an essential contemporary implication of it. The old adage still wheeled out by some Christian commentators that 'the Bible doesn't prescribe any particular form of government' is a lazy attempt to evade the cumulative claims of the tradition's reflection on its authoritative texts and historical experience. A Christianity that *merely* says 'Christians can be faithful under any form of government' is exactly the kind of faith the Chinese government wants Christians in Hong Kong to embrace (which many of them are not doing). As Luke Bretherton puts it, 'Christians do not need democracy to practice their faith, but democracy enshrines some central Christian commitments, and so, as a judgment of practical reason, democracy should be an aspirational feature of political order for Christians.'[2]

Historically, a wide variety of considerations in favour of democracy have been advanced on Christian grounds.[3] Amid this diversity, three distinct justifications of democracy had crystallized by the mid-twentieth century. *Consent* theories affirm that God is the final source of authority but holds that God has also granted to the people rights to determine who should occupy the office of political authority. Divine authorization is compatible with, indeed requires, the expression of popular consent to those officeholders. *Participatory* theories are concerned not so much with the people's rights as with their capacities. They endorse the principle of popular election and influence as an expression of the general human potential for responsible cooperative action. Democracy is a conduit for the fulfilment of a capacity rooted in created human nature. *Defensive* theories are driven not mainly by a concern with people's rights or capacities but by a fear about their vulnerabilities. Popular influence is necessary as a check on the unavoidable tendency of sinful holders of political authority to abuse their office and oppress the people. Democracy is one vital constitutional restraint on the corruption of power. I will show how these theories strongly endorse democracy, but not as a stand-alone aspiration. Rather they locate it within a larger understanding of the purpose of the political community and the institutional and constitutional requirements for that purpose to be properly pursued. They favour not just democracy but 'constitutional democracy'. I offer glimpses of the historical sources from which they emerged, while focusing on the content of their claims.

Consent theories

What I am calling consent theories had already begun to take shape by the late middle ages but were most powerfully developed in the Reformation.[4] These theories give a theological grounding for popular consent and representation but always within a wider view of just government limited by divine and natural law. The theory rejects both an authoritarian 'divine right of kings' and, implicitly, the later doctrine of untrammelled 'popular sovereignty'.

Consent theory starts from the long-standing Christian conviction of the ultimately divine origin of the office of political authority. The right to exercise coercive legal authority over other humans derives finally from God's supreme authority over all things. A role for the people is, however, necessary in the authorization of those who will exercise it. Joan Lockwood O'Donovan identifies a 'dual appointment' theory affirming both divine appointment of rulers and popular endorsement of such appointment.[5] This in turn reflects a theory of 'dual representation'. On the one hand, the ruler acts as representative ('vicar') of God, ensuring respect for divine authority in the human community, while always holding such authority conditionally upon his conformity to basic injunctions of divine and natural law. On the other hand, the ruler also represents the whole community: 'His acts had to embody the common judgment of the people, as handed down in custom and statute law, in communal traditions of right that protected not only personal life, sustenance and property, but other divinely prescribed moral and religious duties, and the freedoms and privileges of the church.'[6] The 'common judgment of the people' must therefore be attended to.

This understanding of dual authorization was developed in contrasting directions. In a conservative version, the 'designation' theory, popular consent is seen as essential to the legitimation of political rulers, but amounts to no more than a recognition (designation) of their divine appointment. Through consent, however expressed, the people confirm, rather than confer, the authority of those in office.[7] The designation version does not yet prescribe a specific method either of divine appointment or of the expression of popular consent. It is, for example, compatible with recognition of an immediate divine appointment (on the model of the Israelite monarchy, where prophets anointed kings), or with popular acclamation of a monarch claiming title through a providentially guided operation of heredity. But it is also compatible with modern popular election.

A more radical 'transmission' (or 'translation') theory also asserts the ultimately divine origin of political authority but holds that God has transmitted the inherent right of self-government to the people. This version of the theory holds that the people's right to exercise political authority exists prior to the formation of any particular polity. While still ultimately deriving from God, such authority is held by the people collectively, until they transfer it to an approved agent. This does not imply that the only permissible method of choosing successive rulers is popular election: the people may decide to institute (or recognize) a monarchy, an aristocracy or some 'mixed' polity. The implication, however, is that the people retain the right to change either the form of the polity or, if they were to violate the polity's divinely prescribed purpose, the current office-holders. But such rights are always pursuant to, and derive their force from, that purpose: 'God invests self-sufficient human associations with the right to establish governments *to serve the common good* ...'[8]

Sixteenth- and seventeenth-century Calvinists and Puritans developed a highly influential reading of the transmission theory that appealed to Old Testament accounts of the covenant between God and Israel.

An explosive version appeared in the Huguenot tract *Vindiciae Contra Tyrannos.*[9] This proposed a double covenant: the first holding between God on the one hand and ruler and people on the other; the second holding between ruler and people. In the first, God invests rulers with authority to rule, and the people with authority to choose their ruler, both conditional upon their obedience to divine and natural law. In the second, the ruler promises to govern the people justly and the people to obey God's just laws. As *Vindiciae* puts it, strikingly: 'It is the people that establishes kings, gives them kingdoms, and approves their selection by its vote. For God willed that every bit of authority held by kings should come *from the people, after Him* ...'[10] Modern democrats might note that this was written in 1579, a century before John Locke's *Two Treatises of Government* and two centuries before Jean-Jacques Rousseau's *Social Contract.*

In Christian consent thinking, popular consent is not merely a desirable but also a necessary condition for the legitimacy of particular office-holders (on the designation theory), or of a particular polity (on the transmission theory). The former can be expressed by means of periodic elections, while the latter case is exceptional and is called for only when a new polity is founded. In either case, the authority of the *office* of political authority does not proceed from popular will itself but is grounded finally in divine authority, however that has been mediated. The obligation to obey derives its moral force ultimately from this transcendent source – even if mediated via humans. The consent theory does not assert that the people possess a 'radical constituent power': the office of political authority is not conjured from autonomous human will. The political community is a natural institution rooted in creation and harbouring an intrinsic normative purpose to which the people are bound (as I argued in the previous chapter). The people are assumed to be consenting to this purpose when they establish a new polity, choose officers within an existing one or give shape to the central purpose and specific policies of the polity. A just constitution, then, must be framed so as to provide for the people's voice, to direct that voice towards the proper end of the political community and to steer it away from corruption, self-interest or other vices.

Participatory theories

The participatory and defensive justifications for democracy are neatly summed up in the two clauses of Reinhold Niebuhr's celebrated maxim: 'man's capacity for justice makes democracy possible; but man's inclination to injustice makes democracy necessary'.[11] Participatory theories proceed from the first clause. They endorse democracy as an implication of a general human potential for the exercise of responsible freedom and social cooperation. The opportunity for political participation, including the expression of consent to political authority, is viewed as an arena in which one dimension of a divinely created human nature – our capacity to work collaboratively towards the common good – comes to expression. Because human nature is not only individual but social, the shared exercise of that capacity is itself a condition of the common good. It is not that the people simply lend their support to some account of the common good given by others (such as rulers or clergy), but that the common good consists partly in them discerning what it is. The common good is not only a destination but a journey.

I noted that the consent theory is compatible with very different conceptions of the method by which popular consent might be expressed. That includes different conceptions of the extent of the electorate. The participatory theory reaches a more radical conclusion by affirming the *equal* possession of the capacity for justice by all human beings. This implies not simply a generalized 'spiritual equality' or 'equal dignity' but the existence of concrete rights to share in the exercise of political power.[12] The logic of the theory calls for a substantial suite of rights and opportunities for citizens not only to vote but also to exercise meaningful, continuous influence on the government via numerous means. Its logic leads to support both for universal franchise and for multiple avenues for popular influence on state policy. The theory does not, however, imply a radical model of direct democracy in which 'the people' assumes the role of legislation and policymaking through a continuous process of popular referendums. That would effectively collapse 'the government' into 'the people' – a fatal flaw in the Leavers' 'will of the people' argument. Nor does it imply that the demands arising from popular participation are assumed to be automatically just. It recognizes that the people, and not only the government, needs to be restrained.

Among the theological arguments typically advanced in support of the participatory theory, two are prominent. One is the doctrine of human beings as equal bearers of the *imago Dei* – where 'imaging' means 'representing God in creation' – and so equally endowed with a vocation to exercise social responsibility. The more formative source turned out to be the vision of the Church as a spiritual community of equals – in which that equal divine image is being restored. This, participationists argue, was practically enacted in the egalitarian organization of the early Church and later communities modelled on it.[13] In the middle ages, however, the memory of the Church as a participatory fellowship of equals was pushed to the margins in favour of what has been called the 'descending theme' of hierarchical authority.[14] But it was never entirely absent and it continued to be appealed to as an alternative source of participatory ideas, especially in the monasteries. Such an appeal was powerfully revived in Protestant covenant theology.[15]

Following a long and tortuous journey, the conviction eventually began to emerge that each person stands equally responsible before God for the proper discernment of justice and the common good and is thus equally entitled to participate in political affairs. Historians have often remarked that the Reformation served to infuse European society with ideas such as the equality of callings (for which the initial cue was the Reformers' insistence on 'the priesthood of all believers'), individual freedom of conscience and the right to participate in church governance. When such notions started to spill over into politics, they served to nurture trends strongly conducive to democracy. The story of the Puritan contribution to local democracy in New England has been well told. More forceful Protestant affirmations of the participatory idea appear in radical egalitarian movements such as the Levellers and the Diggers.[16] Graham Maddox captures the emerging vision thus:

> In the Puritan congregation each person was worthy of full participation in discussion not merely out of respect for her or his worth before God, but also because each person in a gathering in Christ's name could be a vessel for the outpouring of the Spirit – each could be moved by God to add something genuinely revealing, or revealed, to the collective understanding ...[17]

Robert Dahl draws out the political upshot of such a view: 'all men were equal not only in the eyes of God but equally qualified to understand the word of God, to participate in church government, and by extension to govern the commonwealth'.[18] Bretherton shows how the New Testament injunction that 'There is neither Jew nor Gentile, neither slave nor free, nor is there male and female, for you are all one in Christ Jesus' (Gal. 3.28, NIV), served to corrode the hierarchical foundations of pagan society, and later (especially in the Reformation) the inherited ranks of medieval society.[19] Membership of the political community could no longer be conditional upon property holdings, kinship, ethnicity, class, status, gender or other characteristics irrelevant to the shared pursuit of common goods:

> Democratic politics entails the radical extension of who is considered capable and worthy of being political agents, aiming as it does to form a common life through ensuring that political agency is distributed as

widely as possible. [It] thereby extends politics from being the preserve of the few to something undertaken by the many for the good of the whole.[20]

A distinctive modern source of the participatory theory is the Catholic movement known as 'Personalism' flourishing in early twentieth-century France. Founded by Emmanuel Mounier, it was influential on the social philosophy of Jacques Maritain and other Neo-Thomist political philosophers and left a distinct imprint on papal social thought, including that of John Paul II. Personalism affirms equal human dignity, the human rights flowing from that dignity and the humanizing potential of widespread popular participation in society generally – in social movements and trades unions, for example. In dry prose that conceals its far-reaching claim, *Gaudium et Spes*, influenced by Personalism, offers the most explicit official endorsement of democracy by the Catholic Church to date:

> It is in full conformity with human nature that there should be juridico-political structures providing all citizens in an ever better fashion and without any discrimination with the practical possibility of freely and actively taking part in the establishment of the juridical foundations of the political community and in the direction of public affairs, in fixing the terms of reference of the various public bodies and in the election of political leaders.[21]

Democracy, in other words, is a mandate of divinely created human nature. The participatory theory suggests a position that might plausibly be termed 'populist'. But in view of the upsurge of divisive nationalist and nativist variants of populism today,[22] it is essential to make clear that the theory resists any attempt to narrow 'the people' down to 'people like us' ('real people'): those sharing our culture, economic interests, ethnicity, race, religion – or to define our identity in terms of common enemies. Such populisms effectively deny the equal standing of all citizens within the political community. My notion of the political community champions the dignity and authority of the whole *populus* and asserts its radically inclusive character.[23]

Defensive theories[24]

Whereas the participatory theory appeals chiefly to the enduring potential for goodness in human nature – 'man's capacity for justice' in Niebuhr's words – the defensive theory places equal or greater emphasis on human fallenness and corruptibility – 'man's inclination to injustice'. Democracy is justified as a necessary check on the inescapable tendency of fallible office-holders to abuse their power. Niebuhr, still the best modern representative of the theory, states it succinctly:

> If men are inclined to deal unjustly with their fellows, the possession of power aggravates this inclination. This is why irresponsible and uncontrolled power is the greatest source of injustice. The democratic techniques of a free society place checks upon the power of the ruler and administrator and thus prevent it from becoming vexatious.[25]

Niebuhr's view of the function of democracy is not wholly negative. He recognizes its positive social role as 'a permanently valid form of social and political organization which does justice to two dimensions of human existence: to man's spiritual stature and his social character'.[26] His concern is to detach it from the failed liberal idealism by which it was defended in the first part of the twentieth century.[27] One of Niebuhr's central claims in his most influential work, *Moral Man and Immoral Society*,[28] was that human collectivities, especially larger bodies in possession of significant power, greatly amplify the tendency of individual humans to exploit each other. Government, holding the greatest concentration of power, must therefore be brought under the restraint of, among other things, the 'disciplines of democracy'. Such disciplines '[arm] the individual with political and constitutional power to resist the inordinate ambition of rulers, and to check the tendency of the community to achieve order at the price of liberty'.[29]

It has often been thought that defensive arguments lend themselves most readily to the support of conservative or authoritarian political theories driven by fear of anarchy. Yet Niebuhr's account shows how the doctrine of human sinfulness can equally challenge conservative, classical liberal and state socialist conceptions. Conservatives – 'undemocratic constitutionalists' – 'appreciate the necessity, but not the perils, of strong government' and thus 'allow the fear of anarchy to bear the fruit of connivance with tyranny'.[30] Niebuhr certainly endorses characteristic features of modern liberalism. Freedom of expression, for example, is important to allow the flourishing of human creativity, which would be stunted if the changing conceptions of justice engendered by different societies were allowed to rigidify.[31] The minimal state of classical liberalism, however, is as naive about the corruptions of human nature as is centralized socialism.[32]

According to the defensive theory, democracy is an indispensable constitutional restraint on the perennial temptation of political authorities to abuse their power. It is not the only one; advocates typically argue in favour of a wide range of such restraints. As with the two previous theories, an argument for popular consent serves as one element of a larger constitutional theory. The 'democracy' that Niebuhr seeks to 'vindicate' in *The Children of Light* is really a whole political system including the protection of a wide range of civil, political and economic rights. Understood thus, the theory argues that to establish democratic elections *alone*, without further constitutional checks, would carry serious dangers since the people are, like their rulers, also subject to corruption.

Another important feeder of the defensive theory is liberation theology. It is true that liberation theology also favours a radical variant of participationism, flowing from its commitment to transformative, even revolutionary, popular political action. Resisting the widespread economic and political oppression of late twentieth-century Latin American states, the movement advanced a radical conception of the people – exemplified paradigmatically in 'the poor' – and called for a new assertion of popular participation in which the people would take their destiny in their own hands. The grassroots 'base ecclesial communities' in which the movement was originally birthed pressed for maximum lay participation within the Catholic Church. Liberationists accordingly demanded maximum participation for the people in politics, both to resist oppressive rule and to construct a new political order reflective of equality, justice and the common good.

Yet liberationism can equally be seen as fed by a desire to defend the people against oppressive political systems. Such a desire comes to the fore in the work of South African liberation theologian Charles Villa-Vicencio as he reflects on the political structures of apartheid.[33] While earlier liberationists seemed impatient of impediments to the execution of popular democratic mandates (as the story of Nicaragua under the Sandinistas shows), Villa-Vicencio is fully alert to the need for such restraints. It is precisely the systematic abuse of governmental powers by the apartheid regime that leads him to espouse a robust framework of constitutional limitations on the will of the democratic 'majority' in parliament – which was, of course, the will of the white minority, ruthlessly enlisted by the National Party for racist ends. Having experienced first hand the degeneration of the doctrine of 'parliamentary sovereignty' into a brutally effective executive sovereignty in pre-democratic South

Africa, Villa-Vicencio argues that the establishment of the rule of law is indispensable to any just democracy.[34]

Towards an integrated account of constitutional democracy

All three justifications of democracy grasp core insights that remain eminently valid today. The consent theory shows how the people have a formal right to share in the appointment of political rulers (the 'divine right of citizens'). The participatory theory also proposes a normative theory, appealing not to the concept of authority but to the God-given human capacity for responsible political agency. The defensive theory, by contrast, mounts a prudential case for the people to be granted democratic rights in order to reduce the likelihood of tyranny, though without any illusions about the people's political virtues.

These three theories are mutually complementary. We might say that each makes up for limitations in the others. On its own, the consent theory fails to rule out an unacceptably restricted electorate. Equally, neither the participatory nor the defensive theory alone is able to generate an account of the source of political authority. The theories need to be integrated into a wider account. Such an account advocates a just, constitutional, fully representative and maximally participatory democracy. Popular consent to and influence upon particular office-holders are an essential ingredient, but the people as much as the government are conceived as standing under the duty to promote justice and the common good. The authority of this community ultimately derives from such a duty, against which the performance of both the institutions of state and the people is to be judged. Democracy, even standing on all three pillars, remains but one component, not the fount from which everything else springs.

The modern doctrine of 'popular sovereignty' plays no role in my account. I have affirmed the collective right of the people to appoint governing office-holders (or, exceptionally, to establish a new polity where one does not exist or has collapsed) and to share in the ongoing shaping of government policy. But it is misleading and unnecessary to refer to this as an expression of sovereignty. I am inclined to follow Maritain's exhortation, issued in the aftermath of fascism, that the term sovereignty has been so abused in modern political systems that it is probably best to lay it to rest.[35] The indispensable role of the people is adequately championed by affirming the importance of robust and representative processes of consent and participation.

Guidelines for constitutional democracy today

What implications might such an integrated account have for the shape of a contemporary constitutional democracy like the UK? If the central purpose of the political community is to be realized, there must be an ensemble of politico-legal institutions, forums and processes organized to that end, whereby state and people work together to discern and implement the requirements of (what I am calling) public justice. What might such an ensemble look like? Here are some suggested guidelines, offered not as straightforward deductions from the three theories just considered but as indicative prudential applications that comport well with them.

1 The ensemble of political-legal institutions, forums and processes making up the political community must be framed by an enforceable *constitution* that establishes, authorizes and limits them.[36] Such a constitutional order makes possible the pursuit of public justice by the various agents within the political community (the institutions of state and the people). It must also itself be just; it must embody principles of 'constitutional justice'.[37] The most fundamental of these is 'the rule of law', which means that all institutions of state are subject to the law (both constitutional law and other kinds) and can be effectively held to account if they breach it. It is impossible to overestimate the importance of this principle for a just constitutional democracy. To grasp its vital contribution to political justice, one only has to look at nations where the principle is weakly embedded – where there is widespread corruption, breaches of due process, or tax evasion; or where it is routinely set aside – where political opponents are silenced, jailed or assassinated.

2 Constitutional justice calls for a robust suite of *individual civil and political rights, liberties and duties*, as well as other protections against unjust treatment either from government or from elsewhere. Consider simply rights. These include 'political rights' (the rights of the people in their role as citizens): the right to vote, to stand for office, to campaign to change law or policy, and so forth. They also include 'civil rights', such as rights to freedom of conscience, expression, movement, assembly or association. Various other rights safeguard people's interests that derive from social standings other than citizenship, such as the right to marry or receive welfare benefits ('social rights'), the right to property and the right to trade ('economic rights'), and the right to have one's ethnic identity recognized for certain purposes ('cultural rights'). Many such rights need to be legally protected by the political community. Some deserve to be elevated to the status of 'constitutional rights'.

3 Among the political rights of citizens, the *right to vote* is of special importance. It affirms that the voice of every (eligible) citizen counts in deciding who will exercise the offices of legislator and governor within the political community. It is the point at which the people entrust to designated representatives the role of leadership in the pursuit of public justice. On my 'faith-attentive' model of democracy, what is being represented via the right to vote is not only the citizen's will nor even their 'interests', but their political convictions. If governing is about pursuing justice, the process of choosing governors must adequately reflect the people's convictions about justice. Indeed, it should encourage them to clarify such convictions if they lack them and then to express them in relevant forums. The process should not feed a self-referential politics of interest; in most liberal democracies, however, that is exactly what it currently does.

This point carries two important implications. First, it is the indispensable role of *political parties* to provide conduits for the articulation of the people's political convictions. Parties are not to be seen merely as 'coalitions of interests', electoral machines or instruments by which to organize a government (though they perform all such functions). If parties are to make their unique contribution to the political community's pursuit of public justice, they must position themselves first as associations of political conviction. This certainly involves them being attentive to a wide range of voices inside and outside the party as they formulate what those convictions are. That will require careful processes of listening, rather than the quick fixes of focus groups or opinion polls. Christian democratic pluralism enthusiastically endorses Margaret Thatcher's call for a 'conviction politics' (if not all her actual convictions). Parties should not constantly tack towards 'what the people want' – an inchoate idea that will forever elude their grasp – but declare openly what they believe and let the people decide whether they endorse those beliefs.

Second, a fundamental feature of the UK system systematically frustrates this objective. The first past the post (FPTP) *electoral system* used in the UK does not reward parties according to the clarity of their convictions but, to a considerable degree, according to the arbitrary fact of the geographical dispersal of their support.[38] The system has a built-in tendency to grossly distort actual votes cast by rewarding parties that enjoy high concentrations of support in individual constituencies with seriously disproportionate numbers of seats in the Westminster parliament. This is currently true for the Conservative and Labour parties in England and the SNP in Scotland. The system drastically under-represents parties whose support is dispersed across the country, such as the Liberal Democrats, the Green Party and UKIP/Brexit Party.

For example, in the general election of 2015, FPTP delivered the following egregious distortions. UKIP won 12.6 per cent of the vote but one seat; with proportional representation (PR) they would have won about 80. The Liberal Democrats won 8 per cent of the votes but 1.2 per cent of the seats (= 8); on PR they would have won about 50. The Greens won 3.8 per cent of the votes. On PR that would have given them about 25 seats; they won one. The Conservatives won 37 per cent of the vote but 51 per cent of the seats (= 331), giving them an overall parliamentary majority of 12; on PR they would have won about 240 seats, leaving them the largest party but unable to form a government alone. Labour won 30 per cent of the vote, but 36 per cent of the seats (= 232). On PR they would have won about 195. In Scotland, the SNP won 50 per cent of the votes but 95 per cent of the seats (= 56); on PR they would have won about 27.

This is a 'winner takes all' system in which securing a mere plurality (or the barest majority) of votes cast can be enough to secure the totality of government power. The result is that the political convictions of the millions of citizens who support parties whose voters are not geographically concentrated (including Conservatives and Labour in Scotland) are seriously under-represented in parliament. This is to treat such citizens with profound contempt. It is a fundamental violation of the norm of an inclusive political community. The solution is to introduce a form of PR ensuring that seats won are proportionate to votes cast. This is what most of the rest of Europe has done for decades and what the Scottish Parliament, Welsh Senedd and Northern Ireland Assembly have done for over 20 years. Given the value that continues to be attached to a link between MP and geographical constituency, a system should be chosen for the UK Parliament that retains such a link.[39]

PR would mean that parties could take the risk of declaring their convictions and be fairly rewarded (or punished) for doing so. Instead parties face powerful structural pressures either to concentrate on their 'core vote' (as in populisms of right or left), or alternatively to tack to 'the centre' (wherever that is), in order to squeak 'past the post' on the basis of a minority of the people's actual votes (as occurred in 2019 when an 80-seat Conservative majority was won with a mere 44 per cent of the vote). Under PR, every party's 'core vote' would be represented fairly. The outcome of the 2015 election (and most others) under PR would have radically changed the make-up of parliament and forced a coalition government, with likely very different – and undoubtedly much less divisive – outcomes regarding a possible EU referendum. This is standard fare in much of Europe, in most cases producing governments as stable as in the UK. A coalition outcome is, in effect, the majority of voters saying to parties: 'We can't trust any one of you to dominate government and insist you share power with someone else.'

The point of PR is not to satisfy some abstract arithmetical formula but to do justice to the convictions actually represented in the votes of real people – our fellow citizens. This is the only way to treat people's convictions with due respect and thus to signal that every citizen does, in fact, enjoy equal voice in the political community at this crucial moment of decision. PR is not a mere technical enthusiasm but the route by which a democratic system can truly respect the convictional diversity of the people.

4 Constitutional justice also calls for a far-reaching *diffusion of political power*. The defensive theory is especially alert to the dangers of an undue concentration of power in any part of the political community, whether executive, legislature, judiciary or any of their sub-units (such as the military or the bureaucracy); or in central national institutions, as against territorial sub-units; or in unrestrained popular majorities. Equally, the participatory theory affirms that such diffusion substantially increases the potential channels for positive citizens' influence. The consent theory, too, allows for multiple sites of popular consent and not simply a single plenary forum of 'the people' engaged in dramatic acts of collective self-assertion (such as a general election or referendum). Insofar as civil society organizations, political parties, professions, trades unions or towns and cities are accorded opportunities for effective representation, they also confer an indirect form of legitimacy on the system. The idea of a diffusion of power thus receives robust support from each pillar of democratic theory. It turns out to have wide-ranging implications.

a) First, there is the *vertical diffusion* of political authority across terri- torially distinct bodies. These might be regional: the three devolved administrations of the UK; American states; Canadian provinces; German *Lände*; and so forth. Or they might be local: various levels of municipal or 'parish' governance. In federal systems such as the USA, Canada, Switzerland or Australia, the powers of regional authorities are entrenched in the constitution (meaning they cannot be limited by ordinary statute). The constitution allocates specific powers to such tiers, as well as to central government. In unitary systems, the powers of lower tiers, such as those of devolved administrations in the UK, Dutch provinces and municipalities, or French regions, depart- ments and communes, are statutory. This means they are less secure and could in principle be revoked, yet they still serve to deconcentrate governmental power and offer platforms for political resistance to overweening central control. In the UK there is a strong case for further transfers of powers to devolved or regional governments and, especially, to local authorities or other conduits of popular representation (such as Citizens Assemblies). In the UK, local governments have been successively denuded of powers since the mid-twentieth century and that trend is urgently in need of reversal (as the high-handed and incompetent response of central government to COVID-19 testing and tracing revealed).

The case for a vertical diffusion of power is that each tier serves to inform, balance and restrain the others. Such a diffusion constrains potential abuses of power (the defensive case) and affords wider avenues of meaningful political participation than the national electoral level alone can (the participatory case). It can also be supported by two other arguments. One is that different sub-units can serve as sites of policy experimentation that might lead the way for others – 'innovations in public justice'. The other more radical one is that the political community itself can be seen as constituted out of the agreement of lower tiers. This latter argument often appeals to the empirical fact that, because the relevant lower unit – city, region, 'nation' – might have possessed a distinct political or cultural identity prior to the formation of the larger political community, it merits recognition and a degree of self-government.[40]

b) Second, there is the *functional diffusion* among the three main branches of state: executive, legislature and judiciary. This is known as the *separation of powers*, a modern application of what in classical thought is termed a 'mixed constitution'.[41] This also asserts the need for the three principal institutions of state to inform, balance and restrain each other. Each has a distinctive and necessary role to play in the processes whereby the purpose of the political community is advanced. The degree and manner of 'separation' varies widely across democratic constitutions. Here I focus on the British parliamentary tradition, noting four further implications.

The first implication tends to be the least remarked upon: the *leading role of the executive* in presenting legislation to parliament and in actually governing. This is *its* distinctive role in the larger constitutional arrangement. Parliament is a legitimating, deliberating and scrutinizing body, not a governing one – as became excruciatingly clear in the UK parliament's fraught attempts between 2016 and 2019 to prevent the government from ending up with a 'no deal' outcome in the first phase of Brexit negotiations (over the Withdrawal Agreement). It is essential that a polity can act decisively, cohesively and consistently and not be paralysed by endless constitutional gridlock, thereby frustrating its proper leadership of the political community's very purpose. The proper scope of executive power in this process must, however, be carefully circumscribed. Where such power is deployed oppressively, it is bound to evoke destabilizing counter-reactions – as in the Brexit process.

The second is that executive initiative in law-making must be subjected to the consent of popular representative assemblies (elected legislatures) – the principle of *parliamentary accountability*. Laws must be made by parliament not executive decree. This insistence was one of the fundamental achievements of the English Bill of Rights of 1689, although it has parallels in the history of other constitutional democracies.[42] It responds to the classical Christian injunction that rulers are not permitted to legislate in their own right or to construct novel laws out of their own head. Rather, such law (common and statute) should be representative of and expressive of the people's own sense of its common good and traditions of justice, insofar as these can be discerned.

The third implication of the separation of powers is that parliamentary accountability also applies to executive acts: the *accountability of government*. As the UK Supreme Court put it in the 'prorogation' case lost by the government in September 2019, this is the means whereby 'citizens are protected against the arbitrary exercise of executive power'.[43] It was just such executive overreach that Lord Hailsham, a prominent Conservative critic of the Labour government of the 1970s, had in his sights when he described the UK government as an 'elective dictatorship'.[44] The same principle was at stake in the UK Supreme Court case in 2017 over whether the executive could (on the basis of a supposed 'prerogative' power to conclude treaties) invoke the 'Article 50' procedure for withdrawal from the European Union on its own authority. The court ruled that it could not. True, only the government can govern; only it could convey the letter invoking Article 50 to Brussels. But the manner and scope of its executive actions must be effectively accountable to parliament.

The fourth implication of the separation of powers is the subjection of the executive and, in some jurisdictions, the legislature, to the scrutiny of the judiciary. *Judicial review* can mean, first, the subjection of *executive acts* to assessment by the courts: this was what was occurring in the two UK Supreme Court cases mentioned. It can also mean, second, the subjection of *laws* passed by elected legislatures to judicial assessment. This provision exists in, for example, the USA, where the Supreme Court determines whether a statute is in conformity to the constitution, and in a more limited way in Canada, where the Supreme

Court is empowered declare a law compatible with the constitution, such as the Charter of Rights and Freedoms. The UK Supreme Court can issue a 'declaration of incompatibility' of a law with the European Convention on Human Rights but this is rarely used and does not invalidate a law. Something like the Canadian model might, however, be entertained here.[45]

5 The two senses of 'diffusion of power' discussed so far – 'vertical' and 'functional' – refer to a differentiation of authorities *within the political community*. This is why I referred to them as examples of 'constitutional justice' – justice in the constitutional design of the polity itself. A just constitutional order establishes the nature, rights, powers and limits of the political community, its parts and its members. If it realizes the principles outlined so far, it will thereby contribute to, if not guarantee, a just and democratic political community.

There is a distinct sense of the diffusion of power that is no less important, namely the diffusion of power *between the political community and that which is outside it* – the many other institutions, associations and communities of society. In this larger category we can include families or households, schools and universities, churches and other religious organizations, voluntary associations, NGOs, trades unions, vocational and professional associations, cultural and artistic associations, campaigning groups, political parties, the media, business organizations and the many markets in which they interact, and much more.

As already noted, a core conviction of Christian political thought is that the polity is one human institution among many needed for a flourishing human society, not an all-embracing whole of which all other bodies are derivative or subordinate parts. The weight of the tradition resists the conferral of inordinate power upon, or its acquisition by, any single human collectivity, whether a state, nation, tribe, ethnic group, religious community, class, party, corporation or market, or some perverse alliance of these. Nor does the state possess any ontological or moral priority over those other bodies. This conviction radically relativizes the status of the polity vis-à-vis other institutions. Such a conviction originally had Christian provenance. It was birthed from the epochal confrontation between overweening Greco-Roman political orders, notably the Roman empire, and the Christian Church. The Church made its unprecedented appearance as a self-governing, counter-cultural community answering to its own 'Lord'.[46] This conviction was maintained in the middle ages by means of an intricate set of differentiations between multiple (and partly overlapping) 'temporal' and 'spiritual' communities and jurisdictions (churches, monasteries, universities, cities, sodalities or guilds) – generating what John Milbank calls 'complex space'.[47] It was brought to greater clarity in various streams of modern Christian thought as they reflected on, and promoted, the advancing process of differentiation between these and other kinds of institution.[48]

The theological argument for this differentiation can be summarized as follows. Given the multiple needs, capacities and powers of human persons as divinely created – for intimacy, fellowship, work, culture, worship and so forth – there must be a corresponding pluriformity in the structural design of a society that wishes to honour humans thus created. Each type of institution, association, community or relationship offers a distinctive conduit for the fulfilment of one or other set of human needs, inclinations and capacities. The political community does not itself create them and must discern, defer to, protect and support such social bodies. Each social body thus lays claim to its own valid, if limited, right to self-government and to freedom from subjection to, or instrumentalization by, any other. Given a modern political context in which political agency is progressively being reduced either to the individual or to the state, we urgently need to retrieve this theologically grounded vision of a diffusion of institutional power.[49]

Conclusion

In this and the previous chapter I have argued that if we wish to understand the appropriate role of faith in democracy we must begin by properly discerning the nature and purpose of the political community of which democracy is one component. Today, these are far from self-evident. In the previous chapter I argued that the purpose of democracy is not first to express the collective 'will of the people' but to advance the causes of public justice (my term for the defining normative purpose of the political community). In this chapter I have argued that the Christian political tradition has over the centuries yielded powerful theological grounds for asserting, today, a clear 'preferential option' for constitutional democracy. This does not guarantee that the political community will pursue its central purpose (there are no such guarantees) but it is a necessary condition if it is to do so. In a constitutional democracy, numerous channels of popular representation and participation must be powerfully affirmed alongside a range of other equally essential requirements. These work to secure just, constitutional government, such as the rule of law and limited, accountable and diffused political authority and an independent civil society. This, I propose, is what Christian political thinkers and activists should be guided by as they work, via democratic

49

processes, to promote public justice in the political communities in which they find themselves. In doing so, they will, of course, find many allies among adherents of other political visions.

I close by reiterating that, whether at the level of basic constitutional principle or specific policy outworking, the impact of deep diversity will also continue to reveal itself in such a democracy – and, indeed, over the very nature of constitutional democracy itself. The political community as I have envisaged it affirms a decisive role for 'the people', but does not see it as a homogenous whole with a cohesive single will or a unified vision of the common good. Rather it reckons with the people as it presents itself in the political arena in all its messy and shifting convictional plurality. A just constitutional democracy must be one in which such plurality is visibly embraced, harnessed for good ends where possible and limited only where necessary. The question to which I now turn is whether, and in what senses, 'secularism' is capable of satisfying that requirement. Can 'secularism' protect convictional 'pluralism'?

Notes

1 Remainers often pointed out that the referendum result expressed the will of only 37 per cent of eligible voters. Leavers retorted that this was a bigger number than normally express their will in general elections.

2 Luke Bretherton, *Christ and the Common Life: Political Theology and the Case for Democracy* (Grand Rapids, MI: Eerdmans 2019), 12.

3 See Donald W. Norwood, *Democracy and the Christian Churches: Ecumenism and the Politics of Belief* (London: I. B. Tauris, 2019); Graham Maddox, *Religion and the Rise of Democracy* (London: Routledge, 1996); John De Gruchy, *Christianity and Democracy* (Cambridge: Cambridge University Press, 1995).

4 Brian Tierney, *Religion, Law and the Growth of Constitutional Thought 1150–1650* (Cambridge: Cambridge University Press, 1982).

5 Joan Lockwood O'Donovan, 'Political Authority and European Community: The Challenge of the Christian Political Tradition', *Scottish Journal of Theology* 47.1 (1994), 1–17.

6 Lockwood O'Donovan, 'Political Authority', 6–7.

7 Robert Song, *Christianity and Liberal Society* (Oxford: Clarendon Press, 1997), 198.

8 Lockwood O'Donovan, 'Political Authority', 8. Emphasis added.

9 In Julian H. Franklin, ed. and trans., *Constitutionalism and Resistance in the Sixteenth Century* (New York: Pegasus, 1969), 142–99.

10 Franklin, *Constitutionalism*, 158. Emphasis added.

11 Reinhold Niebuhr, *The Children of Light and the Children of Darkness* (New York: Charles Scribner's Sons, 1944), vi.

12 On Christian accounts of equality, see Duncan Forrester, *On Human Worth: A Christian Vindication of Equality* (London: SCM Press, 2001); Oliver O'Donovan, *Ways of Judgment* (Grand Rapids, MI: Eerdmans, 2005), chapter 3.

13 De Gruchy, *Christianity and Democracy*, 49–53.

14 Walter Ullmann, *Principles of Government and Politics in the Middle Ages* (London: Methuen, 1961).

15 See William Johnson Everett, *God's Federal Republic: Reconstructing Our Governing Ideal* (New York: Paulist Press, 1988).

16 Andrew Bradstock, *Radical Religion in Cromwell's England: A Concise History from the English Civil War to the End of the Commonwealth* (London: I. B. Tauris, 2010).

17 Maddox, *Religion and the Rise of Democracy*, 150–1.

18 Robert Dahl, *Democracy and its Critics* (New Haven, CT: Yale University Press, 1989), 32.

19 Bretherton, *Christ and the Common Life*, 400–16.

20 Bretherton, *Christ and the Common Life*, 445.

21 Pope Paul VI, *Gaudium et Spes* (1965), www.vatican.va/archive/hist_councils/ii_vatican_council/documents/vat-ii_const_19651207_gaudium-et-spes_en.html (§75).

22 Roger Eatwell and Matthew Goodwin, *National Populism: The Revolt Against Liberal Democracy* (London: Pelican, 2018); Daniel Nilsson DeHanas and Marat Shterin, eds, *Religion and the Rise of Populism* (Abingdon: Routledge, 2020).

23 For theological readings of populism, see Joshua Ralston and Ulrich Schmiedel, eds, *The Spirit of Populism: Political Theologies in Polarized Times* (Leiden: Brill, forthcoming 2021); Bretherton, *Christ and the Common Life*, chapter 14; Anthony Reddie, *Theologizing Brexit: A Liberationist and Postcolonial Critique* (Abingdon: Routledge, 2019).

24 On 'defensive power', see Stephen Charles Mott, *A Christian Perspective on Political Thought* (New York: Oxford University Press, 1993), 15.

25 Niebuhr, *Children of Light*, vi.

26 Niebuhr, *Children of Light*, 10.

27 Niebuhr, *Children of Light*, 15.

28 New York: Charles Scribner's Sons, 1960.

29 Niebuhr, *Children of Light*, 38.

30 Niebuhr, *Children of Light*, 38.

31 Niebuhr, *Children of Light*, 53.

32 Niebuhr, *Children of Light*, 80.

33 Charles Villa-Vicencio, *A Theology of Reconstruction: Nation-building and Human Rights* (Cambridge: Cambridge University Press, 1992).

34 Villa-Vicencio, *Theology of Reconstruction*, 49–116.

35 Jacques Maritain, *Man and the State* (Chicago, IL: Chicago University Press, 1951), 29. See Joel Harrison, 'Sovereignty', in Nicholas Aroney and Ian Leigh, eds, *Christianity and Constitutionalism* (Oxford: Oxford University Press, forthcoming 2021).

36 Aroney and Leigh, eds, *Christianity and Constitutionalism*.

37 See Jonathan Chaplin, 'Justice: Constitutional Design and the Purpose of the Political Community' in Aroney and Leigh, eds, *Christianity and Constitutionalism*. A constitution need not be 'codified' (or 'written'); untypically, the UK constitution is not.

38 Technically, the system is known as the 'single-member constituency plurality system'. A parliamentary seat is won by the candidate who secures a plurality of

votes (more than anyone else) cast within a constituency, in which there is a single seat. Such a plurality, not even a majority, is all that is needed to get 'past the post'.

39 For example, the Single Transferable Vote (as in Northern Ireland), which operates with multi-member constituencies; or the Additional Member System (as in Scotland and Wales), which uses single-member constituencies but tops them up with seats elected by party lists in order to secure overall proportionality.

40 This is the argument deployed in Canada in favour of the recognition of devolved powers both for the province of Quebec (recognized as a 'distinct society') and for aboriginal 'First Nations' (where the clue is in the name).

41 John Milbank and Adrian Pabst invoke this idea in *The Politics of Virtue: Post-Liberalism and the Human Future* (London: Rowman & Littlefield International, 2016), chapter 6.

42 On the Magna Carta's role in holding rulers accountable, see Thomas Andrew, *The Church and the Charter: Christianity and the Forgotten Roots of the Magna Carta* (London: Theos, 2015).

43 *R (on the application of Miller) v The Prime Minister* [2019] UKSC 41, para. 46.

44 'Elective Dictatorship', BBC Richard Dimbleby Lecture 1976, *The Listener* (21 October 1976), 496–500.

45 Some fear this would lead to 'judicial activism'. See Jonathan Sumption, *Trials of the State: Law and the Decline of Politics* (London: Profile, 2019).

46 John Courtney Murray, 'Are There Two or One?', in John Courtney Murray, *We Hold These Truths: Catholic Reflections on the American Proposition* (Kansas City, MO: Sheed & Ward, 1960), 197–217; Sheldon Wolin, *Politics and Vision: Continuity and Innovation in Western Political Thought*, expanded edn (Princeton, NJ: Princeton University Press, 2004), chapter 4.

47 John Milbank, 'Complex Space', in *The Word Made Strange: Theology, Language, Culture* (Oxford: Blackwell, 1997), 275.

48 For a Protestant case, see Jonathan Chaplin, *Herman Dooyeweerd: Christian Philosopher of State and Civil Society* (Notre Dame, IN: University of Notre Dame Press, 2011).

49 Adrian Pabst, *The Demons of Liberal Democracy* (Cambridge: Polity, 2019), chapter 4; Patrick J. Deneen, *Why Liberalism Failed* (New Haven, CT: Yale University Press, 2018), chapter 2.

PART 2

Secularism: Rights and Wrongs

3

Secularism *or* Pluralism?

Introduction

We are secular judges serving a multicultural community of many faiths sworn to do justice to all manner of people … We live in this country in a democratic and pluralist society in a secular state, not a theocracy. Sir James Munby (President of the Family Division)[1]

Only a 'secular state', Sir James suggests in this 2013 lecture to an assembly of the nation's lawyers, will deliver us from the terrors of 'theocracy'. His language echoes Janet Daley's stark opposition between 'doctrines of faith' and 'secular law' with which I opened this book. They are insisting that something called a 'secular' state or 'secular' law is the only way to fend off imposed uniformity and defend a 'pluralist society' populated by many faiths. But what does it mean for judges, or any organ of state, to be 'secular'? Sir James did not think it necessary to define the term closely.

The claim has, however, been contested, as an empirical assertion, in another high corner of the establishment. In 2003, a House of Lords Select Committee on Religious Offences in England and Wales had declared, to the contrary, that, in view of the established status of the Church of England, 'the UK is not a secular state'.[2] The claim has also been contested, as a theological assertion, by advocates of the 'Christian nation' position. Former Anglican Bishop Michael Nazir-Ali, for example, asserted in 2008 that Britain must recover an awareness of its distinctive Christian origins if it is to understand itself as a nation at all:

Christian faith has been central to the emergence of our nation and its development. We cannot really understand the nature and achievements of British society without reference to it. In a plural, multi-faith and multicultural society, it can still provide the resources for both supporting and providing a critique of public life in this country … [Christian faith] is necessary to understand where we have come from, to guide us to where we are going, and to bring us back when we wander too far from the path of national destiny.[3]

Moreover, if the influence of non-Christian faiths, notably Islam, continues to grow, then, 'Instead of the Christian virtues of humility, service and sacrifice, there may be honour, [public] piety and the importance of "saving face".'[4]

Across Europe there is also vigorous debate on these questions.[5] The European Court of Human Rights (ECtHR) has been called on to adjudicate on them in two highly controversial cases. In a 2003 case, the court upheld the Constitutional Court of Turkey's right to dissolve an Islamic party, the Refah Partisi (The Welfare Party), on the grounds that it was 'a centre of activities contrary to the principles of secularism'.[6] It concluded that 'the principle of secularism' was a necessary presupposition of 'democracy',[7] and that 'sharia is incompatible with the fundamental principles of democracy, as set forth in the Convention'.[8] It declared in effect that even to *campaign* for the introduction of Islamic personal law was incompatible with the liberal democratic principle of a religiously impartial state.[9]

However, in a 2011 case, *Lautsi v Italy*, the ECtHR reached a decision that on its face stands in tension with its judgment in *Refah Partisi*. The court defended the right of the Italian state to require the display of crucifixes in public schools. The case had been initiated in 2004 by a parent of secular convictions, Soile Lautsi, who claimed that the policy violated her and her children's Convention rights to religious freedom and the principle of secularism of the Italian constitution. The case worked its way through the national courts, culminating in a decision of the Supreme Administrative Court that the crucifix was permissible, in part because, after all, it now represented Italian cultural values such as tolerance, respect, individual rights and freedom of conscience. That decision was initially overturned by a lower tier of the ECtHR, which ruled that the crucifix was indeed incompatible with the principle of secularism. But in 2011 the Grand Chamber eventually resolved it in favour of the Italian state. The court conceded that the crucifix was indeed a Christian symbol, even if representing secular values, but that it was a 'passive' one, involving no indoctrination, no breach of state neutrality and no breach of Convention rights.[10] The case elicited Europe-wide controversy over the meaning of secularism, national identity and public religion. In *Refah Partisi*, the ECtHR had argued that 'secularism' permitted a curtailment of another fundamental principle of liberal pluralism, that of free political speech, while in *Lautsi*, it argued that a Christian symbol in a very prominent public place was compatible with secular values like state neutrality.[11] The meaning of 'a secular state' and whether it secures something called 'pluralism' remains far from clear in Europe as well as in the UK.

This chapter offers a theological defence of 'jurisdictional secularism' as the best guarantor of convictional pluralism. Jurisdictional secularism holds that the state should adopt an official stance of impartiality towards the plural faiths of its people and guarantee extensive religious freedom for all. It frames public space so that citizens adhering to a wide diversity of faiths have maximum freedom to manifest their convictions in public and participate on equitable terms in democratic politics. Jurisdictional secularism facilitates the expression of a plurality of faiths. It is the most important thing that is 'right with secularism'. I will argue that protecting convictional pluralism is one essential way of 'doing justice to all manner of people', as Sir James Munby aptly puts it. First, however, we must define some key terms in the debate.

A 'secularism toolkit'

'Secular'

The origin of the term 'secular' as used in the modern West is the Latin term *saeculum*, literally meaning 'age'. Of Roman origin, the term came to be used during the Christendom era to refer to 'this present age' – the period of history between the first coming of Christ (the incarnation) and the second (the *eschaton*).[12] It was a thoroughly theological idea. A 'secular' matter was an affair of 'this age' rather than of 'the age to come'. But both were under the providential and redemptive ordering of God, and both were indispensable spheres of divine action and Christian faithfulness – the latter because 'eschatology' concerned not only the future (the 'last things') but also the shape of Christian behaviour now. A 'secular priest' was one who exercised his ministry 'in the world' rather than retreating to a monastery where he would devote himself to preparing for the age to come (which, of course, included very 'this-worldly' activities such as learning or caring for the poor). Similarly, 'secular' (or 'temporal') government, for example, was necessary to maintain order and establish a measure of justice in this age, an age that remained 'fallen' even though it was the theatre of the unfolding work of divine redemption. But secular government would be superseded in the next. Under Christendom, 'secular' carried a temporal not an ontological reference: it was an epoch within the larger plan of divine redemption, not a zone of human conduct standing over against a 'sacred' or 'religious' zone, or zone of 'grace'. The secular was already in process of being 'graced', primarily through the medium of the Church. With this sense in mind, Oliver O'Donovan speaks without contradiction of a 'Christian secular political order', one that anticipates in this age something of the redemptive influence of the age to come – for example, by 'tempering justice with mercy'.[13]

In the modern world, however, 'secular' has overwhelmingly come to refer to just such a spatially defined zone of human conduct in which God, and religion, are absent; or, at least, to which they are irrelevant. This is a stance also adopted by 'self-secularizing' religious believers, who voluntarily align themselves fully with the expectations of secular culture. The story of how this sense of 'the secular' achieved dominance in Western culture has been told most magisterially by Charles Taylor in *A Secular Age*. Taylor charts how 'the secular' in this sense came to be seen as the 'natural' condition of the world, a condition laid bare to modern people now that religion had been 'subtracted' from our culture's taken-for-granted account of the world. Not only has religion been 'subtracted', it has also been given a radically novel 'construal' in which it is reduced to a matter of individual, subjectively chosen private belief. It may, perhaps, have implications for private behaviour. But it is no longer seen as a body of thick communal commitments and practices that have shaped, and may shape, the public realm. Secular modernity has come to construe 'religion' as a carefully demarcated sector of human life and, moreover, one (so some critics suggest) with an uncanny resemblance to modern, individualistic liberal Protestantism. But because most secular moderns maintain an uncritical presumption of the rational objectivity of their world view, they are unable to recognize this as *one* construal among many. They are, as John Milbank puts it, incapable of seeing that 'once there was no "secular"'.[14] A rising chorus of critics of secular modernity have, however, shown that this is indeed a contestable, Western – indeed colonialist – construal of religion.[15]

Of course, many who assume this modern construal of 'the secular' obviously recognize that something called 'religion' still survives (indeed revives), and that it continues to be a source of significant subjective meaning for some citizens, perhaps a respect-worthy source – even, for a few, an enviable source. Yet they mostly assume that religion is 'unnatural', an alien presence in the public world that must, so to speak, carry a visa certifying its right to act on the public stage. Such a visa is granted subject to certain conditions of good behaviour. Religion thus needs to be managed in suitable ways so as not to obscure the objectivity of public reasoning or disrupt the stability of the public realm. I won't attempt further summary of Taylor's account because the focus in this book is the narrower institutional question of 'political secularism'. We shall see, however, that how 'religion' and 'the secular' get construed is highly important to that question.

'Secularism as faith'

Up to now I have spoken in passing of religious and secular 'faiths' but not explained what, admittedly, is a highly contentious imputation. In what sense might 'secularism' be plausibly construed as a 'faith'? Quite understandably, the suggestion will be objectionable to many secular humanists, atheists and agnostics. Many who identify as such regard their basic convictions as premised entirely on 'reason' and hold that any claim premised on faith is at best epistemologically suspect and at worst irredeemably irrational – as requiring a groundless 'leap of faith' that could lend credibility to all kinds of publicly dangerous superstitions.[16]

Instead of 'faiths', one might speak of religious and secular 'world views', 'ideologies' or, in postmodern currency, 'meta-narratives'. Equally I could have invoked John Rawls's widely adopted term 'comprehensive doctrines' – broad conceptions of the human good that can be religious or secular. In *Political Liberalism*, Rawls himself recognized that the Kantian moral philosophy he had relied on in his earlier *A Theory of Justice* after all amounted to a controversial comprehensive doctrine that could not reasonably serve as the shared foundation of a liberal conception of justice acceptable to all.

Each of these terms has strengths and weakness. My central claim is that *any* sustained rational argument about matters of great human significance will inevitably disclose the tacit or explicit influence of some underlying 'faith-like' perspective (or perhaps an amalgam of more than one). Such a perspective will often function as a presupposition, sometimes unacknowledged, of the reasoning process rather than as its conclusion – as what gets reasoning going rather than the destination towards which it travels. Thus Mark Lilla, while conceding that political theology can indeed be a 'rational' exercise, holds that the reasoning it engages in always rests finally on some faith commitment: 'Covenant and law [for example] are products of speech; there are reasons behind them. But behind the last reason there is only revelation.'[17]

I submit that behind the last reason in any chain of substantive argumentation about the human good is a prior commitment either to religious 'revelation' or to some secular substitute. Such a commitment will concern things as the nature of truth, the purpose of human life, the source of morality, the nature of justice, the meaning of history, the prospects for human progress or 'salvation', the rationale of political community – or, perhaps, the inscrutability or absence of all such things. In turn, such commitments will be shaped by what Taylor calls visions of 'fullness' – a sense of what a 'fuller, richer, deeper, more worthwhile, more admirable' life would be, providing moral and spiritual 'orientation' in the world.[18]

Such commitments, and the visions behind them, may not be made explicit in public discourse. For example, advocates of the legalization of assisted suicide normally do not defend their stance explicitly in terms of the assertion of a vision of fullness such as 'the primacy of individual autonomy as the essence of human meaning'. But some deep commitment like this will often be 'behind the last reason' they do proffer; and such a commitment cannot itself be generated solely from the exercise of 'reason'. Drawing on Taylor, the editors of an important volume on secularism allow that 'all normative orientations, even those that claim to be entirely rational, in fact depend on some higher-order values'. And sometimes these can seem thoroughly 'secular':

> Being completely rational can be one such value. Some higher-order values are very this-worldly, as, for example, in economic discourses in which either some indicator of utility or some hedonic principle of human happiness is clearly the utmost good by which the entire analytic framework is organized and which has a standing apart from any merely incremental values. So it is not clear that reference to higher values clearly demarcates religious from secular reasons.[19]

Or, as Craig Calhoun puts it in the same volume: 'Both religious orientations to the world and secular, "Enlightened" orientations depend on strong epistemic and moral commitments made at least partly prerationally.'[20] I am claiming that secularism is a 'faith' insofar as it rests, like religion, upon some such 'pre-rational' (not irrational) commitments.[21] We should not, however, think of such commitments as regrettable baggage that, alas, we just can't shake off. Rather, as Terry Eagleton puts it, 'it is only if reason can draw upon resources and energies deeper, more tenacious and less fragile than itself that it is capable of prevailing, a truth which liberal rationalism for the most part disastrously overlooks.'[22]

'Secularization'

Under Christendom, the idea of 'secularization' had a precise meaning, referring, for example, to the process whereby a 'religious' priest left a monastery and became a 'secular' priest, or, after the Reformation, to the transfer of property from the Church to secular institutions such as the state. It did not imply the loss or marginalization of faith. In the modern world, however, 'secularization' has come to assume the proportions of a comprehensive narrative of universal 'modernization' in which religion is progressively displaced from the public realm by reason, science and individual autonomy. Among social theorists, 'the secularization thesis' asserted a series of distinct processes that, it has now become clear, have been wrongly conflated. This is the central argument of José Casanova's *Public Religions in the Modern World*.[23] Casanova's account sheds valuable light on what I mean by jurisdictional secularism.

Casanova distinguishes three different processes captured by secularization theory and shows how theorists had long tacitly assumed that these necessarily travelled in convoy in modernity. The first is the *decline* of religion: the progressive loss of personal belief and practice and the weakening of organized religion. The second is the *privatization* of religion: the confinement of religion to the private sphere and the resultant diminution of its social significance. But Casanova shows that, apart from the case of Western Europe,[24] it is clear that religion has not undergone precipitous decline in all modernized countries (as is shown by the USA or South Korea, for example). Moreover he observes that, in many settings, even in secular Europe, there is mounting evidence of 'deprivatization', of a growing refusal by religions 'to accept the marginal and privatized role which theories of modernity ... [and] secularization had reserved for them'.[25]

The third process is the *differentiation* of religion from other spheres of society such as market, state, academy, the arts, and so forth.[26] It refers to the 'differentiation and emancipation of the secular spheres from religious institutions and norms'.[27] This is the momentous process, stretching from the sixteenth to the nineteenth centuries, by which the moral authority of religious norms was progressively undermined and the legal jurisdiction of religious institutions pegged back.[28] The process allowed institutions like states, corporations, markets and universities to 'come into their own' by asserting their independent normative authority over against that of the Church (and each other): business corporations, for example, were no longer directed by religious norms such as 'charity' or 'solidarity'. Religion also 'comes into its own', occupying its own demarcated social sphere.[29] Casanova argues that this claim about differentiation remains the single valid element of the secularization thesis. Differentiation is fundamental to liberal democracy and it is not about to be reversed. But it has no necessary connection with either religious decline or privatization.[30]

Casanova is on to something very important here. The idea of a differentiation of distinct institutional spheres comports well with the theology of institutional plurality I outlined in Chapter 1.[31] But while his analysis is helpful, it underplays a distinction central to my argument. This is the distinction between, on the one hand, the differentiation of institutional *jurisdictions* and, on the other, the differentiation of the *norms* guiding them. It is indeed true that the norms properly guiding, for example, state-craft, business and medicine are not identical: 'justice' cannot be conflated with either 'efficiency' or 'care', even though they are not essentially in tension. So a clarification of distinct institutional norms properly follows from a differentiation of institutional jurisdictions. But this does not imply that differentiated institutions like states, businesses or hospitals will or must then be immune from the influence of either 'religion' or 'ethics' (as if 'efficiency', for example, were necessarily deaf to justice). The questions religion and ethics raise emerge in *every social sphere*, whether acknowledged or not. While we can rightly speak of the 'autonomy' of these spheres, what that should be taken to mean is the *distinctive modulations of religion and ethics within such spheres*, not that religion and ethics now must be confined to (private) 'spheres' of their own.

It is true, however, that the specific way institutional norms *actually* came to be differentiated in the modern West did have the effect of insulating 'secular' institutions like these from religious and ethical norms. Here, differentiation was indeed accompanied by privatization. But this was a contingent matter, not a necessary element of differentiation. It was the unique pathway that institutional differentiation took in the West (and some Westernized societies elsewhere) but is not the necessary route for all modernizing nations elsewhere, nor the one that must always prevail in the West.

My account of jurisdictional secularism will explain theologically why institutional differentiation should allow religious (as well as secular) faiths, and their ethical implications, to contribute to the shaping of the public realm – to what Casanova calls its 'renormativization'.[32] Differentiation need not and should not lead to the triumph of 'secularist' norms in politics or other spheres of society. It need not require that the state be dominated by bureaucratic norms, business by the motives of profit maximization, or hospitals by the imperatives of medical technology. Insights of religion and ethics can be reintroduced – or perhaps rediscovered (they were never entirely lost) – within all the spheres and institutions making up the modern public realm. This could include the redeployment of formerly discarded 'classical' norms of justice and the common good in politics – one of the goals of this book.

'Post-secular'

Social theorists are reporting mounting evidence of 'desecularization' and 'deprivatization' in modern secular societies. Does this suggest that we are now steaming confidently towards a new condition called the 'post-secular'?[33] Some argue that we are now moving towards a 'post-secular' age in which many of the fundamental assumptions shaping secular modernity are increasingly being put into question. They observe that the hitherto dominant construal of 'the secular' as 'natural', as 'the way things are', is now under formidable challenge from sources as varied as postmodern philosophy, radical feminism, postcolonial theory, Green political thought, indigenous political movements and, of course, resurgent public religions.

'Signs of the post-secular' do seem to be appearing and, by questioning the undisputed hegemony of secularism, are evidently conducive to an argument for Christian democratic pluralism. Yet we would be wise to heed the cautionary account offered by Elaine Graham. Graham registers many such signs and welcomes some of them but warns against assuming that 'the secular', or 'secularism', are on their way out. While the resurgence of interest in religion, or at least 'spirituality', poses questions to the dominant rationalism of modernity, she notes that 'contemporary discourses founded on the continuing triumph of reason and science continue to maintain a vigorous defence of secularism'.[34] The 'post-secular' is no sunny upland but an 'awkward and contradictory space'.[35] There is no compelling evidence in the West of religious revival. But nor, as some secularists think, is the return of public religion merely a 'blip on an otherwise undisturbed trajectory of modernity'. The picture is complex: 'Religion is both more visible and invisible: more prominent and more vicarious; more elusive institutionally (and intellectually, theologically), and yet more cited, more pervasive.'[36] The lesson for faith-based organizations and political institutions alike is that we must learn to navigate a path between the 'rock' of religious revival and the 'hard place' of secularism, with little in the way of rules of engagement to guide us.[37] Graham's account of the landscape is helpful; this book is a sketch of one religiously informed account of such rules of engagement.

Jurisdictional secularism

So much for 'the secular', 'secularization', 'secularism' and the 'post-secular'. All that was preparatory to a positive case for *jurisdictional* secularism, which concerns the way *the state* relates to religion; it is a species of 'political secularism'. Political secularism has been defended from a variety of standpoints. For example, the religiously impartial state is widely defended by liberal secularists on the basis of individual freedom and the right not to have any controversial 'conception of the good' (or 'comprehensive doctrine') imposed on one by the state.[38] Political secularism can also be defended in more pragmatic terms as a means to mitigate civil conflict in religiously divided societies; this was a major motivation behind the Indian model of secularism established after independence in order to transcend 'communal' hostilities between Hindus and Muslims (it is now being aggressively undermined by prime minister Modi). But there are several variants of political secularism, some of which are more congenial to the argument of this book than others. I will not survey them all here but rather specify the form I favour and then offer a theological account of it.

When people speak of a 'secular state', they sometimes simply mean one that has undergone what Casanova terms 'differentiation' – one in which there is a clear distinction between the spheres of jurisdiction of the state and those of churches or other religious organizations. Often this is what they are recommending when they defend 'secularism', or when they express appreciation that the modern state has been 'secularized'. Some who favour 'a secular state' *also* mean by this that the state must be governed by a 'secularist faith' and religious faith pushed to the margins of public life – a stance I have called 'exclusivist secularism'. But 'a secular state' does not necessarily imply this sort of secularism. Advocates of a 'secular state' may only be proposing that the state should be 'jurisdictionally secular'. What this means is that it does not officially favour any one faith over others but aspires to relate to all of them 'even-handedly' or 'impartially'; or, in standard legal parlance, 'neutrally'.[39]

A state committed to jurisdictional secularism acknowledges that it has no jurisdiction to adjudicate among competing claims regarding ultimate truth. As the ECtHR puts it: 'the State's duty of neutrality and impartiality [among beliefs] is incompatible with *any power on the State's part to assess the legitimacy of religious beliefs* ... and ... requires the State to ensure mutual tolerance between opposing groups.'[40] I would add that neither does the state have any power to assess the legitimacy of 'secular beliefs'. It is important to note that this does not mean that the state is *empirically unable* to attempt such an assessment; in practice states often do just this. An officially Islamic state 'assesses the legitimacy' of Islam and judges it to be true, perhaps even mandatory (and renders an adverse judgement on 'secularist faith'). The French state affirms the legitimacy of a robustly secular republicanism. Even the British state, by retaining the established status of the Church of England, by implication judges Anglicanism to be true (for England, at least – its epistemological competence somehow stops at the borders of England).

Jurisdictional secularism claims, rather, that the state should not *assume to itself the authority* to assess the legitimacy of religious beliefs. If the state has no valid claim to such authority, it has no licence to favour or disfavour any faith, or all faiths. Jurisdictional secularism requires the state to deal even-handedly (not necessarily identically) with whatever faiths may be present within its territory: majority or minority; traditional or recent; indigenous or migrant; familiar or strange. How far it actually succeeds in doing so is a contested question I pick up at various points. The core of jurisdictional secularism is the institutional *intent* to treat plural faiths impartially and the existence of principles and procedures that make that outcome more likely than not.

This stance of jurisdictional restraint on the part of the state is the first of the 'twin tolerations' identified by Alfred Stepan as defining the quite specific and limited senses in which a liberal democratic state must be 'secular'.[41] This means that the state must not inhibit the proper remit of religion by inserting the blunt instrument of its coercive power into matters pertaining to the search for ultimate truth. The second is that neither must religion inhibit the proper remit of the state by seeking to control or illegitimately influence its laws and policies.[42] But, Stepan holds, a 'secular state' need not be committed to exclusivist secularism. It can permit or even strongly affirm the place of faith in the forums of liberal democracy. As Cécile Laborde puts it, 'The state should be secular so that citizens do not have to be secular.'[43]

Recognizing the incapacity of the state to determine what counts as true faith is the fundamental basis of religious toleration, of religious freedom and, more broadly, of 'freedom of conscience' – a term embracing many varieties of 'secular conscience' as well. The twin tolerations are mutually constitutive and supportive. On the twin tolerations, Christians will often find themselves in alliance with secular liberals, and against those, such as Islamists, theocratic Christians, Hindu or Buddhist nationalists or atheistic communists, who construe the jurisdictions of the state and faith communities very differently.

The establishment of a religiously impartial state and freedom of conscience is an enormous achievement of the modern world, and Christians and many other religious believers today, as well as secularists, have powerful principled and pragmatic reasons for supporting it: all have a stake in the public protection of convictional plurality. A religiously impartial state presupposes that citizens, who may adhere to faiths claiming comprehensive implications for all of life, nevertheless agree to maintain limited expectations of the kind of unity properly secured by the political community. As American exponent of 'principled pluralism' James Skillen puts it:

> The extent to which people of incompatible religions can, with some
> degree of peace, share a political order in common depends ... on what

they demand of the political order. An overlapping *political* consensus of some kind may be possible not because of an overlapping religious consensus ... but because people of diverse religions agree to keep a pluralistic and constitutionally restricted political order subservient to their deepest and prior commitments ... But political schism is entirely possible ... if people with incompatible religious commitments choose to fight for exclusive control of the body politic.[44]

I have stated that jurisdictional secularism must be clearly distinguished from 'exclusivist secularism' – a form of secularism bent on keeping religion on the margins of public life.[45] On such a view, the state may, perhaps, uphold wide private religious liberty and equality and be officially committed to upholding a pluralism of faiths in civil society. This is certainly one way to treat faiths 'equally' – as equally irrelevant. It strives to keep the actual influence of religious faith out of political debate, political institutions and public policy. The French model of *laïcité* is often cited as the leading European instance of exclusivist secularism, although 'exclusivist' impulses are increasingly operating in a number of European states that in other ways are 'inclusivist'.[46] More radical examples include Kemalist Turkey and post-independence Egypt, where the state made concerted attempts to keep religion (in these cases Islam) under its firm control. The British organizations National Secular Society and Humanists UK are often attacked by religious critics for espousing an aggressive form of secularism. In fact, they uphold some of the most important planks of jurisdictional secularism, while also espousing positions that on my account amount to exclusive secularism.[47]

Political secularism generally (of which jurisdictional secularism is one example) is not intrinsically hostile to religion. However, when it is driven by an exclusivist secular ideology, it places the impartiality of the state in serious jeopardy. As Casanova puts it:

Political secularism falls easily into secularist ideology when the political arrogates for itself absolute, sovereign, quasi-sacred, quasi-transcendent character or when the secular arrogates for itself the mantle of rationality and universality, while claiming that 'religion' is essentially nonrational, particularistic, and intolerant (or illiberal) and, as such, dangerous and a threat to democratic politics once it enters the public sphere.[48]

This danger is all the more difficult to resist, even identify, if political secularism is construed in the public mind as a mere 'absence' – a public realm devoid of religion – rather than a 'presence' – a specific *regime* of secularism sustained by substantive and controversial views of 'religion', of the 'public' and 'private' spheres or of 'public rationality'. Even well-intentioned versions of political secularism often end up discriminating against minority faiths that do not conform to an assumed conception of what 'religion' must look like. As the editors of *Rethinking Secularism* put it:

> Nondominant religions may actually be disadvantaged by apparently neutral regimes that in some ways mask tacit assumptions about what constitutes legitimate religious identity ... the secular realm is sometimes constructed in a manner that implicitly privileges one type of religion, while more or less delegitimizing other sorts of religious engagement.[49]

As we shall see, this has also been true of those Western liberal democracies formed by what Elizabeth Shakman Hurd calls 'Judeo-Christian secularism'.[50]

Of course, simply invoking the general principle of 'jurisdictional secularism' does not resolve any of the specific religion–state tensions confronting a country like the UK. Everything depends on how the relevant jurisdictions are defined and circumscribed (and on that I have no complete set of bright lines to propose). As I note in Chapters 6 and 7, this in turn reflects the ways contested terms like 'the religious' and 'the secular' are defined. The term 'jurisdictional secularism' does, however, help concentrate minds by keeping debate focused on a determinate set of political and constitutional questions. It presses us always to ask: 'To which *institutional jurisdiction* does this question properly belong?', thereby steering the discussion away from questions that may be culturally momentous but are constitutionally 'off-piste'. For example, it is not the task of the state to answer a question such as whether the Qur'an – or the Bible for that matter – is 'inherently peaceful' or 'inherently undemocratic'. Those are matters for scholars of religion. By contrast, it is entirely proper, indeed necessary, for the state to be able to identify sources of potential subversion or criminality, and on *that* question religious experts might well be consulted.[51]

A theology of jurisdictional secularism

Let me now offer a theological justification for jurisdictional secularism. Such a justification could be mounted from various starting points.[52] In this chapter I draw on the often neglected but pathbreaking insights of the dissenting Protestants of the sixteenth and seventeenth centuries.

The first 'dissenting Protestant' communities often found themselves in trouble with the better-known 'magisterial' Reformers such as Luther, Calvin and Zwingli. They were the first to make a sustained theological case for the principles of religious tolerance and religious freedom, principles that were later to be almost universally accepted across modern Europe. The context in which they arrived at their case was turbulent and complex. But one of its dominating features was the long-standing conviction held widely among both Catholics and magisterial Reformers that a temporal ruler is entitled, indeed obliged by God, to enforce the true faith in his territory. Rulers were bound under God to protect 'true religion' and root out religious falsehoods. As Perez Zagorin observed, this was seen as 'necessary not only for religion's sake but for the preservation of political unity and peace'.[53] What this meant on the ground could differ widely from region to region, but it essentially mandated uniformity in the public manifestation of belief and worship across the whole of a ruler's territory – the 'territorial principle'. The idea had taken root centuries earlier following the conversion to Christianity of the Roman emperor Constantine in 312 (which led for the first time to religious toleration for Christianity) and the subsequent imposition of Christianity across the entire empire by his successors Theodosius I, Valentinus II and Gratian. Their jointly promulgated Edict of Thessalonica in 380 made Nicene orthodoxy the official state religion, effectively criminalizing both paganism and Christian 'heresy'. Until then, the early Church had almost unanimously rejected the use of state power to give public privilege (as distinct from protection) to Christian faith.[54] The Edict, however, reasserted the long-standing Roman practice whereby an emperor governed the religion of the state. The territorial principle was not an implication of a biblical view of the divine authority of the state but an 'unredeemed' hangover from this pagan Roman political theology.

There were minority voices in the middle ages that questioned imposed religious uniformity.[55] But it was only in dissenting Protestantism that it came to be systematically challenged on theological grounds and new foundations laid for a defence of the religiously impartial state and religious freedom. This was the achievement not principally of the magisterial Reformation but of free churches, sects and spiritualists, ranging from the Puritans to the Quakers.[56] In the dominant narrative of modernity, these achievements are presented as uniquely the consequence of the secular Enlightenment's breaking out of the iron grip of archaic religious reaction. Such a narrative overlooks the 'minority report' of how such achievements arose from the struggle of persecuted Protestant minorities for religious toleration – often against their fellow Protestants. Public toleration of diverse theologies was itself birthed in theology. As Zagorin puts it, the Dissenters' arguments for toleration 'were the work of profoundly Christian if also unorthodox thinkers, not of minds inclined to religious indifference or unbelief'.[57]

Religious toleration was first openly advocated by the early sixteenth-century pacifist Anabaptists who, persecuted by Catholics and Protestants alike, declared themselves firmly against all religious coercion. But the first explicit exponent of a *theory* of religious toleration was Sebastian Castellio.[58] Originally a close associate of John Calvin, he was incensed by Calvin's consent to the burning of Servetus in 1553, and argued passionately for religious freedom and against the use of force to suppress heresy. The most forceful theological arguments for religious freedom emerging in this period came from the radical Puritan Roger Williams, who migrated with the Puritans to Massachusetts in 1631 and founded the new colony of Rhode Island in 1636, later serving as governor. His vigorous polemic against intolerance, *The Bloudy Tenent of Persecution*, published in 1644, argued, strikingly, for universal religious toleration, freedom of religious speech and a full jurisdictional separation of Church and state, on theological grounds.[59] It was, Zagorin asserts, 'not only the most sweeping indictment of religious persecution thus far written by any Englishman but one of the most comprehensive justifications of religious liberty to appear during the seventeenth century'.[60]

Following the devastation of a century of religious warfare, dissenting Protestant arguments began to acquire greater momentum. They were to be substantially reinforced and extended, while also cast into a more 'rationalist' language, by Enlightenment thinkers and statesmen. In England the classic case for religious toleration was John Locke's decisive *Letter Concerning Toleration* (1689), which anticipated Enlightenment rationalism but still drew heavily on biblical arguments. But the theological origins of the right to religious freedom confirm John Witte's wider observation that 'the Enlightenment was not so much a wellspring of Western rights as a watershed in a long stream of rights thinking that began more than a millennium before.'[61]

The subsequent history of the expansion of religious toleration and freedom in modern Europe, and the flowering of religious pluralism, was, to say the least, no smooth passage. But this history was launched by an explicitly Christian political theology. Commitment to religious toleration and freedom was not to be accepted on mere modus vivendi grounds as a temporary, pragmatic adjustment to lost ground but was a compelling mandate of Christian faith. What was that mandate?

The dissenting Protestant case

The case emerging from the Dissenters can be summed up in four mutually supporting arguments. Their fundamental *spiritual* argument was that the only worship God finds acceptable is one born of voluntary love rather than inducement or coercion. The inner orientation of the conscience, the 'heart', of human beings may not and cannot be compelled.[62] Not only was forced conversion a contradiction in terms (in fact it was rare), but every individual should be free to choose and manifest her faith without outward constraint or disadvantage. Genuine faith is a wholly free response to the grace of God.

This claim was often combined with an *epistemological* argument that while there may be certainty on the 'fundamentals' of the faith, this certainly was lacking in respect of 'secondary' (or 'indifferent') matters of belief and practice; and in any case, the distinction between the two was itself incapable of objective resolution. It was therefore impossible to appeal, as defenders of intolerance frequently did, to any notion of 'truths that must be known to all' and that could only be denied perversely. Others grounded the epistemological claim more broadly in a theology of the created nature of humanity. Since all human beings, not only Christians, are created in the image of God, all possess not only an identical dignity and worth but also an equal capacity to seek and acquire knowledge of God, whatever they might do with that capacity. To restrict the entitlement to religious freedom only to Christians (or only to a certain type) would be an arbitrary frustration of a universal, divinely bestowed human possibility.

A third argument was *ecclesiological*. Dissenting Protestants may have severed ties with dominant religious institutions but this was only in order to reconstitute themselves as a distinctive ecclesial community liberated to practise more faithful communal obedience. The freedom to believe was both an individual and a collective entitlement; the former could only be authentically realized through intense participation in a believing fellowship, one that might impose high expectations of conformity to communal belief and behaviour. While most Protestant Dissenters saw the Church as a voluntary association, most also rejected spiritual individualism – a view implying that corporate religious practice was incidental to true faith. The Church would almost inevitably become a 'contrast society', standing against 'worldly' practice in many areas of private and public life.

This brought with it a powerful new argument regarding the place of the Church in society. Membership of the Church generated among its members a compelling new loyalty that undermined any fusion of political and religious identities. Nicholas Wolterstorff has restated this as the claim that, in New Testament theology, the Church 'cannot express the shared religious identity of [a whole] people, since there is no such identity ... Whenever the church enters a society, it destroys whatever religio-ethical unity that society may have possessed. Now there is only religious pluralism.'[63] That is not only a factual assertion but a normative one: those who deny that the Church could express such an identity are bound to deny that the state may try to make it do so. Some Dissenters reinforced this claim with a wider argument about the character of the Church under the New Covenant. While, in biblical Israel, God had covenanted exclusively with the Jewish people, now the people of God have become a transnational, non-territorial, global fellowship of believers united in allegiance to Jesus Christ and in the mission to 'proclaim the gospel to all the nations'. This did not imply that the mission is now *non-political* (although Dissenters at times implied that) but rather that it is *non-territorial*, no longer channelled through any particular geographically bounded political communities.

Fourth, the culmination of the Dissenters' case for religious toleration and freedom was a cluster of *political* arguments building to the claim that government is simply not authorized to impose any type of civil penalty upon those who uphold or reject any particular faith. One of these arguments was the 'Pauline' claim that God had given government no such authority. Most dissenting Protestants held – here in keeping with much of the tradition – that rulers have a distinctive but limited mandate from God to establish an external ('worldly', 'temporal' or 'secular') civil order of peace and justice and were therefore deserving in principle of obedience. The classic Pauline passage, Romans 13, was invoked to justify such a mandate. But it was also used to show that since even the pagan Roman empire was 'God's servant' it was inconceivable that Paul could have thought God had authorized it to impose religious uniformity. This argument challenged head-on the long-standing Christendom assumption that there could be officially Christian territorial nations. The Dissenters were, in effect, anticipating the ECtHR's repudiation, over four centuries later, of the competence of the state to 'assess the legitimacy of religious belief'.

This denial to the state of the authority to assess the truth of religion was often shored up by observations regarding the arbitrariness of the religious judgements of particular rulers. Roger Williams, for example, argued that if Protestant Queen Elizabeth was entitled to 'persecute according to her conscience', so was Catholic King James. Indeed, the absurd implication was that if one ruler is entitled to persecute the 'heretic and schismatic', another might be entitled to 'persecute the Son of God, instead of the son of perdition'.[64] Because different rulers frequently reach conflicting judgements on what religious beliefs may be publicly (dis)advantaged, to permit them to rule on the matter created a persistent uncertainty that was inherently damaging to civic order.

This argument supported the wider conclusion that religious intolerance did not, after all, safeguard civil peace but inevitably subverted it. As Williams puts it, it was persecutors not dissenters who sowed the divisions:

> [T]he worship which a state professes may be contradicted and preached against and yet no breach of civil peace [occur]. And if a breach follow, it is not made by such doctrines but by the boisterous and violent opposers of them. Such persons only break the cities' or kingdoms' peace who cry out for prison and swords against such who cross their judgment or practice in religion.[65]

This claim was powerfully reinforced, Dissenters argued, by the fact that the life and teaching of Jesus and the consistent practice of the early Church demonstrated a stance of universal neighbourliness and peace-ableness, and eschewed religious hatred or coercion. They were painfully aware of how religious coercion, not only against themselves, invariably fed public strife. Peace would emerge not by believers abandoning or moderating their truth-claims but by propagating them solely by means of respectful, if forceful, persuasion.

Contrary to the supposed imperatives of the territorial principle, then, it turned out that a plurality of faiths could indeed peacefully coexist within the same territory. Where temporal government confined itself to the establishment of civil order, dissenting beliefs might indeed flourish – indeed, even non-Christian ones: Roger Williams tolerated the religion of the Native Indians in Rhode Island. But, astonishingly, this would itself pose no threat to civil stability.

Jurisdictional secularism or a 'Christian nation'?

To conclude this chapter, I briefly reflect on the implications of jurisdictional secularism for the contemporary iteration of the 'Christian nation' position. Defenders of this view hold that it is both possible and desirable for a nation to be corporately 'Christian' and that it is part of the mission of the Church to look to the state to defend the Christian character of the nation. On this view the state is not at all bound to be religiously impartial between faiths but may endorse Christianity as its official faith and confer certain privileges on it – without, however, compromising the civil and political rights of non-Christians. Part of the argument for the Christian nation view is historical: advocates assert that liberal democracy did not arise in Europe by accident but grew organically out of distinctive elements of Christian culture and that its future sustenance depends on contemporary culture being replenished by these Christian sources. I think such a historical claim could be partly vindicated. It would draw, among others, on the theological arguments for political community, constitutional democracy and religious toleration and freedom I have canvassed in this and the previous two chapters.[66] My main concern here is with the theological arguments for it.

The Christian nation stance does not imply 'theocracy', which literally means 'the rule of God'. Indeed, not even the ancient Israelite polity was a literal theocracy, since God's rule was always mediated by some human office-holder, whether a Moses, a Samuel or a David, whose task was to apply or interpret the law. What is really meant by 'theocracy' is the rule of the Church or the clergy, which would be more accurately (if less elegantly) termed ecclesiocracy or clerocracy.[67] Contemporary Iran would be an example of sorts, where a council of senior Islamic clerics functions as a type of supreme court, assessing the compatibility of legislation with Islamic law. Christian nation advocates (at least in the UK) do not advocate anything resembling such an arrangement.

For some, however, a Christian nation view can imply some form of church 'establishment' as an essential bulwark of the Christian character of the nation; for English defenders, that of the Church of England. Michael Nazir-Ali claims that the ceremonial public expression of this character in, for example, the coronation service, daily prayers in parliament or the national anthem, 'have the purpose of weaving the awareness of God into the body politic of the nation'.[68] Others defend Anglican establishment as a way of maintaining a 'transcendent' reference point at the heart of the constitution and so reminding government that it is accountable to a higher authority. Still others claim, on the assumption that a state will inevitably privilege *some* faith, that it should opt for one that will be conducive to human flourishing. Yet others defend it as a means to retain a respected place for religion at the centre of public life and thus to resist exclusivist secularism.[69]

My argument, however, questions the existence of any public privilege granted by the state to one or other faith. Jurisdictional secularism excludes not only egregious cases of religious coercion or discrimination by the state, such as those widespread in early modern Europe, but also the enjoyment by any faith (religious or secular) of any state privilege at all, however modest or seemingly inoffensive. It thus excludes, for example, a religious confession or preamble in a constitution (as in Ireland or Poland), and 'strong establishments' such as Greece. It would equally exclude both an 'establishment of secularism', and a provision like that in the Malaysian constitution that 'Islam is the religion of the federation'.

Of course, there are more or less troublesome deviations from jurisdictional secularism. A 'weak' establishment like that of the Church of England does not create any substantial injustices at the level of faith, even though it does accord unique, if rather modest, public privileges to the Church that create in some citizens a sense of 'symbolic exclusion'.[70] It has been shown that weak establishments like this are entirely compatible with maintaining extensive religious freedom for other faiths.[71] But if the central argument for jurisdictional secularism is convincing, even weak establishments should be dismantled. This would involve progressively ending the remaining legal or political privileges enjoyed by the Church of England, such as the automatic right of 26 diocesan bishops to sit in the House of Lords, or a sacral coronation presided over by the Church. The same applies to Christianity generally, of course. Thus, for example, the statutory duty on most maintained schools in England and Wales to offer collective worship of a 'mainly' Christian character should be abandoned as a plain breach of jurisdictional secularism.[72] Equally, the inclusion of Christian (in fact, any) prayers in the official business of local councils or the Westminster parliament should end (they can be retained as a voluntary practice).[73]

Advocates of a Christian nation position may regard the reluctance by Christians to seek official declarations in favour of Christianity as a 'failure of nerve' or a 'concession to secularism'. Christian supporters of jurisdictional secularism see it instead as a result of a proper view of the limits of the state – theologically mandated limits.

Conclusion

This chapter has sought to clarify various meanings associated with secularism – 'the secular', 'secularization', 'the post-secular' and 'political secularism' – in order to clear the ground for an account of one species of the latter, jurisdictional secularism. This is the commitment of the state to treat the diverse faiths extant in its territory, as far as possible, with impartiality and to guarantee extensive religious freedom. It is the most important example of 'what is right' with secularism. I have presented a theologically grounded case for jurisdictional secularism indebted to the dissenting Protestants who first came up with a fully fledged account of it.

Jurisdictional secularism is a key constitutional baseline for my model of democratic pluralism. It places a restraint on the jurisdiction of the state, concurring on this point with the ECtHR that the state is not entitled to 'assess the legitimacy of religious belief'. Such a state leaves the task of assessing ultimate truth-claims to the jurisdiction of others – individuals, universities, churches or other faith-based bodies. It does not imply a commitment to secularism as a 'faith', nor to a general 'secularization' of the public realm. By accepting the restraint of impartiality it secures equitable space for plural faiths to manifest themselves in the public realm. Jurisdictional secularism thus stands opposed to an 'exclusivist secularism', which seeks to keep religion to the margins and impose a secularist faith across public space. That is one of the chief 'wrongs' of secularism. In the next chapter I critique an instance of exclusivist secularism applying to religious reasoning in political debate.

Let me reiterate that jurisdictional secularism also flows naturally from the idea, introduced in the Conclusion to Chapter 2, that 'the people' consists of the entire body of citizens in all their sprawling differences, each enjoying equal civil and political rights within a political community that strives to respect all. This inclusive notion of the political community requires that we reckon with the people as they present themselves, not as they might feel obliged to appear in order to be 'presentable'. A just political community committed to jurisdictional secularism will allow the convictional diversity that *actually* exists among the people to come to public expression (within essential legal limits). Unlike exclusive secularism, it facilitates public pluralism.[74] It does not at all prevent religious faiths from engaging extensively in democratic activity and exercising substantial influence over public debate, public policy and law-making – on the same terms as others. That is what Part 3 will be about.

Notes

(Websites accessed 8/12/20)

1 'Law, Morality and Religion in the Family Courts'. Keynote address given by Sir James Munby at the Law Society's Family Law Annual Conference, 'The Sacred and the Secular: Religion, Culture and the Family Courts', London, 29 October 2013.

2 House of Lords Select Committee on Religious Offences in England and Wales, 2003, para. 132.

3 Michael Nazir-Ali, 'Breaking Faith with Britain', *Standpoint* Issue 1 (June 2008), 47.

4 Nazir-Ali, 'Breaking Faith', 47. See also Michael Nazir-Ali, *Triple Jeopardy for the West: Aggressive Secularism, Radical Islamism and Multiculturalism* (London: Bloomsbury, 2012); George Carey and Andrew Carey, *We Don't Do God: The Marginalization of Public Faith* (Oxford: Monarch, 2012).

5 Olivier Roy, *Is Europe Christian?* (London: Hurst & Co, 2019); Lorenzo Zucca, *A Secular Europe: Law and Religion in the European Constitutional Landscape* (Oxford: Oxford University Press, 2012).

6 *Refah Partisi (Welfare Party) v Turkey* (2003) 37 EHRR 1, para. 12. See Kevin Boyle, 'Human Rights, Religion and Democracy: The Refah Party Case', *Essex Human Rights Review* 1.1 (2004), 1–16.

7 *Refah Partisi*, para. 93.

8 *Refah Partisi*, para. 123. In concurring opinions, three judges attacked this unqualified generalization.

9 *Refah Partisi*, paras 40, 47, 125, 128.

10 *Lautsi v Italy* (2012) 54 EHRR 3. See Dominic McGoldrick, 'Religion in the European Public Square and in European Public Life – Crucifixes in the Classroom?', *Human Rights Law Review* 11.3 (2011), 451–502.

11 In my view, it was right for the court to deem such a matter to be within the 'margin of appreciation' it may grant to national governments. However, as an Italian citizen I would have campaigned democratically for the removal of the crucifixes from public schools.

12 This is the first of three senses of 'secular' distinguished by Charles Taylor in *A Secular Age* (Cambridge, MA: Harvard University Press, 2007), 1–4.

13 Oliver O'Donovan, *The Desire of the Nations: Rediscovering the Roots of Political Theology* (Cambridge: Cambridge University Press, 1996), 195.

14 John Milbank, *Theology and Social Theory: Beyond Secular Reason* (Oxford: Blackwell, 1990), 1.

15 See, for example, Talal Asad, *Formations of the Secular: Christianity, Islam, Modernity* (Stanford, CA: Stanford University Press, 2003); Saba Mahmood, *Religious Difference in a Secular Age* (Princeton, NJ: Princeton University Press, 2016).

16 A binary view of faith and reason is sometimes unreflectively assumed among secular thinkers who are not necessarily hostile to religion. Medical lawyer Elizabeth Wicks, for example, asserts without explanation that religious views are 'unique … in depending on faith rather than reason. They may not always, therefore, be susceptible to a reasoned explanation' ('Religion, Law and Medicine: Legislating on Birth and Death in a Christian State', *Medical Law Review* 17.3 (2009), 413).

17 Mark Lilla, *The Stillborn God: Religion, Politics, and the Modern West* (New York: Alfred A. Knopf, 2007), 30.

18 Taylor, *A Secular Age*, 5–6.

19 'Introduction', in Craig Calhoun, Mark Juergensmeyer and Jonathan Van-Antwerpen, eds, *Rethinking Secularism* (New York: Oxford University Press, 2011), 19.

20 Craig Calhoun, 'Secularism, Citizenship, and the Public Sphere', in Calhoun et al., eds, *Rethinking Secularism*, 83.

21 See Roy Clouser, *The Myth of Religious Neutrality: An Essay on the Hidden Role of Religious Belief in Theories*, rev. edn (Notre Dame, IN: University of Notre Dame Press, 2005).

22 Terry Eagleton, *Reason, Faith, and Revolution: Reflections on the God Debate* (New Haven, CT: Yale University Press, 2009), 110. See also William E. Connolly, *Why I Am Not a Secularist* (Minneapolis, MN: University of Minnesota Press, 1999).

23 José Casanova, *Public Religions in the Modern World* (Chicago, IL: University

of Chicago Press, 1994). Casanova has since refined his analysis in 'Rethinking Public Religions', in Timothy Samuel Shah, Alfred Stepan and Monica Duffy Toft, eds, *Rethinking Religion and World Affairs* (New York: Oxford University Press, 2012), 25–35.

24 See Grace Davie, *Europe: The Exceptional Case. Parameters of Faith in the Modern World* (London: Darton, Longman & Todd, 2002).

25 Casanova, *Public Religions in the Modern World*, 5.

26 Casanova, *Public Religions*, 7.

27 Casanova, *Public Religions*, 6. The notion derives from Max Weber's idea of 'the internal and lawful autonomy of the individual spheres' in 'Religious Rejections of the World and Their Directions', in *From Max Weber: Essays in Sociology*, ed. H. H. Gerth and C. Wright Mills (New York: Oxford University Press, 1946), 323–59.

28 On the differentiation of Church and state in Britain since the seventeenth century, see Julian Rivers, *The Law of Organized Religions: Between Establishment and Secularism* (Oxford: Oxford University Press, 2010), chapter 1.

29 Casanova, *Public Religions*, 19.

30 José Casanova, 'The Secular, Secularizations, Secularisms', in Calhoun et al., eds, *Rethinking Secularism*, 56.

31 For a Protestant defence of differentiation as an expression of the historical 'unfolding' of created order, see Jonathan Chaplin, *Herman Dooyeweerd: Christian Philosopher of State and Civil Society* (Notre Dame, IN: University of Notre Dame Press, 2011), chapter 5.

32 This is a possibility occasioned by 'deprivatization', which leads to the 'repoliticization of the private religious and moral spheres and renormativization of the public economic and political spheres' (Casanova, *Public Religions*, 5–6).

33 Jürgen Habermas, 'Notes on a Post-secular Society', *Signandsight.com* (18 June 2008), www.signandsight.com/features/1714.html.

34 Elaine Graham, *Between a Rock and a Hard Place: Public Theology in a Post-Secular Age* (London: SCM Press, 2013), 64.

35 Graham, *Between a Rock and a Hard Place*, 53.

36 Graham, *Between a Rock and a Hard Place*, 64.

37 On the limits of the concept of 'post-secular', see Veit Bader, 'Post-Secularism or Liberal Democratic Constitutionalism', *Erasmus Law Review* 5.1 (2012), 5–26.

38 Rex Ahdar and Ian Leigh, *Religious Freedom in a Liberal State*, 2nd edn (Oxford: Oxford University Press, 2013), chapter 3.

39 For a helpful account of 'even-handedness', see Joseph H. Carens, *Culture, Citizenship, and Community: A Contextual Exploration of Justice as Evenhandedness* (Oxford: Oxford University Press, 2000).

40 *Refah Partisi*, para. 91. Emphasis added.

41 Alfred Stepan, 'The Multiple Secularisms of Modern Democratic and Non-Democratic Regimes', in Calhoun et al., eds, *Rethinking Secularism*, 116.

42 Rajeev Bhargava expresses this as the state's adopting a stance of 'principled distance' from all faiths. 'Rehabilitating Secularism', in Calhoun et al., eds, *Rethinking Secularism*, 92–113. We might equally characterize it as implying a stance of 'principled proximity' to all faiths.

43 Cécile Laborde, *Liberalism's Religion* (Cambridge, MA: Harvard University Press, 2017), 125. She proposes a 'minimal secularism' that has affinities with my notion of 'jurisdictional secularism' (*Liberalism's Religion*, chapter 4). In a similar

vein, Tariq Modood espouses a 'moderate secularism' in *Multiculturalism: A Civic Idea* 2nd edn (Cambridge: Polity, 2013), chapters 4, 8. See also Tariq Modood, *Essays on Secularism and Multiculturalism* (London: Rowman & Littlefield International, 2019), chapter 8.

44 James Skillen, *Recharging the American Experiment: Principled Pluralism for Genuine Civic Community* (Grand Rapids, MI: Baker Books, 1994), 45. See also Richard Mouw and Sander Griffioen, *Pluralisms and Horizons: An Essay in Christian Public Philosophy* (Grand Rapids, MI: Eerdmans, 1993). For a critique of 'pluralism', see James K. A. Smith, *Awaiting the King: Reforming Public Theology* (Grand Rapids, MI: Baker Academic, 2017).

45 As noted, this is similar to what Rowan Williams calls 'programmatic' secularism, but my term accentuates its discriminatory effects.

46 See, for example, Silvio Ferrari and Sabrina Pastorelli, eds, *Religion in Public Spaces: A European Perspective* (Farnham: Ashgate, 2012).

47 See https://humanism.org.uk/campaigns/secularism/ and *Quality and Equality: Human Rights, Public Services and Religious Organisations* (https://humanism.org.uk/wp-content/uploads/BHA-Public-Services-Report-Quality-and-Equality.pdf); *Rethinking Religion and Belief in Public Life: A Manifesto for Change* (London: National Secular Society, 2019). See also Andrew Copson, *Secularism: Politics, Religion and Freedom* (Oxford: Oxford University Press, 2017).

48 Casanova, 'The Secular', 69.

49 'Introduction', in Calhoun et al., eds, *Rethinking Secularism*, 16.

50 Elizabeth Shakman Hurd, 'A Suspension of (Dis)Belief: The Secular-Religious Binary and the Study of International Relations', in Calhoun et al., eds, *Rethinking Secularism*, 166–84.

51 For example, Philip Lewis and Sadek Hamid point out that the fallout from the UK government's 'Prevent' counter-extremism strategy, 'has produced the problematic spectacle of the instruments of state, police and media arbitrating on matters of Islamic theology as Salafi and Islamist readings of the faith are judged to be a "distortion" and efforts continue to support moderate, Liberal Muslims who are deemed secular, progressive and government-friendly' (*British Muslims: New Directions in Islamic Thought, Creativity and Activism* (Edinburgh: Edinburgh University Press, 2018), 165).

52 The most important Catholic source for such support is the *Declaration on Religious Liberty* (*Dignitatis Humanae*) issued by Pope Paul VI at Vatican II in 1965. See www.vatican.va/archive/hist_councils/ii_vatican_council/documents/vat-ii_decl_19651207_dignitatis-humanae_en.html.

53 Perez Zagorin, *How the Idea of Toleration Came to the West* (Princeton, NJ: Princeton University Press, 2003), 82.

54 See Timothy Samuel Shah and Allen D. Hertzke, eds, *Christianity and Freedom: Vol. 1: Historical Perspectives* (Cambridge: Cambridge University Press, 2016), chapters 1–5.

55 See Cary J. Nederman and John Christian Laursen, eds, *Difference and Dissent: Theories of Toleration in Medieval and Early Modern Europe* (Lanham, MD: Rowman & Littlefield, 1996).

56 Magisterial Reformers did, however, establish a theology of 'Christian freedom' that proved essential to the Dissenters' case. See Martin Luther, *The Freedom of a Christian* (1520).

57 Zagorin, *How the Idea of Toleration*, 9. 'Unorthodox' should be read here

as 'dissenting from the majority view', rather than 'questioning core orthodox doctrines'. Many Dissenters were thoroughly orthodox in this sense.

58 Zagorin, *How the Idea of Toleration*, chapter 4. Castellio's argument was denounced by both Calvin and Theodor Beza, Calvin's successor as leader of the Genevan church.

59 See James Calvin Davis, ed., *On Religious Liberty: Selections from the Works of Roger Williams* (Cambridge, MA: Harvard University Press, 2008), Introduction, 1–45; Teresa M. Bejan, *Mere Civility: Disagreement and the Limits of Toleration* (Cambridge, MA: Harvard University Press, 2017), chapter 2.

60 Zagorin, *How the Idea of Toleration*, 196.

61 John Witte, *The Reformation of Rights: Law, Religion, and Human Rights in Early Modern Calvinism* (Cambridge: Cambridge University Press, 2007), 23.

62 This claim was widely affirmed prior to the Reformation (e.g. by Augustine and Aquinas). Its logic – freedom to manifest one's faith – was, however, obscured by the 'territorial principle'.

63 Nicholas Wolterstorff, *The Mighty and the Almighty: An Essay in Political Theology* (Cambridge: Cambridge University Press, 2012), 123.

64 Davis, ed., *On Religious Liberty*, 122.

65 Davis, ed., *On Religious Liberty*, 106.

66 See also Tom Holland, *Dominion: The Making of the Western Mind* (London: Little, Brown, 2019); Larry Siedentop, *Inventing the Individual: The Origins of Western Liberalism* (London: Allen Lane, 2014); Nick Spencer, *Freedom and Order: History, Politics and the English Bible* (London: Hodder & Stoughton, 2011).

67 Ahdar and Leigh, *Religious Freedom in the Liberal State*, 90.

68 Nazir-Ali, 'Breaking Faith', 45.

69 These and other defences are voiced in Mark Chapman, Judith Maltby and William Whyte, eds, *The Established Church: Past, Present and Future* (London: T & T Clark, 2011). They are echoed by supporters of establishment among other faiths. See Tariq Modood, *Church, State and Religious Minorities* (London: Policy Studies Institute, 1997); Therese O'Toole et al., *Taking Part: Muslim Participation in Contemporary Governance* (Bristol: Centre for the Study of Ethnicity and Citizenship, 2013), 50–1.

70 For a nuanced treatment of this question, see Laborde, *Liberalism's Religion*, 132–43.

71 Ahdar and Leigh, *Religious Freedom*.

72 Jonathan Chaplin, 'Statutory School Worship: Managing Post-Christendom Pluralism', *Law and Religion UK* (5 August 2019), https://lawandreligionuk.com/2019/08/05/statutory-school-worship-managing-post-christendom-pluralism/. See Peter Cumper and Alison Mawhinney, eds, *Collective Worship and Religious Observance in Schools: An Evaluation of Law and Policy in the UK* (London: Arts & Humanities Research Council, 2015).

73 See Jonathan Chaplin, 'Why the Bideford Ruling on Council Prayers is a Setback for Secularism', *The Guardian* (13 February 2012), www.theguardian.com/commentisfree/belief/2012/feb/13/bideford-council-prayers-secularism; *Time for Reflection: A Report of the All-Party Parliamentary Humanist Group on Religion or Belief in the UK Parliament* (London: APPG Humanist Group, 2019–20).

74 See Jonathan Chaplin, 'Liberté, Laïcité, Pluralité: Towards a Theology of Principled Pluralism', *International Journal of Public Theology* 10.3 (2016), 354–80.

4

Beyond Secular Esperanto

Introduction

Until such time that she can establish, after years of therapy and demonstrated conduct, that she is no longer a lesbian living a life of abomination (see Leviticus 18:22), she should be totally estopped from contaminating these children.[1]

So intoned one Justice Henderson of the South Dakota Supreme Court in a 1992 case involving a child custody dispute between former spouses. The father had objected to a court order allowing the mother, a lesbian, to have unsupervised overnight visitations with her daughter. The court took the father's side, overturning the order and requiring an investigation of the home circumstances. Justice Henderson offered his concurring opinion. It is not only the judge's assumption that a mother who was a lesbian could not be trusted with her own daughter in her own home that causes us to recoil at this judgment. It is also his citation of a biblical text to support his legal reasoning: it is 'see Leviticus 18:22' that most painfully offends our democratic sensibilities, especially our commitment to the principle of the religious impartiality of the state.

Modern British courts have rarely if ever lapsed into such overt breaches of the principle. But we should not conclude too hastily that this is a purely American question. Anxieties about the use of religious arguments to justify state actions are also very much alive here.[2] Public alarm that religious convictions might be shaping the content of law has been expressed for several decades in the UK. They have been triggered, notably, by debates on laws regulating bioethics, such as the Human Fertilisation and Embryology Act 2008 and the Assisted Dying Bills of 2003 and 2020.[3] That such fears are serious is shown by the fact that even the leading (Anglican) moral philosopher, the late Baroness Mary Warnock, chose in 2010 to devote an entire book to opposing that possibility. It carried the blunt title *Dishonest to God: On Keeping Religion Out Of Politics*. In it she argues that while law is properly subordinated to morality, morality must be separated from religion. This is because religiously based morality comes claiming the 'special authority' of a sacred text or institution, appealing to mystical and dogmatically held notions like the 'sanctity of life' rather than scientific evidence, and circumventing the individual (rational) conscience of the legislator.[4] When religious advocates, under pressure, are required to fall back on secular arguments, they do so 'dishonestly'.[5] Permitting religious reasons to shape legislative debates is to allow the 'godly' to wield 'undue power' over the 'godless'.[6] With religious members of the House of Lords particularly in her sights, she urged that we must, therefore, 'fend off the forces of theocracy'.[7] Given such shots across the bow, it is not surprising to hear a professor of health care law report that while religious people are not excluded from the public forums of bioethics, 'their voices are strangely constrained', with the result that 'Explicitly religious ideas and values have largely disappeared from the language and concepts used in debates.'[8]

Warnock's anxieties were shared by others. Jackie Ashley was one of many commentators incensed by efforts of Roman Catholic cardinals in 2007 to influence the consciences of Catholic MPs over abortion law. Ashley objected, understandably, to the 'ferocity' of Scottish Cardinal Keith O'Brien's claim that the current rate of abortion in Britain amounted to 'two Dunblane massacres a day'. But her response was startlingly intolerant:

> If any MP really thinks their personal religious views take precedence over everything else then they should leave the House of Commons. Their place is in church, mosque, synagogue or temple. Parliament is the place for compromises, for negotiations in a secular sphere under the general overhead light of the liberal tradition. So liberalism is privileged, is it? Yes. For without it, none of these religions ... would have such an easy time. Cardinals, come to terms with the society we live in ...[9]

It may seem surprising that occasional invocations of religious arguments like these should evoke such intense opposition. They are so contentious, however, because what is at stake is not just rhetorical style (secular critics of British opposition to the Iraq war of 2003 could match Cardinal O'Brien's florid prose) but constitutional fundamentals: can we be subjected to coercive laws on the grounds of religious reasons held by only a minority of citizens?

In this chapter, I address the question of the legitimacy of invoking religious reasons in deciding matters of law and public policy. This is a key anxiety not only of adherents to exclusivist secularism but also of some who embrace more moderate versions of political secularism. In Chapter 3, I offered a theological defence of jurisdictional secularism, at the heart of which is a commitment to a religiously impartial state and to extensive religious freedom. Such freedom allows believers (religious or secular) to say pretty much whatever they like in political debates (within the law). Driven by anxiety at the supposed dangers of this prospect, many secular-minded liberals have argued that certain kinds of (otherwise legal) utterances – especially religious ones – should either be excluded from such debates or, at least, labelled with a civic health warning.

This position has its own name: *justificatory secularism* – broadly, the position that only 'secular' reasons fully pass muster in publicly justifying laws and public policies.[10] Religious reasons, the argument goes, can't do that kind of justifying work. Such reasons run up against a so-called 'doctrine of restraint' on the kind of reasons deemed proper to political debate. They may, perhaps, be freely voiced in certain public settings but they must be excluded from the repertoire of reasons that are able to justify the laws we live under – whether on embryology, economics, ecology or anything else. In this chapter, I rebut that idea, defending the rights of citizens and their representatives to invoke such reasons where they see them as necessary to arguments about some important matter of justice or the common good. I will argue that the doctrine of restraint stands in basic tension with a fundamental liberal democratic principle: the safeguarding and encouragement of free speech for all lawful political visions.

To prepare for the argument, let me clarify the distinctions between *jurisdictional* secularism, *justificatory* secularism and *exclusivist* secularism. While jurisdictional secularism is a matter of what the political community does, or refrains from doing, towards citizens of faith, justificatory secularism is a matter of how it speaks publicly about what it does. Exclusivist secularism certainly implies justificatory secularism (as applied both to citizens and to state officials). But it is often mistakenly assumed that jurisdictional secularism also implies justificatory secularism – that the state cannot treat religions impartially unless public debates over law and public policy are consistently secularized. This is a prejudicial and dangerous error, the consequence of which is the risk of marginalizing those citizens for whom faith is a broad and deep source of normative guidance for their public lives. I will argue that while justificatory secularism does apply to state officials, it does not apply to citizens and their representatives.

Reasons and respect

In assessing the 'doctrine of restraint' on religious reasons, we enter a long-running debate about the place of religious arguments in what liberal political philosophers call 'public reason', a debate set going especially by John Rawls's influential work *Political Liberalism*, first published in 1993.[11] The ensuing discussion over the meaning of public reason has produced an industry of argumentation that is still alive today.[12] This chapter seeks to capture what is essentially at stake in these arguments. By framing them in terms of the account of constitutional democracy developed in Chapters 1 and 2, I hope to shed new light on their significance.

The scholarly debate has moved a long way since the first edition of *Political Liberalism* appeared. In that work, Rawls adopted a fairly exclusivist stance towards religious reasoning in political debates. Since then, however, he and many other liberals have come to adopt a range of more 'inclusivist' positions, permitting a wider invocation of religious reasons than before. A few have abandoned the insistence on any restraints on religious reasoning in public at all. Some have also begun to acknowledge the positive contribution of religious reasoning to the functioning of constitutional democracy in the past – names like Abraham Lincoln, William Gladstone, Martin Luther King or Desmond Tutu are typically cited here – and its potential to contribute in the future. William Galston, for example, argues for a 'liberal pluralism' that creates space for many different public voices, including religious ones.[13] Jeffrey Stout, in *Democracy and Tradition*, presents a powerful case for including religious voices in political debate in order to preserve their capacity to inject robust critical thinking into democratic discourse. Stout praises Lincoln's momentous second inaugural address – an explicitly theological interpretation of the American Civil War in terms of divine providence and judgement – as a 'paradigm of discursive excellence'.[14] Even secular modernist Jürgen Habermas now affirms the potentially constructive role of religious reasoning in 'the public sphere'.[15] A thoroughly exclusivist position today is defended only by a small minority of liberal political philosophers. But it remains the case that in wider debates in the media or on the floor of many Western parliamentary chambers, a more exclusivist position – 'We don't do God' – remains the default stance.[16] I begin, then, with a brief sketch of the early Rawlsian liberal version of this stance.

Such Rawlsian liberals hold that the only form of reasoning in political debate that can truly pass muster is 'public' reasoning. Stated thus, the claim might seem innocuous. But these liberals propose a very precise definition of what counts as 'public'. Public reasoning is not simply reasoning that takes place in some public forum (say, the media, or parliament) or is addressed in a general way to 'the public' – and thus not just to 'the choir'. For them, what makes political reasoning legitimate is not the scope of its audience but its actual content, in particular the sources of justification it appeals to in support of state action. The central anxiety among these liberals is about the *justification* of laws and the public policies grounded in them. Their primary concern is not so much with any particular laws that might be introduced as a result of the influence of religion – say, a restrictive abortion law, or a radical policy on climate change – but rather with the nature of the reasons offered to justify them. This position accordingly became known as 'justificatory liberalism' (hence the term 'justificatory secularism').

Justificatory liberals don't deny that all kinds of disputed substantive reasons will be thrust forward in the bear pit of democratic debate. For example, the debate over Brexit has turned on whether membership of the European Union is an enhancement or an abandonment of British 'sovereignty', and thus over what in fact 'sovereignty' itself means. Disagreements like these, such liberals accept, are the stuff of normal democratic contestation. But they proceed to set an extremely demanding threshold for what is to count as an acceptable form of justification for any policy. They do so because of a very specific understanding of the relation between *reasons* and *respect* – of what it means for reasoning citizens to respect one another as 'free and equal'.

We might be forgiven for supposing that we have adequately respected our fellow citizens in political debate if we have listened to them – given them a decent hearing – and granted them an equal right to vote when the debate has reached its conclusion.[17] For example, a Christian may profoundly reject radical libertarian arguments for complete freedom of choice for women over their pregnancies or of corporations over their investment decisions. Yet she will, one hopes, wish to show such libertarians the courtesy of hearing them out when a debate is under way and to respect their equal right to determine its political outcome. But the liberals I have in mind set the bar of respect much higher than this. It is not enough, they hold, that laws must be passed only after proper public debate, and by a democratic decision procedure in which every citizen is equally free to speak or vote. It is not only the *constitutional procedure* that must respect citizens' freedom and equality. The *proffered justification* of the law also has to meet a stern test of acceptability. For a reason to count as 'public' it must appeal to political principles that are available to all reasonable citizens. What might this mean?

By 'available to all reasonable citizens', these liberals don't mean that public reasons must in fact be *accepted* by all citizens (that they are thought to be the right substantive reasons), but only *acceptable in principle* (that they are thought to be the right kind of reasons). The right kind of reasons must be both intelligible to any reasonable citizen, and recognizable as based on public canons of validity. A public reason will be one that makes sense to any reasonably informed citizen and that is open to inspection by any such citizen regardless of their religious or secular perspective. For example, a public argument for the expansion of faith schools would have to appeal to reasons like 'expanding choice' or 'improving performance' rather than supposedly esoteric, 'in-house' considerations such as 'preparing students for a life of religious faithfulness'. A public reason, crucially, cannot depend on any private, esoteric knowledge – such as the precise meaning of an ancient Near Eastern sacred text. Only reasons that meet this stern test truly honour the freedom and equality of our fellow citizens. To offer them a reason we know they can never make sense of or assess for themselves is in effect to say to them, 'Don't think – trust me.' It is to wield authority over them arbitrarily, to disrespect them in a very fundamental way. So the original Rawlsian argument went.

Now, on the one hand, from a Christian standpoint a commitment to public explanation is exemplary. Religious believers should surely want to communicate effectively and respectfully to their fellow citizens. If we accept the theological conception of democracy I outlined earlier – one that champions the deliberative role of 'the people' in the search for principles of justice and the common good – then of course it is highly desirable that as many citizens as possible be encouraged to grasp the rationale behind the laws being imposed upon them, and, if possible, to affirm that rationale. If many citizens have to submit to laws based on reasons they find inherently irrational or arbitrary, then the legitimacy of the law, and perhaps of the political community itself, may be called into question. Religious citizens, like anyone else, should certainly seek to offer convincing defences of their favoured policies that reach as wide a public as possible. So let us call a 'public explanation' one that sincerely aims to be intelligible and persuasive to as large a proportion of one's fellow citizens as possible. It may in fact fail to persuade some, perhaps many, but so long as a conscientious effort has been made, the religious citizen has discharged her responsibilities. Christopher Eberle calls this 'the ideal of conscientious engagement', requiring citizens at least to attempt a public justification of their favoured policies.[18] It is a demanding principle, requiring considerable efforts of imagination, empathy and communicative skill. Merely declaring one's faith-based convictions will not do as a contribution to democratic deliberation. As if we needed any reminder today, many citizens and political leaders – religious and secular – often fall short of it.

Respect and equality

The Rawlsian liberals I am discussing, however, insist on something more demanding than this ideal. They hold that to offer a reason for a law or policy that cannot be 'available' or 'accessible' to all citizens is to commit a breach of 'civic virtue'.[19] It is not enough for us to *attempt* public justification; we must *succeed*, and if we can't, then we cannot responsibly support the proposed law or policy. To offer such a reason as justification for a coercive public law is to disrespect many of the citizens who will be subject to that law. Hence, the exclusion of religious reasons. The argument is deceptively simple. It goes roughly like this:

1 A liberal democracy is based on the principle of political equality.
2 Political equality means that citizens should adopt a duty of respect towards one another in political debate.
3 The duty of respect requires that citizens only offer reasons for the public policies they advocate that everyone equally can in principle find intelligible and acceptable.
4 Religious (or other faith-based) reasons can only be found intelligible and acceptable by some citizens, and indeed are repudiated by many.
5 Therefore, religious reasons should not be employed to justify public policies, and:
6 To employ religious reasons to justify a policy – to seek 'justification by faith alone' – is disrespectful and inadmissible.

Put more simply, the argument says: 'To respect each other as equals, we have to speak in a shared language; if you lobby for policies based on reasons I can't possibly agree with, you sweep my views aside and thereby diminish and disrespect me.' The assumption is that 'our' common language is also 'my' language. If it isn't, then that is my shortcoming which I should strive to overcome. But notice the curious twist in this argument. From a seemingly innocent and widely accepted principle of equal respect, these Rawlsian liberals claim to derive a principle that justifies unequal treatment of different kinds of political speech. A religiously based argument for a public policy ends up facing additional discursive burdens that other kinds do not.

Such liberals think they can generate out of the principle of respect what political scientists call a 'gag rule' – a rule restricting the kinds of reasons that can properly be used in political debate. Now, it actually *is* the case that some important gag rules can be derived from the idea of equal respect. Indeed, such a rule follows from my own conception of the people as a deliberative community of equals. If we respect our fellow citizens as equals, we won't ignore them, dismiss them as of no account, misrepresent them, slander them or incite hatred against them (and there are laws against the latter two kinds of disrespect). But the gag rule that the first wave of Rawlsian liberals tried to derive from the equality principle seems straightforwardly discriminatory. If imposed it would amount to a significant constraint on the freedom of expression of those citizens whose political views reflect religious convictions – their freedom and equality would be seriously compromised. Not only would religious citizens find themselves swimming against the discursive stream, they would find themselves accused of offending against the very rules of proper political discourse – of being 'bad citizens'. At this point, such liberals seem stand accused of the very same 'exclusivism' with which they charge religion.

In his later writings, however, Rawls qualified his earlier exclusivism and argued for what he calls a 'wide view of public reason' in which religious believers are quite entitled to bring forward religious reasons in political debate. In fact, he suggested that they may do so *at any time*. That was a significant concession. But then he entered what turned out to be a potentially debilitating 'proviso': if citizens bring religious reasons into public debate, they must *also* find arguments that every other citizen will consider reasonable – 'public reasons'.[20] Robert Audi (himself a Christian) proposes another version of the same idea: religious citizens can introduce religious reasons in public debate, so long as they *also* bring with them at least one self-respecting 'secular reason'.[21]

We may receive these proposals as sincere efforts to show greater respect to religious reasons than had been the case by more exclusivist approaches. Yet such proposals nevertheless end up adopting what is in effect a patronizing attitude towards religious reasons. They treat them essentially as minors who can't enter adult political debate unaccompanied. They need to be chaperoned by grown-up 'public' or 'secular' reasons. It is not enough, for such liberals, for citizens to *pursue* the 'ideal of conscientious engagement'. They must *succeed* in coming up with reasons any citizen could find acceptable (in principle).

Why might this be problematic for citizens wishing to bring to bear a religious faith in democratic debate? What, after all, is the problem with simply accepting the prevailing terms of discourse of the society we find ourselves in, confining ourselves to what society deems to be 'public'? Isn't Christianity, after all, an 'incarnational' religion that immerses itself in its inherited culture and speaks the lingua franca of that culture?[22] Why the insistence on speaking publicly in one's own religious language?

The problem is identified by Oliver O'Donovan in the course of a response to Jacques Maritain's call in the early 1950s (cited earlier) for religious believers to reason politically on the basis of a shared 'demo-cratic secular faith'.[23] O'Donovan notes correctly that Christians will, as a matter of fact, sometimes find themselves sharing common political prin-ciples with others. But he issues this caution: 'Granted, the church may always make the best of any coincidence of political doctrine between Christians and non-Christians that it lights upon; but "making the best" means *making the evangelical content of the doctrine clear, not veiling it in embarrassment.'*[24] The argument is that if 'evangelical public reason-ing' can't go out unchaperoned, Christian citizens will be compelled to veil it in the interests of consensus and acceptability. If they succumb to an obligation to offer justifying reasons in a secular public vernacular alongside any religious one, they will undermine the authenticity of their religious reasoning. For those whom Wolterstorff calls 'religiously integrated citizens' – for whom faith has implications for the whole of life and thought – this will require them to live a compartmentalized life, to lapse into religious 'dis-integration'.

Equality of persons, not reasons

The injunction that religious reasons must always be chaperoned in political debate by 'public' or 'secular' ones trades on a subtle but prob-lematic shift in the meaning of political equality. The principle of political equality quite properly applies to *persons* – each should have an equal standing in the political community and an equal voice in political debate. The principle is hugely important to constitutional democracy and, as I have shown, Christians have powerful reasons of their own to support it, as do other religious (and secular) citizens. When political equality was first fought for in early modern Europe it was seen as the enemy not of faith but of feudalism, of a natural social hierarchy that trapped people in a condition of inherited subordination. Contemporary Rawlsian liberals have, however, tried to apply the principle not just to persons but to *reasons*, and in a strikingly counter-intuitive way. We might think that the natural way to extend the principle of equality to reasons would be to say that, like persons, all reasons shall be given equal status in political debate. That would have the effect of opening up political debate to new ideas, including those offering radical challenges to conventional wisdom. But in this strand of liberalism the extension careens off in an entirely different direction. Instead, the argument is that only those reasons that are equally accessible to all citizens can be admitted to political debate. But this has the unintended effect of closing it down, excluding ideas that cannot pass this artificially stringent test.

This is a distortion of the original meaning of political equality. Consider this. When we offer our fundamental reasons for (or against) a policy, of course we necessarily reject other people's fundamental reasons against (or for) it. One might even say that we 'disrespect' those *reasons* because we think they are harmful to the public good. Just as the law should be 'no respecter of persons', so political debate should be 'no respecter of reasons'. In both cases, while they get an equal hearing, they should get what they deserve – which might be praise or blame. But in disrespecting a fellow citizen's reasons we don't disrespect *them*. On the contrary, we actually show them more respect by critically engaging with their political reasons than we do by ruling their reasons out of order in advance (or at least deeming them second class). Equally, we show them greater respect by offering them *our* deepest reasons for a policy than we would by presenting reasons we can't fully identify with ourselves or that we only use for tactical reasons. In both ways, we demonstrate that we take our fellow citizens with full seriousness. And we expect them to return the compliment. This is true civic reciprocity among free and equal citizens. A Christian perspective summons us back to an older meaning of political equality. As Stephen Carter puts it:

> What is needed is not a requirement that the religiously devout choose a form of dialogue that liberalism accepts, but that liberalism develops a politics that accepts whatever form of dialogue a member of the public offers ... What is needed ... is a willingness to *listen*, not because the speaker has *the right voice* but because the speaker has *the right to speak*.[25]

The Rawlsian liberals I have been discussing run the unintended risk of closing down legitimate political debate rather than opening it up to diverse voices. This is because they are preoccupied with the *epistemological grounding* of reasons offered as public justifications for laws or policies. Behind this preoccupation is a misconstrual of the principle of equality. The principle calls for equal treatment for persons, and I have suggested that this at least implies a commitment to 'conscientious engagement' by all sides. It does not, however, require that reasons should in fact be equally accessible to all hearers. That is an impossible demand in a society marked by deep convictional diversity. In political debate persons should be accorded proper respect, but reasons should be prepared to take whatever drubbing (or praising) they deserve in the bear pit of democratic contestation. The restraint that this strand of liberalism would impose on religious reasons is morally discriminatory (if not legally so).

Can religious reasoning be 'public'?

But can religious political reasoning, even if *legitimate* (it doesn't breach any civic norms), actually speak successfully beyond its host community and into wider society? Can it after all be *public*? What would it look like if it pursued the 'ideal of conscientious engagement'?

Let me explain further why the Rawlsian liberals I have so far been considering interpret political equality in this counter-intuitive way. The fundamental reason is that they take it as self-evident that religious reasoning is inescapably private, while secular reasoning is inherently public. They think that while religious reasons necessarily exclude some people, secular arguments can embrace everyone, since religious citizens can also accept them. A religious justification for a law or policy will necessarily alienate many, but a secular justification will be just fine with everyone, religious citizens included. A twofold response to this assumption is required: first, that secular reasons are inherently no more or less tribal than religious ones; second, that religious reasons can indeed sometimes meet a proper test of 'publicness'.

On closer inspection, it turns out that what counts as a 'religious reason' or a 'secular reason' is not as clear as has been supposed. Many assume that a reason is 'religious' if it mentions God or some transcendent religious authority, and 'secular' if it does not. Or consider Robert Audi's definition: a secular reason is 'one whose normative force ... does not evidentially depend on the existence of God (or on denying it) or on theological considerations, or on the pronouncements of a person or institution qua religious authority'.[26] That is, a secular reason not only won't *mention* religious sources but won't *depend on* them. Audi's concern here seems to be that someone might offer a political reason that does not mention God but does after all (covertly perhaps) rest upon a religious source. But what might it mean for a political reason to 'rest upon' a religious source? Consider the following two statements:

A. Governments must abide by the principle of the rule of law.
B. 'Jesus is Lord.'

The second – the earliest recorded Christian confession – is obviously a religious statement, but is the first one 'secular'? Suppose we combine them:

C. Governments must abide by the principle of the rule of law ultimately because 'Jesus is Lord'.[27]

This is also a religious statement, and it would now clearly be false to say that its *first clause* is 'secular' just because it shares the same wording as statement A. Now suppose a parliamentarian who believes statement C asserts, during a debate, statement D:

> D. The UK government's Internal Market Bill of 2020 (designed to address alleged shortcomings in the 2019 Withdrawal Agreement with the EU) must be resisted because it amounts to an intentional and serious breach of the principle of the rule of law, and governments must consistently abide by that principle.[28]

Suppose the parliamentarian is a Christian (a 'religiously integrated' not a 'nominal' or 'self-secularizing' one). Has she uttered a 'secular' statement? Surely not. For *this* speaker, *that* statement is ultimately religiously grounded, even though no 'religious' words were spoken. And this is the case even if the religious sub-clause 'because "Jesus is Lord"' didn't enter her mind at that moment, for on reflection she would indeed recall that the deepest reason why she believed statement A was statement B.

This may seem counter-intuitive to many secular-minded liberals. The idea that the confession, 'Jesus is Lord', might play any role whatsoever in the thinking of a Christian MP on something as seemingly 'secular' as a bill regarding technical aspects of a foreign treaty might come as a surprise to them. Yet this is indeed how some Christian MPs – and many Christian citizens – actually think. It is also similar to how some Muslim political activists think, even (perhaps especially) those who are sometimes patronized as 'moderates'. Many Muslims are now searching their own sacred texts to see how principles like the rule of law or accountable government or religious toleration might be theologically warranted. But while secular liberals may not have exact parallels to 'sacred' texts, they still think on the basis of what I earlier argued are faith-based commitments, such as 'the moral autonomy of the rational individual', or 'the sovereign will of the people'. It will probably come as less of a surprise to religious citizens that secular liberals approach questions even as mundane as the Internal Market Bill in the light of such commitments (even unawares).

We should observe, of course, that for the secularist MP sitting next to our Christian parliamentarian, statement D probably might well be heard as secular. But that only means that this hearer is quite naturally slotting it into his own conceptual framework (or would do on reflection). In his framework, governments must abide by the rule of law, not 'because Jesus is Lord' but ultimately 'because the supreme moral autonomy of the individual requires it' (or some similar reason). These two MPs happen to agree on statement A. But A means something interestingly different to the one than to the other. So is statement A 'secular'? The answer is that this depends on who is uttering it and who is listening to it. We cannot tell whether a statement is 'religious' or 'secular' just by examining the words that make it up. We have to consider what the speaker intends, what the hearer receives, and how each relates the statement to their larger world view.

But here a highly important corollary follows, often missed by resolute defenders of religious speech. Religious speakers who want to avoid 'secularist' language – to speak in public from their own faith – do not have to lead with their deepest religious reasons in order to live faithful (religiously integrated) lives. To employ principles like 'the rule of law' or 'human rights' is not, after all, to 'veil' one's deepest beliefs, only to refrain from putting them on display at that moment. In Britain today, for the majority of purposes, citizens or politicians who want to defend the rule of law can do so just by invoking that principle on its own, as a widely accepted and constitutionally embedded element of our political culture. So our Christian parliamentary speaker can criticize the Internal Market Bill just by appealing to 'the rule of law' without the slightest loss of integrity. 'Because X violates the rule of law' is a sufficient public reason. It is both intelligible and testable by any of her fellow citizens. She need not, to be 'faithful', add 'because Jesus is Lord'. This means that when she says in parliament, 'government must uphold the rule of law', she is speaking no less authentically as a Christian than when addressing the group Christians in Parliament she says, 'Government must uphold the rule of law because, ultimately, "Jesus is Lord".'

Levels of reasons

This is not to say that she *may not* utter that fuller, unchaperoned statement in parliament, as secular liberals insist. It is only to say that if she does not, she is not necessarily 'veiling her convictions in embarrassment'. This is so because there are actually two levels of 'reasons' at work in these utterances. 'Because Jesus is Lord' is a faith-based reason. Or, as Mark Lilla puts it, it is the 'revelation behind the last reason'.[29] 'Because governments should uphold the rule of law', in contrast, is not an ultimate reason. It is a proximate constitutional reason valid in this political system. For a religiously integrated Christian, the reason 'Jesus is Lord' ultimately grounds the principle of the rule of law,[30] while *that* principle then grounds the specific conclusion, 'The Internal Market Bill must be resisted.' This conclusion thus enjoys a two-tiered grounding.

We could if we wanted spell out other intermediate or parallel levels of reasons, such as 'because abiding by treaties is the bedrock of international order', 'because the Manifesto committed the party to strengthen the rule of law', and so forth. Each of these supports more specific ones above it, or buttresses ones next to it. The many component parts of any chain of ethical reasoning are complexly (and not always coherently) related, and no one needs reminding that this applies as much in political debate as anywhere else. Precisely which reasons are best advanced in any particular deliberative context depends on a wide variety of factors. But the fact that ultimate religious reasons are not articulated during deliberation does not thereby make the reason or the policy conclusion actually offered 'secular', in the sense of being uninfluenced by or indifferent to or antithetical to faith.

What, then, is a truly 'secular reason'? Let me define it simply as one that proceeds from secularist faith convictions, whether or not stated explicitly. We can, then, apply exactly the same logic to the public reasoning of secularly minded citizens or politicians. Suppose the secularist MP mentioned above intervenes in the debate. Suppose he utters statement D. He has clearly uttered a public reason, one that all his hearers can in principle recognize as such. And from his point of view it is also 'secular'. But it is not public *because* it is secular. It is public for the same reason it would have been public when uttered by his Christian colleague, namely that it is widely acknowledged in British political culture. It is public more because of its context than because of its content. Reasons are 'public' for sociological not epistemological reasons. This means it would be wrong of him to turn to his Christian colleague and say: 'Thank you for joining the club and speaking in a secular language the rest of us can make sense of.' Her response should be: 'I wasn't speaking in a secular language, only a public one.' Conversely, she wouldn't then be justified in retorting: 'And by the way, thank you for keeping *your* secular humanist beliefs to yourself.' To which his response should be: 'I was doing no such thing, I just didn't articulate them at that moment.' In this case it is not that the faith basis is *not present in* the justifying reason, only that it is *not presented*.

Reasons: public, but not secular

Secular liberal Julian Baggini comes close to endorsing this position. He echoes familiar Rawlsian anxieties, insisting that 'Secularism is the most powerful bulwark against sectarianism we have', but also acknowledges the importance of integrity:

Because it demands that we only discuss in the civic sphere what we share and leave out the personal beliefs that divide us, it forces us to the common ground ... it does not require us to leave behind our personal convictions to do so: everyone brings their personal beliefs to the secular table. The trick is that we find a way of expressing them in universalist and not particularist terms.[31]

Now, if by 'common ground' or 'in universalist terms' Baggini simply means that we should strive to make ourselves understandable to as many of our hearers as possible – that, pursuant to 'conscientious engagement', we should *strive for* public justification – then no one should object. However, he means more, as becomes clear when he goes on to discuss the question of abortion:

A devout Catholic is obviously going to be strongly influenced by her religious beliefs on the subject, and when she is speaking in Parliament, these beliefs will come through. But, vitally, she must find some way of expressing them in terms that everyone can understand and appreciate. If she says, 'we should not allow abortion because it is against the teachings of the Roman Catholic Church' she has failed to make an argument that has any purchase beyond her own faith. If she argues for the sanctity of human life in terms which are not specific to the tenets of Roman Catholicism, then she is making a contribution to the secular debate, *even though at root her basic commitments are grounded in religion.*[32]

We can appreciate Baggini's recognition that a religious MP's basic commitments may legitimately be 'grounded in religion'. He accepts that such an MP may argue for 'the sanctity of human life'. But he insists that the MP may do so only 'in terms that everyone can understand and appreciate'. Admittedly, a bare appeal to 'the teaching of the Roman Catholic Church', while perfectly intelligible, does not go very far in meeting the requirement of public explanation. That said, Catholic MPs rarely rely *only* on that reason, and most do not invoke it at all. The problem with Baggini's argument is his insistence that any argument for the 'sanctity' of human life must be presented in 'universalist terms'. For who is to decide what qualifies as 'universal'? As Mary Warnock rightly recognizes, 'sanctity' is a religiously loaded word.[33] It means 'holiness', specifically a holiness conferred by God. It does not simply mean, 'of very high human value'. It is not clear how any self-respecting secular humanist could sincerely invoke it. Genuine secularists should not accept it as 'universal'.

The valid point Baggini is trying to make can, perhaps, be made with another word. Unlike 'sanctity', the term 'dignity' does seem to have wide purchase for both religious and secular believers. So it is no surprise that this is the term commonly invoked by Catholic MPs in bioethical debates. Papal social encyclicals since Vatican II are replete with the term. Suppose we were to say that our MP must 'argue for the *dignity* of human life in terms which are not specific to the tenets of Roman Catholicism'. Would that be too confining? For the majority, in most settings, probably not. For some, however, it still might be. It could be that a speaker reaches a point in debate at which he finds he has no finally compelling way of explaining what 'dignity' means other than stating that it is, finally, a gift of God. Their situation would be exactly parallel to a secular humanist MP who would have reached a juncture at which 'dignity' could only be explained by appealing to a belief in, for example, 'the supreme moral autonomy of the rational individual'. So to impose a rule in political debate against confessing that 'dignity' is a divine gift – or is grounded in rational autonomy – would be needlessly exclusionary.

But, as noted, appeals to 'human dignity' or 'rational autonomy' still remain widely intelligible and acceptable in our political culture, even if many citizens can no longer offer a strong foundation for them. Neither term is (yet) 'sectarian'. Like 'the rule of law', 'human dignity' can often successfully be appealed to without also declaring the faith basis on which it is held. Different citizens may read different particularist meanings into it – while some secular materialists would reject it in the same breath as 'sanctity' – but it is not an esoteric language that would leave half our hearers baffled or 'disrespected'. So we can now see why it is misleading to designate 'dignity' a 'secular' language, as Baggini implies when he refers to the need for Catholic MPs to 'make a contribution to the secular debate'. It is, rather, an eminently 'public' language. Here we meet a phenomenon that secular liberals might not have reckoned with: a reason can be *public* yet without being *secular*.[34]

It is worth noting that this possibility is well understood, and increasingly practised, by Muslim participants in democratic forums. Even Michael Nazir-Ali, a defender of the 'Christian nation' idea and prominent critic of Islamism, does not rule out the possibility of such faithful Muslim speech:

> There is no place for coercion where the relationship of the state to religion is concerned. But there is room for persuasion; to argue our case in terms of the common good and human flourishing, and to show how these depend on our spiritual vision ... Religious leaders, for their part, will seek to guide their peoples in the light of their faith and to seek to make a contribution to public life on the same basis ... it should be possible for Muslims to contribute to the development of a common life by bringing *maqasid*, or principles of the sharia, to bear on the discussion.[35]

Nazir-Ali is referring here to the idea that Muslims, while not seeking to implement literal injunctions of Islamic law, might appeal to widely recognizable 'higher ethical purposes of the law' (*māqaṣid-al-sharī'a*), such as the 'public good' (*maslahah*).[36] This is a promising mode of faithful Muslim speech that is not abandoning authentic Islamic commitments merely in virtue of employing public language. It parallels what Jews or Christians routinely do in appealing to general moral principles embedded within notions of *torah* ('instruction') or *agape* ('love').

What, then, of the other side of the coin? Can we also identify a *public reason* that is not just 'not secular' but actually *religious*? Nigel Biggar proposes just such an argument against euthanasia premised upon a series of theologically grounded assertions, including:[37]

- 'the value of the life of a human individual is conceived in terms of responsibility to created goods and to a vocation from God';
- 'the hope that there is a more-than-human power – God – who will turn evil to good where human creatures either cannot or may not';
- 'the conception of a humane society as one whose members normally support each other in adversity is shaped by [the theological assumption] that in the light of the resurrection of Jesus suffering is to be viewed without ultimate despair ...'[38]

It is hard to see why most thoughtful secular-minded people, even those with little exposure to theology, would find assertions such as these unintelligible or inaccessible, even though they might reject their content.

Now consider the language of Desmond Tutu, universally respected as a religiously inspired contributor to constitutional democracy. Tutu routinely justified his opposition to apartheid by appealing to the status of human beings as 'made in the image of God'. Here we have a justifying reason being offered in public for a specific and controversial policy stance (the abolition of apartheid), one that would imply radical changes in the law affecting every South African citizen and which would be enforced by the coercive apparatus of the state. Quite clearly, Tutu's reason is not only religious but *eminently public*. His reasoning was intelligible to virtually every citizen in the land – not least the white Christian defenders of apartheid who did all in their power to silence him.

Did his reasoning satisfy the liberal secularist norm of civic respect? Tutu's decisive reason was that apartheid had to be abolished because it denied the image of God in black South Africans (and whites, he would always add). Was such a reason one that all citizens could in principle recognize as the sort that honoured their freedom and equality? Few Western secular liberals would have denied that. Could all citizens in principle recognize its 'rational validity'? Not at all. Non-Christians, and especially non-theists, would have thought the biblical doctrine of the image of God irrational and in principle untestable. They would have offered different (even if politically convergent) reasons for opposing apartheid. Why, then, did they not resist Tutu's theologically laden reasoning as objectionable in principle?

The answer is surely that they respectfully acknowledged it as a perfectly legitimate rhetorical resource for mobilizing people behind a political change they desired. It was the authentic public language of a significant section of the citizenry because the great majority of black South Africans at the time had been formed by Christianity. How could it have been disrespectful for black Christian citizens to address their fellow secular citizens in the language most naturally expressing their highest political aspirations and their deepest public identity? It turns out, then, that not only are there public reasons that are not secular, but there are also religious reasons that are quite clearly public in the relevant sense: not as 'testable in principle for rational validity by all citizens', but as authentic articulations of a community's vision of justice.

We might then ask why secular liberals uniformly affirm Desmond Tutu as a hero of liberal democracy but uniformly denounce Catholic cardinals who appeal to the very same biblical doctrine in opposing what they see as another form of legalized violence: abortion. I cannot discern a convincing answer to that question – other than that they happen to support anti-racist positions and oppose pro-life ones. Justificatory secularism is thus invoked when it works in support of one's favoured causes but quietly set aside when it does not. My point, however, is not to impale secular liberals on the stake of their own public inconsistencies – they could quite easily return the compliment on religious believers. Rather it is to draw the obvious conclusion from the foregoing: the Rawlsian liberal insistence that a legitimate political justification must meet their artificial definition of 'public accessibility' cannot stand. Whether a justifying reason is in principle recognizable by all citizens as intelligible or accessible or testable is largely a contingent matter depending on the circumstances in which it is presented. These liberals suggest it is an epistemological question: it depends on the inner cognitive content of the reason. I submit that it is a sociological question: it depends on what the audience happens to know or understand or be willing to accommodate.

Living with dissensus

In his celebrated dialogue with (then Cardinal) Joseph Ratzinger, Jürgen Habermas offered a compelling historical reason why religiously inflected reasoning is not inherently unintelligible or inaccessible to Western publics. He argued that Christian thought has been deeply interwoven with Western philosophy for two millennia, leaving its traces on a formative legacy of powerful concepts:

> [T]he mutual compenetration of Christianity and Greek metaphysics ... promoted the assimilation by philosophy of genuinely Christian ideas. This work of assimilation has left its mark in normative conceptual clusters with a heavy weight of meaning, such as responsibility, autonomy, and justification; or history and remembering, new beginning, innovation, and return; or emancipation and fulfilment; or expropriation, internalization, and embodiment, individuality and fellowship. Philosophy has indeed transformed the original meaning of these terms, but without emptying them through a process of deflation and exhaustion ... One [philosophical translation of Christian ideas] that salvages the substance of a term is the translation of the concept of 'man in the image of God' into that of the identical dignity of all men that deserves unconditional respect.[39]

While Habermas's historical observation is valid as far as it goes, his requirement that religious concepts must get 'translated' into a secular language nevertheless risks subjecting religious concepts to a process of 'deflation' whereby the theological meaning is so muted or distorted as to be effectively suppressed.[40] This is why, as I noted earlier, the term 'dignity', while having more public purchase today than 'sanctity', still remains contested. The Christian meaning of 'dignity' as grounded in human beings as 'images' of God speaks of humans exercising the dynamic vocation of being God's 'representatives' within a creation structured for flourishing and pregnant with possibility. Most of this is 'lost in translation' if it is rendered abstractly as 'unconditional respect accorded to autonomous individuals'. It is true that, as O'Donovan puts it, Christians must 'make the best' of whatever convergences between Christian and secular language are still available to them. But we must reckon with the fact that as soon as notions like 'dignity' get fleshed out and applied, significant differences of meaning will surface. If we are to fulfil the norm of mutual respect among citizens, this will require a form of public dialogue in which we are prepared to listen attentively to the deeper reasons for others' political objectives, if they choose to present them. As Biggar puts it:

> If we are to have public dialogue where citizens have the possibility of learning something new and important, then ... [m]oral concepts should be allowed to own and display their roots, even if those roots are strange and controversial, and whether they be Marxist or Nietzschean, Christian or Muslim ... Public discourse, if it is to be genuinely plural, cannot prescribe translation ...[41]

The consequence of this is that as societies become ever more religiously and morally plural, we should ready ourselves not for a growing consensus on the most important justifying reasons but for a growing dissensus. One of the ironies of the secular liberal position is that while it ostensibly defends the rights of dissenters to be heard in public debate, what really drives it is a hidden premium placed on consensus. This assumption is exposed by Wolterstorff in an instructive exchange with Audi. Audi proceeds on the assumption that publicly accessible reasons are in principle available to all citizens of a liberal democracy who are 'fully rational people in possession of the facts'. But as Wolterstorff points out, the extent and intensity of disagreements in a morally plural society make this an unattainable goal, since in every case there will, as a matter of fact, be *some* fully rational citizens with all the facts at hand who will reject those justifying reasons.[42] Indeed, in some cases there will be many. The very concept of the 'fully rational citizen' is mythical, an idealized fiction pressed into the service of an unwarranted prejudice towards public religion. Wolterstorff observes that secular liberals often use terms like 'rational', 'rationality', 'reason' or 'reasonable' in an uncritical Enlightenment sense, taking it for granted that the outputs of 'rational' thinking will be universally endorsable.[43] But 'rationality' will not, as he puts it, 'winnow out diversity' or 'leave sufficient consensus to serve as the basis of [political] decisions'.[44] The quest for a 'common set of political principles to which all rational citizens can in principle assent' is misguided:

> [T]he reasonable thing for [us] to expect, given any plausible understanding whatsoever of 'reasonable and rational', is *not* that all reasonable and rational citizens would accept those principles, but rather that *not all* of them would do so. It would be utterly unreasonable for [us] to expect all of them to accept them ... What is reasonable for [us] to expect is that [our] proposals will stir up controversy and dissent ...[45]

The possibility of a universally accepted set of secular political principles is still entertained by some liberals. But this reveals a naive aspiration towards 'the politics of a community with a shared perspective', whereas 'we must learn to live with a politics of multiple communities'.[46]

In an early critical review of Rawls, radical democratic theorist Sheldon Wolin warns of the monistic logic of such liberalism: '[Rawls's model of] "reasonable pluralism" converts differences from a threat to an accomplice of stability, co-opting them so that in the end they are eviscerated, absorbed into a consensus that requires smoothing off the rough, possibly irrational edges of differences.'[47] Christian democratic pluralism requires a democratic arena in which those supposed 'irrational edges' (religious or secular) can still find a voice. They might, perhaps, turn out to be voices of a deeper reason than conventional wisdom expects.

Conclusion

The aims of this chapter were two. The first was to cast doubt on a defining claim of an important strand of secular liberalism: that religious reasons are either inadmissible as justifying reasons for public policy, or at least need chaperoning, because they are intrinsically private and inaccessible, whereas secular reasons are inherently available to all. The second was to show how religious reasons can, after all, be eminently public – whether or not they show their colours. Both religious and secular reasons might be more or less public depending on the context in which they are presented. If so, then the foundation for justificatory secularism, as applied to citizens, collapses. We do not disrespect our fellow citizens by presenting religiously based justifying reasons to them. On the contrary, for any citizen to present their deepest reasons for a policy to their fellow citizens is to treat them as grown-ups, capable of responding in a mature and respectful way to the reality of deep difference.[48] That, I submit, is what it means to dignify our fellow citizens as 'free and equal'.[49]

In the next chapter, I set out a constructive idea of 'faithful speech'. I develop the idea by asking two questions evoked by the foregoing defence of faith-based political reasoning. Even if religiously based justifying reasons do not necessarily breach the norms of constitutional democracy, in what contexts are they *appropriate*? And *who* is entitled to utter them?

Notes

1 Cited in Sanford Levinson, 'Abstinence and Exclusion: What Does Liberalism Demand of the Religiously Oriented (Would Be) Judge?', in Paul J. Weithman, ed., *Religion and Contemporary Liberalism* (Notre Dame, IN: University of Notre Dame Press, 1997), 81.

2 See, for example, Steve Kettell: 'On the Public Discourse of Religion: An

Analysis of Christianity in the United Kingdom', *Politics and Religion* 2.3 (2009), 420–43.

3 For an account of debates on the first two, see Elizabeth Wicks, 'Religion, Law and Medicine: Legislating on Birth and Death in a Christian State', *Medical Law Review* 17.3 (2009), 410–37. See also Martin H. M. Steven, *Christianity and Party Politics: Keeping the Faith* (Abingdon: Routledge, 2011), which cites these issues as an example of 'the power of the Christian lobby' (chapter 6).

4 Baroness Mary Warnock, *Dishonest to God: On Keeping Religion Out Of Politics* (London: Continuum, 2010), 11. Baroness Warnock was a member of the Archbishop of Canterbury's Medical Ethics Advisory Group from 1993 to 2006.

5 Warnock, *Dishonest to God*, 127.

6 Warnock, *Dishonest to God*, 108.

7 Warnock, *Dishonest to God*, 166. As she put it during the 2008 embryology bill debate, 'we are not a theocracy but a democracy … it is parliament alone that gives law the authority' (*New Statesman*, 10 April 2008).

8 Jonathan Montgomery, 'Public Ethics and Faith', *Theology* 117.5 (2014), 343.

9 *The Guardian*, 4 June 2007.

10 For one account, see Cécile Laborde, 'Justificatory Secularism', in Gavin D'Costa et al., eds, *Religion in a Liberal State* (Cambridge: Cambridge University Press, 2013), 164–86.

11 I will refer to a later edition (New York: Columbia University Press, 1996).

12 See Paul Billingham and Jonathan Chaplin, 'Law, Religion and Public Reason', in Russell Sandberg et al., eds, *Research Handbook on Interdisciplinary Approaches to Law and Religion* (Cheltenham: Edward Elgar, 2019), 127–48; Paul Billingham, 'Can My Religion Influence My Conception of Justice? Political Liberalism and the Role of Comprehensive Doctrines', *Critical Review of International Social and Political Philosophy* 20.4 (2017), 403–24.

13 William Galston, *Liberal Pluralism: The Implications of Value Pluralism for Political Theory and Practice* (Cambridge: Cambridge University Press, 2002).

14 Jeffrey Stout, *Democracy and Tradition* (Princeton, NJ: Princeton University Press, 2004), xxx.

15 Jürgen Habermas, 'Religion in the Public Sphere', *European Journal of Philosophy* 14.1 (2006), 1–15.

16 The phrase was used by Alastair Campbell, Tony Blair's head of communications, when a religious question came up in an interview. In fact, Tony Blair 'did quite a lot of God' (as I show in Chapter 7). See Nick Spencer, *'Doing God': A Future for Faith in the Public Square* (London: Theos, 2006).

17 See Nicholas Wolterstorff, 'Liberal Democracy as Equal Political Voice', in *Understanding Liberal Democracy: Essays in Political Philosophy*, ed. Terence Cuneo (Oxford: Oxford University Press, 2012), 113–42.

18 Christopher Eberle, *Religious Conviction in Liberal Politics* (Cambridge: Cambridge University Press, 2002), 104–8.

19 They do not say it should be illegal.

20 John Rawls, 'The Idea of Public Reason Revisited', in John Rawls, *Collected Papers* (New York: Columbia University Press, 1999), 584, 591–3.

21 Robert Audi, 'Liberal Democracy and the Place of Religion in Politics', in Robert Audi and Nicholas Wolterstorff, *Religion in the Public Square: The Place*

of Religious Convictions in Political Debate (Lanham, MD: Rowman & Littlefield, 1997), 25.

22 See David Hollenbach's appealing notion of 'intellectual solidarity' in *The Common Good and Christian Ethics* (Cambridge: Cambridge University Press, 2002), chapter 6.

23 Jacques Maritain, *Man and the State* (Chicago, IL: University of Chicago Press, 1951), 108–14.

24 Oliver O'Donovan, *The Desire of the Nations* (Cambridge: Cambridge University Press, 1996), 219. Emphasis added.

25 Stephen Carter, *The Culture of Disbelief* (New York: Basic Books, 1993), 230. Emphasis original.

26 Audi and Wolterstorff, *Religion in the Public Square*, 26.

27 This is shorthand for what would need to be a longer argument, including premises such as 'governments are accountable to God for ensuring just governance' and 'an essential requirement of just government is abiding by the rule of law'.

28 Ronan Cormacain shows how serious it actually is: 'The United Kingdom Internal Market Bill and Breach of Domestic Law', *UK Constitutional Law Association Blog* (23 September 2020). In December 2020 the government withdrew the offending clauses.

29 Mark Lilla, *The Stillborn God: Religion, Politics, and the Modern West* (New York: Alfred A. Knopf, 2007), 30.

30 See, for example, Julian Rivers, 'Government', in Michael Schluter and John Ashcroft, eds, *Jubilee Manifesto* (Leicester: Inter-Varsity Press, 2005), 138–53.

31 Julian Baggini, 'The Rise, Fall, and Rise Again of Secularism', *Public Policy Research* 12.4 (2006), 210.

32 Baggini, 'The Rise, Fall, and Rise Again of Secularism', 210. Emphasis added.

33 Warnock, *Dishonest to God*, 46, 50–4. See also Andrew Grey, *Dignity at the End of Life: What's Beneath the Assisted Dying Debate?* (London: Theos, 2017).

34 For examples of 'public but not secular' reasoning, see Sherif Girgis, Ryan T. Anderson and Robert George, *What is Marriage? Man and Woman: A Defense* (New York: Encounter, 2012) and Michael Banner, 'Why and How (Not) to Value the Environment', in *Christian Ethics and Contemporary Moral Problems* (Cambridge: Cambridge University Press, 1999), 163–203.

35 Michael Nazir-Ali, 'Breaking Faith with Britain', *Standpoint* Issue 1 (June 2008), 47.

36 See Basma I. Abdelgafar, *Public Policy: Beyond Traditional Jurisprudence: A Maqasid Approach*, IIIT Books in Brief Series (Herndon, VA and London: International Institute of Islamic Thought, 2018); Tariq Ramadan, *Radical Reform: Islamic Ethics and Liberation* (Oxford: Oxford University Press, 2009), chapter 5.

37 Nigel Biggar, '"God" in Public Reason', *Studies in Christian Ethics* 19.1 (2006), 9–19. See also Nigel Biggar, *Behaving in Public: How to do Christian Ethics* (Grand Rapids, MI: Eerdmans, 2011).

38 Biggar, '"God"' in Public Reason', 15.

39 Jürgen Habermas, 'Pre-political Foundations of the Democratic Constitutional State?', in Jürgen Habermas and Joseph Ratzinger, *Dialectics of Secularization: On Reason and Religion*, Florian Schuller, ed. (San Francisco, CA: Ignatius Press, 2006), 44–5.

40 Luke Bretherton, 'Translation, Conversation, or Hospitality? Approaches to

Theological Reasons in Public Deliberation', in Nigel Biggar and Linda Hogan, eds, *Religious Voices in Public Places* (Oxford: Oxford University Press, 2009), 85–109; Nigel Biggar, 'Not Translation But Conversation: Theology in Public Debate about Euthanasia', in Biggar and Hogan, eds, *Religious Voices*, 151–93.

41 Biggar, 'Not Translation But Conversation', 171.

42 Wolterstorff, 'Audi on Religion, Politics, and Liberal Democracy', in Audi and Wolterstorff, *Religion in the Public Square*, 154.

43 See Cécile Laborde, 'Abortion, Marriage and Cognate Problems', *The American Journal of Jurisprudence* 63.1 (2018), 33–48.

44 Wolterstorff, 'Audi on Religion', 161.

45 Wolterstorff, 'Audi on Religion', 99.

46 Wolterstorff, 'Audi on Religion', 109.

47 Sheldon Wolin, 'The Liberal/Democratic Divide: On Rawls's Political Liberalism', *Political Theory* 24.1 (1996), 103.

48 As Biggar puts it, this will lead to a form of public discourse that 'should allow contextually sensitive, dialectical, improvisational, candid conversations about public goods between genuinely different points of view which articulate themselves in their own terms while seeking to be persuasive to others' ('Not Translation But Conversation', 192).

49 A similar conclusion is reached by Bikhu Parekh in *Rethinking Multiculturalism: Cultural Diversity and Political Theory*, 2nd edn (Basingstoke: Palgrave Macmillan, 2006), 295–335.

PART 3

Public Faith: Neither Privileged Nor Pliant

5

Faithful Speech

Introduction

The minutes of a cabinet meeting have been leaked to *The Guardian*. The paper leads with an uncharacteristically large block headline, 'GOVERNMENT DOES GOD', reporting that on the agenda of the meeting were the following items:

- Registrars of marriage: advice to local authorities on how to rebut biblical arguments against equal marriage.
- Reforming the Financial Conduct Authority: presenting an Islamic defence.
- Ministerial media briefing: how to defend the secular humanist case for assisted suicide.

Uproar ensues, led by charges that the government is 'dabbling in religion' and contemplating invoking highly controversial faith-based claims to justify its policies. Within hours, a storm of tweets, Facebook posts and letters also appears. Christian activists supporting 'biblical arguments against same-sex marriage', Islamic scholars explaining the public benefits of the Quranic prohibition on usury, and members of the All-Party Parliamentary Humanist Group (APPHG) espousing a 'secular humanist case for assisted suicide' each vigorously defend their positions. The debate is animated. But in contrast to the visceral opposition to the cabinet agenda, no one objects to these various protagonists making their case – not even to the MPs supporting the APPHG statement.

This improbable thought experiment is designed to remind us that the legitimacy of faith-based political speech is highly context sensitive. The justifications we present for laws or policies in democratic debate depend on what role we occupy and who we are addressing, as well as what we are saying. Before rushing in to defend (or oppose) maximum freedom in the area of 'faithful speech', we need to pay careful attention to the possibilities and constraints of such contexts.

In Chapter 4, I critiqued a version of 'justificatory secularism' that served unreasonably to inhibit the open, faith-based political speech of citizens in democratic forums. This, I suggested, is one of the 'wrongs' of secularism. That discussion issued in a call for a level discursive playing field, supporting the civic legitimacy of faith-based public reasoning. It left open two key questions that need to be addressed in building a constructive picture of such reasoning. In what contexts are religiously based justifying reasons appropriate? And who is entitled to utter them? In this chapter I argue, first, that in 'the representative sphere' citizens and their representatives should be fully free to voice such reasons – to practise 'confessional candour' (of the kind that broke out in the debate following the *Guardian* leak). I will also suggest that even though such people should have democratic permission to practise such candour and not be disrespected if they do, it will not normally be institutionally appropriate for them to do so. I will argue, second, that when *state officials* publicly declare a justification for a law or policy, they should adopt a posture of 'confessional silence' – as my fictional cabinet rather spectacularly failed to do.

Faithful speech and political community

My account of the possibilities and limits of 'faithful speech' follows from the conception of the political community I have been developing throughout the book. Legitimate political reasoning is reasoning orientated to the normative purpose of the political community; not just anything goes. What this implies is not so much a negative *restraint* on political discourse (a prohibition) as a positive civic *duty* (an injunction). The idea is that political reasoning has its own intrinsic rules of appropriateness arising from the *raison d'être* of the political community itself and from the diverse roles we occupy within it.

Consider the powerful expectations arising as soon as we enter the political realm. When speaking within the various forums of the political community, we at least need to *appear* to justify our favoured policy as somehow contributing to the good of the whole public, however that is specifically defined (I defined it as 'public justice'). Otherwise we risk being accused of sectionalism – the enlisting of public power for unjustified private or tribal interest. Even those who enter politics in bad faith, merely seeking the narrow interests of their own kind and simply faking a concern for some public principle, still feel compelled to try to make others believe they are genuine. This is why President Trump's shameless appeals to self-interest – his supporters' and his own – sounded to many so shocking. But politicians cannot indefinitely get away with being seen to act on nakedly transactional motivations without invoking public censure. As soon as we step within the institutional frame of the political community we are under an intangible but real moral pressure *arising from that very context* to argue in terms of the public good, however dishonestly, incompetently or ignorantly we may actually do so.

Responsible political reasoning will, then, intentionally address itself to the state's moral purpose. Thus, legitimate items on the agenda of political debate will be concrete instances of what public justice (as I call that purpose) consists in. This could include, for example, how to attain a more sustainable balance of energy sources: what promotes or obstructs it (carbon taxes or regulation of energy suppliers); what the state is competent to do to contribute to its realization (incentivizing corporate initiative or imposing tougher legislation); and how practically it should discharge the duty for which it is competent (what size of budget or design of administration it needs to pursue any of the above, for example). Salient and effective political reasoning has to 'get with the programme' in the specific sense that it must focus on the purpose and capacity of the state. Political reasoning that diverges from that purpose is to be discouraged as institutionally 'off-piste'. This is not because it is morally or epistemically illegitimate or civically substandard, but because it is inappropriate for the political forum – as revealing a misunderstanding of what the political community is actually for. This applies as much to faith-based political reasoning (religious or secular) as any other.

It turns out that we have now arrived at another implication of jurisdictional secularism, but via another route. If the agenda of legitimate political debate, and legitimate state action, is determined by the requirements of public justice (or some parallel norm), then what is *not* on that agenda is the truth of contending faith perspectives. The formal agenda of the Houses of Parliament, the cabinet and its committees, local authorities, public bodies, and so on, will contain many items relating to particular aspects of public justice. Some items will be mundane, others far-reaching. But they won't contain items like those in the example with which I opened this chapter. John Locke was right to recognize, in his *Letter on Toleration*, that 'Neither the right nor the art of ruling does necessarily carry along with it the certain knowledge of other things; and least of all the true religion.' He was equally right to insist that 'the public good is the rule and measure of all law-making'.[1] This is not to imply that, from a religious perspective, the truths of religion might not affect matters of the public good, only that it is not the official business of *the state* to decide whether, or how, they might.

Candour in representation

May political reasoning that *does* properly focus on the purpose of the political community appeal to faith-based justifications? And how far might such 'confessional candour' legitimately go before the principle of jurisdictional secularism is breached? I want to propose that in the representative sphere of politics, free rein should be allowed for citizens and their elected (or other) representatives to bring their rival faith perspectives to bear on the task of discerning the requirements of public justice – if they wish. 'The representative sphere' includes, first, 'civil society'. This consists, for example, of public forums such as media debates, policy statements of NGOs or churches or the social media world. Most secular-minded liberals do not object (or as strongly) to the articulation of faith-based political reasoning in these forums, because they stand outside the formal arena of policymaking – the realm where legally binding decisions applying to all are made. Rawls, for example, is quite relaxed about citizens appealing to 'comprehensive doctrines' in what he calls 'the background culture'.[2] Jürgen Habermas positively encourages the practice as a potentially constructive democratic resource. I argue, then, that adherents to diverse faiths may, in such settings, justify their favoured laws or policies by appealing to faith-based political reasoning. Indeed, if a statement by a faith-based NGO (religious or secular) did not at some point make the faith basis of their policy statements explicit – at least on its 'vision' page – we might suspect it had lost its identity. To repeat: this is a *permissive* proposal: individuals or organizations *may* invoke faith-based reasoning in the representative sphere if they choose, without breaching any norm of constitutional democracy. Whether it is advisable or effective to do so in such contexts is a matter of discursive prudence: what works for a vision page is unlikely to work when addressing a parliamentary select committee.

Those who do decide to exercise confessional candour in the realm of civil society will need to reflect on the manner in which they do so. No complete set of guidelines could ever be drawn up here, since contexts and personalities are so different. One obvious maxim would be that the manner in which any faith-based statement is made should be consonant with its content. This surely means, at least, that any faith-based pronouncement should be: respectful towards other views even when such views are being severely criticized; accurate in describing opposing positions; modest about the wisdom of those making the pronouncement even when it is asserted confidently; constructive in tone even when attacking some defective or unjust policy; and conducive to further debate and the realization of consensus, rather than shutting these possibilities down.[3]

Placards, loudhailers and tweets are poor transmitters of confessional truth (though they have other uses). Statements that simply assert the truth of a faith-based viewpoint without proceeding to unpack the 'public justice reasons' flowing from it or without acknowledging the presence of other sincerely held perspectives will be less persuasive. Platitudinous or sanctimonious declarations – religious or secular – are always unwelcome. Bare appeals to a specific religious or secular text or authority will rarely impress. What is more, since most citizens actually want their arguments to persuade, they will not lead with their faith-based convictions if they know this will instantly deprive them of all influence over an important and pressing matter of injustice. The victims of such injustice will not thank them for their indulgence.

It goes without saying that we must now reckon with the reality of a discursive world dominated by the insatiable appetites of a 24-hour news cycle that cares less and less for reliability or explanation and a great deal for ratings and revenues. This is compounded by a ubiquitous presence of social media outlets that amplify tribal prejudice, fragment public discourse and feed a 'post-truth' culture. In such a world, all political speakers face immense challenges (even to be heard at all). Those who wish to employ confessional candour face even steeper ones. Skilled, principled and shrewd faith-inspired communicators will be at a premium in such a context, and religious communities, among others, should be working hard to cultivate them.

From civil society to institutions of state

So much for the use of confessional candour in civil society, part of the 'representative sphere'. I want to suggest that this sphere also includes the *deliberative* activities of parliaments, councils or other representative organs of the state. In such contexts, elected politicians are expected to continue to 'represent' the views of those who elected them. Here, too, I argue that faith-based justifying reasons could legitimately be invoked. MPs, when acting in their capacity as representatives, may freely voice their own confessional convictions in political debates if they see fit, without breaching any norm of civic virtue. Indeed, it is hard to see why they should not be permitted to do so at every stage of the deliberative process involving legislation or government policy. For example, during the debate on the Human Fertilisation and Embryology Bill in 2008, Mark Pritchard MP declared (alluding to Psalm 139): 'I believe that the unborn are fearfully and wonderfully made. Terminating a child that has been woven and knitted in the womb should be a choice of last resort, not the latest manifestation of Britain's throwaway society.'[4] One can debate the rhetorical skill of this wording but I would entirely defend its constitutional propriety. The logic of such a position is that elected representatives may not only freely voice their deepest convictions but also freely vote according to those convictions. In addition, they should, of course, also uphold the generic norms of discursive respect I proposed for civil society.

An obvious constraint on such a practice in the British system is the rigorous party discipline enforced from the whips' offices. There is, however, a valuable tradition of allowing MPs greater freedom on certain 'moral' questions ('matters of conscience'). The coalition government allowed its MPs a free vote on the Marriage (Same-Sex Couples) Bill of 2013 (as did the Labour Party); the Labour government had done the same on key parts of the Embryology Bill of 2008 (albeit reluctantly). But Polly Toynbee was quite right to point out during the debate on the latter that the distinction between 'moral' and other issues is, in fact, arbitrary and for governing parties often self-serving. All political issues are 'moral'. The implication she drew from this, however, was that a free vote on that bill should be *disallowed*. The implication of my approach is the opposite: there should be more, not less, scope for MPs to 'vote with their conscience', and not only on the narrow range of issues conventionally classified as 'moral'. My approach implies a substantial relaxation of party discipline, acknowledging that this will make for a rougher parliamentary ride for important pieces of government legislation (part of what I called, in the Introduction, 'slow democracy').

One of the striking features of the Brexit process in parliament was the gaping hole it blew at the time in the traditional conventions of party discipline. It is too soon to tell whether this heralds a new era of independent, conscientious parliamentary voting across a range of issues: the Conservative government's 80-seat majority in 2019 did not augur well for that prospect. The one serious recent attempt to break out of the straitjacket of existing party loyalties, the new party Change UK launched in 2019, ended in futility. But a slackening of loyalties to the major parties would be very healthy for the kind of democratic pluralism I am commending. A system of propositional representation would, by increasing the number of party affiliations available to MPs wrestling with their consciences, also make this more feasible.

The prospect of MPs voting according to their faith-based consciences sometimes scandalizes media commentators ('How dare they impose their religion on the rest of us!'). But on the pluralistic model of representation I am commending it is entirely permissible for an elected representative of the people to appeal to their own faith-formed conscience in deciding how to justify a particular policy – so long as they did not deceive their voters about those convictions when campaigning for election. If, for example, it was right for Christian MPs to rely on their religious conscience in opposing the Iraq war – and secular liberals did not cry foul when some did – it is equally legitimate for them to rely on it in calling for restrictions on abortion or genetic engineering. In any case, secular-minded MPs routinely and inevitably rely on *their* (faith-based) consciences in justifying the policies they favour – sometimes in defiance of the views of their constituents. If political debate is, as Polly Toynbee rightly puts it, a 'contest of moral universes', to lay heavier burdens on some politicians (religious ones) than others (secular ones) is arbitrary.

Julian Baggini accepts that 'There is [no] reason why a senior politician shouldn't acknowledge the importance of her religious faith,' but he is needlessly restrictive when he adds, 'although she would need to be very careful not to invoke these beliefs as justifications for where [she stands] on policy.'[5] That would seem to invite disingenuousness. It implies that politicians can concede that they are motivated by religious beliefs but must conceal where those beliefs actually make a difference. For similar reasons, we should repudiate a proposal reached by the otherwise religion-friendly Jürgen Habermas. Habermas accepts that ordinary citizens are free to invoke religious reasons in political debate in civil society and in 'the public sphere', welcoming such reasoning as a potentially valuable democratic resource for the 'renormativization' of politics. Yet he insists that parliamentarians, as state officials, are under a more stringent duty:

> Every citizen must know that only secular reasons count beyond the institutional threshold that divides the informal public sphere from parliaments, courts, ministries and administrations … However, the institutional thresholds between the 'wild life' of the political public sphere and the formal proceedings within political bodies are also a filter that from the Babel of voices in the informal flows of public communication *allow only secular contributions to pass through*. In parliament, for example, the standing rules of procedure of the house must empower the president to have religious statements or justifications *expunged from the minutes*.[6]

Thankfully, the rules of the British House of Commons confer no such autocratic power on the Speaker: no one is empowered to censor what may go into Hansard. Habermas's drastic proposal would erase religiously inspired parliamentary speech from public memory, effectively branding it constitutionally illegitimate.

I would press the argument yet further: even members of the government may (within the constraints of collective ministerial responsibility) present faith-based justifying reasons during the deliberative process. Consider, for instance, a hypothetical Gaia Party environment minister (perhaps holding office in a coalition with other parties) confessing during parliamentary debates that the deepest reason why she favours the government's proposed radical climate change policy is that 'Earth demands it'. That particular reason may not normally make for very successful persuasion, but this is a question of deliberative skill and judgement, not of civic virtue or constitutional propriety. Equally, even a prime minister, arguing in a debate (say) for a military intervention, may invoke not only the substantive principles of just war thinking (for example, 'non-combatant immunity') but also their deeper theological grounds. Would that Tony Blair – whom a friend later revealed was reading Thomas Aquinas on the matter in the run-up to the invasion of Iraq – had declared his theological sources. He could then have been held to account by others for his (mis)reading of such sources.

Some may fear that all of this will open the floodgates to faith-based deliberative anarchy. But my argument has been *against* arbitrary exclusions of such faith-based speech, not *for* a saturation of political debates with faith-based language. What I am calling 'public justice reasoning' would continue to be the normal fare of democratic debate, confining itself to the institutionally appropriate 'agenda' of politics (while acknowledging that what falls within that agenda will itself be contested). Here, however, it is salutary for British readers to recall that permitting more faith-based political reasoning is hardly entering uncharted territory for a constitutional democracy. The most pervasive example of such reasoning in modern Europe is the Christian Democratic political parties represented in several European legislatures, and governments, for many decades. In the post-war period, such parties routinely included explicitly confessional language in their programme of principles or manifestos, though they have grown shy of doing so in recent decades. Several European democracies (Germany, Austria, Belgium, the Netherlands) have 'laboured' under faith-based political reasoning for decades and yet, amazingly, have survived just as well if not better than the British one (or if they have not it is not on account of confessional speech). Confessional candour in the representative sphere somehow did not precipitate social division or constitutional collapse.[7]

A party elected on such a programme is surely not under any obligation suddenly to lapse into secular Esperanto upon entering office. To be sure, government ministers from such parties will, in deliberative processes, need to strike a prudent balance between expressing their party's own faith-based principles and speaking as representatives of a government responsible for the whole citizenry. Thus, for example, when proposing a reform to human rights legislation, a governing Christian Democratic party would be wise to place at the forefront an appeal to widely understood terms like human dignity and equality rather than 'the image of God' (and this is what they typically do). But there is nothing unusual about the need for such a balancing act between distinctive party principles and language suitable for national governance. It is a demand facing any political party once in office.

'Faithful law'?[8]

The line of argument I have been developing seems to allow that faith-based reasoning may actually shape the *content of the laws* emanating from the representative and deliberative stages of democracy. The prospect has alarmed senior British judges. For example, in 2010 Lord Justice (Sir John) Laws, in the course of delivering judgment in the case of *McFarlane v Relate Avon Ltd*, delivered a striking *obiter dictum* warning against the possibility.[9] His views are especially interesting because he was a practising Anglican (he died in 2020), though in delivering judgment he was not, of course, speaking for any religious body. Sir John was criticizing an impassioned witness statement submitted by former Archbishop of Canterbury, Lord Carey, in support of the appellant Gary McFarlane. McFarlane had lost his job at the counselling service Relate Avon for declining, on religious grounds, to offer sex therapy to same-sex couples. The substance of the case is not at issue here, but Sir John's various strands of argumentation are. He rightly affirms that the state cannot itself determine the truth or falsity of any religious belief – 'the ascertainment of such a truth lies beyond the means by which laws are made in a reasonable society.' He is also right to assert that the state can only justify a law on the grounds that it can be seen 'rationally and objectively to advance the general good' (para. 23) (although what meets that criterion is obviously going to be contested).[10]

Sir John's third claim, however, is ambiguous. He holds that the state cannot officially justify a law solely on the ground that it is founded on a particular religious belief held only by *some* citizens: 'The precepts of any one religion – any belief system – cannot, by force of their religious origins, sound any louder in the general law than the precepts of any other' (para. 23). Now this is valid if it refers to the *de jure* status of such precepts; I have already argued that jurisdictional secularism prevents state officials from invoking religious precepts to justify laws. However, it seems inevitable that some such 'precepts' – including some grounded in religious or secular faiths – will sometimes exercise greater *de facto* influence on legislators or courts than others. Sir John himself seems to allude to this in acknowledging that the Judeo-Christian tradition 'has no doubt exerted a profound influence upon the judgment of lawmakers as to the objective merits of this or that social policy' (para. 23). What he seems to mean is that this tradition has in some sense presented to the minds of lawmakers a justification for a policy that does not in itself depend on that tradition, so that the 'merits' of the policy commend themselves 'in reason', not 'in faith'. This claim assumes that a bright line can be drawn in legal and political discourse between the workings of faith and the operations of practical reasoning. But as I showed in the previous chapter, this is far from clear. Even when ministers and judges work hard, as they should, to respect the principle of jurisdictional secularism when making a case for a law (or ruling) to the public, it is eminently possible that certain faith presuppositions (religious or secular) will have 'weighed more heavily' in their processes of reasoning than others – even if those presuppositions do not, in justificatory statements, 'sound more loudly' than others.[11]

Sir John further claims, also problematically, that if the precepts of faith were (even *de facto*) to 'sound louder' in the law than others, this would leave some citizens feeling 'out in the cold' (para. 24). To that I would simply reply that feeling out in the cold on some issue or other is a regrettable but entirely normal part of the experience of democratic citizenship in conditions of deep diversity. For example, the continuing predominance in British economic policy of a highly contestable neo-liberal philosophy, rooted in a (to me) mystifying faith in the efficacy of spontaneous individual exchange, has left millions feeling 'frozen out' of this area of government action for decades. But it has not left such people 'less than a citizen': rather, they have just lost the democratic argument on this area of policy – for now (the tide seems to be turning).

We encounter, then, the possibility of what might be called 'faithful law'. This is the result of the normal and inevitable operation of faith-based convictions in the dense web of political and legal reasoning that go to justify legislation and, less visibly, legal judgments. If this is so, it is surely better to acknowledge it rather than suppress it, not least so that the faiths in question – religious or secular – can be held up to scrutiny rather than operating unawares.[12]

Public justice reasoning

So far I have argued that faith-based reasoning is in principle *legitimate* in the representative and deliberative stages of democratic decision-making. The term 'faith-based' refers to the presuppositions and motivations of such reasoning. But the content of political reasoning is not *about* faith but about politics: it concerns the normative purpose of the political community. Faith-based reasoning, I propose, should be *directed to the task of discerning the requirements of public justice*. That was my definition of the political community's purpose; others may want to substitute some other idea. But the thrust of the argument to follow would not be much affected by that choice.

A focus on public justice will already steer speakers away from a good deal of institutionally inappropriate faith-based language. For example, the House of Commons is not a suitable venue for a discussion of the doctrine of the Trinity. Nor, for that matter, is the House of Lords, in spite of the fact that the presence of 26 Anglican bishops might actually make for an enlightening (or at least entertaining) discussion of the theme. Speakers should be *free* to invoke such fundamental faith-based themes if they really think it is essential to make their case, and they should not be censured if they do. But in many cases it will be evident that they have strayed 'off-piste' if they do. Exactly the same point applies to secular faiths. The House of Commons is not a suitable venue for a discussion of the truth of secular humanism, Marxism, deconstructionism or the Gaia hypothesis. A Communist MP in the 1930s who treated his fellow parliamentarians to a lengthy disquisition on historical materialism as the basis for a true view of human labour during a debate on a shortening of the working week would have been formally within his rights to do so, but would not have been hugely successful in persuading his colleagues. The rules of assemblies like the House of Commons should permit MPs to use such language, but the imperatives of successful political discourse in that context will generally discourage it.

Faith perspectives, then, may, without breaching any norm of constitutional democracy, be brought explicitly into play in political debates, even in venues like parliament, *insofar as they bear upon public policies that are sincerely intended to promote public justice*. Archbishop Tutu's confession that black South Africans were 'created in the image of God' advanced public justice because it spoke immediately and forcefully to the manifest public injustice of the legislation maintaining apartheid. If a speaker genuinely seeks to explain why her favoured policy advances public justice, then she does not violate any civic duty by *also* explaining how her public justice reasons flow out of her faith-based reasons.

But at this point a tricky question remains: may a faith-based reason be appealed to as the *only* justifying reason? Could there, in other words, be *public justification by faith alone*? Again, given the logic of the model being proposed, it is hard to see how this could be deemed constitutionally illegitimate, even though it will be rare and mostly disadvantageous. There may, perhaps, be occasions where the speaker, perhaps for lack of opportunity to do otherwise, or for failure of imagination, simply cannot come up with any justifying reason at all other than an ultimate faith perspective (religious or secular). Or, where a debate has deadlocked, speakers may find themselves forced back to their deepest motivations to explain their stances. For example, a secular economic libertarian, concluding that a protracted argument with a pro-Brexit Tory nationalist on (say) the reform of the World Trade Organization had run its course, might end up confessing: 'At the end of the day, I oppose this measure because I attach supreme importance in human affairs to the absolute moral right of each individual to enter into any economic exchange they choose. That is why I must vote against it.' Or, on Brexit itself, it might have been helpful, in clarifying what was most fundamentally at stake amid all the technical economic claims and counter-claims, for protagonists to declare, 'I am a Remainer because I have an unshakable conviction that the direction of history is to transcend narrow national loyalties'; or, 'I want to leave the EU because nations are intended by God to govern themselves.'[13] There could, then, be cases of 'justification by faith alone' – not to close down debates, but to illumine why they have become intractable and thus to open up more honest possibilities of compromise.

In recent decades in the UK, such cases have been rare. For the most part, political debate has operated at the level of claims such as: 'New WTO regulations will improve the prospects for a more just and efficient distribution of the fruits of trade.'[14] This is likely to continue to be so. Debates will not often approach the point at which it is necessary to invoke reasons like the 'absolute moral right of each individual' or 'the biblical priority of the poor'. If they do, however, citizens or MPs should not be censured for presenting such a faith-based argument for what they see as the public good.

But my central claim here is that the *only* kind of reasons that it is *obligatory* to present in deliberative political settings are 'public justice reasons' – reasons that articulate some reasonably clear conception of the scope and requirement of public justice (or some similar idea), the principal threats posed to it, why such a conception demonstrably supports the specific legislative or policy proposal in question, and so on. Institutionally effective political arguments should contain sound public justice reasons, and the presentation of such reasons is all that is strictly required in political debate. And that is a demanding task.

Declaratory restraint

I have been speaking so far about deliberation taking place in 'the representative sphere', which I have defined as including both civil society and the representative deliberations of the state. I have defended the possibility of 'confessional candour' in this sphere. The other half of the argument is to call for 'restraint in justification' when representative deliberation has run its course and the state reaches the point of announcing authoritative decisions to the public.

Imagine that our hypothetical Gaia Party, surging to a majority on the back of an explosion of popular anxiety about climate change, proposes a draconian transport policy aimed at slowing greenhouse gas emissions. The policy would ban the use of private cars in major city centres, levy huge taxes on road use and air travel, and lavish large public subsidies on trains and electric coaches, raising the basic rate of income tax by 5 per cent to pay for it all. Suppose the party wins a parliamentary majority, and introduces the policy. The environment minister stands with the prime minister outside 10 Downing Street and solemnly declares: 'This policy is mandated by our faith in Earth as a Living Organism from whose hand we and all living creatures receive life and sustenance and to whom due reverence is owed. If we do not act to preserve the environment, Earth's judgement will surely fall upon us and the human species will rightly be judged for its irresponsibility.'

Let us remind ourselves why many would object to this justification. After all, the party has come to power by legal means and enjoys a working majority in the House of Commons, the practical locus of sovereignty in the British constitution. Some might simply dismiss it as irrational dogma or just gobbledygook, but that may say more about them than the statement itself. A more likely and persuasive reason why people would object is because the reason given seems to be *a confession of faith*, not a sufficient explanation of why the state, given its specific mandate, must take this legal action at this time in response to this threat to the common good. Note that this scenario would be strictly comparable to an argument, say, to abolish same-sex marriage by a hypothetical Christian Nation party, citing Leviticus 18.22 (the text invoked by Justice Henderson from South Dakota) as its clinching reason.

Let me now explain in more detail why the state itself should refrain from officially presenting faith-based grounds in support of the decisions it takes – legislative, executive or judicial decisions. I propose that at moments of constitutional declaration – second readings of bills, or cabinet or council decisions, for instance – states should adopt a posture of 'confessional silence'.[15] This is indeed a principle of restraint, although it is not a concession to exclusivist secularism. In a democratic process there comes a point at which representative deliberation ceases and an executive or legislative decision is taken and then presented to the public as the official position of the political community – the moment at which a justification is publicly declared. At that unique declaratory moment, the state, as it were, clears its throat, straightens its back, and speaks as the state to and on behalf of the entire citizenry. Here a principle of restraint upon state organs and officials indeed comes into play.[16] The representative sphere can and must accommodate a plurality of voices, but when the state speaks qua *state* it necessarily speaks with one voice: the voice of the whole political community, not only of sections of its membership. It should therefore strive to speak as inclusively as possible, though it will never be able to express every citizen's voice equally.

At the executive level, the moment might occur, for example, in cabinet when a vote is taken (or arguments summarized by the prime minister). Cabinet minutes may or may not record the deliberations leading up to a decision, but they will and should record the decision, and ideally the grounds for it which will be presented to the public. The announcement of such a decision should refrain from citing any faith-based convictions – religious or secular – that underlay the arguments presented in its favour during the representative and deliberative process. It may only cite what I am calling the 'public justice reasons' justifying it. This is not to try to divorce a policy decision from the deliberative process that led up to it or to conceal the presence of faith-based justifying reasons operative during that process. If there has been an open debate in which a plurality of voices was heard, that would in any case be impossible. The restraint follows simply from the recognition that a vital limit has been reached – a limit on the kind of reasons the state itself is licensed to approve publicly.

The same principle applies even more clearly at the *judicial* level. Court judgments are also state decisions, and they too must refrain from citing any faith-based considerations that may have played a role in the chain of legal reasoning leading up to the judgment. I noted that Sir John Laws rightly recognized that such a grounding may, in fact, have materially influenced the train of thought of an individual judge. But as long as the published judgment itself relies, as it should, only on the facts of the case and the law, it is not illegitimate for a judge's *interpretation* of both facts and law to be materially influenced by her own moral convictions; so it is hard to see why they also may not be shaped by her faith-based convictions. It is true that the margin for interpretation in judicial reasoning is much narrower than it is when, for example, elected politicians apply their party's broad political principles in public policy. Yet if we were to say that a judge should absolutely cordon off her legal reasoning from any knowledge she may have of, say, biblical morality, then we would equally have to say that she should completely cordon it off from, say, her knowledge of utilitarian, communitarian, positivist or libertarian morality. Even if this were constitutionally desirable, it is hard to see how it could be cognitively feasible. Nonetheless, the publicly recorded court judgment may not itself refer to or explicitly depend on any such faith-based grounding.

When the *legislative* process passes from the deliberative to the declaratory stage, the same restraint is mandated. When members of a legislature vote, there is no official record of the interior reasons why they voted, and nor could there be. Any reasons already voiced in debate will in any case be recorded in Hansard. On the view being proposed here, Hansard would then turn out to contain some quite interesting examples of faith-based political reasoning – both religious and secular.[17] Again, the key question is how the passing of a bill is officially justified to the public as an act of state. That could, perhaps, take place in a preamble, though many preambles are short and platitudinous, and some bills do not have them or need them. More importantly, it will take place as ministers and MPs present justifications of the bill to citizens, whether in parliament, departmental statements, press releases, the media or elsewhere – hopefully not only on the couches of a breakfast TV studio or, worse, on Twitter (which doesn't allow for anything so ponderous as a 'reason'). Such official public justifications of legislation or other policy acts should adopt the norm of confessional restraint I am proposing. They might, perhaps, occasionally take the form: 'While the government recognizes that a great variety of reasons – secular and religious – have served to persuade MPs and Ministers of the merits of this proposal, government claims the authority to approve it because it advances public justice in *this* specific way (for example, it safeguards public health by boosting its capacity to respond to pandemics ...).' Note also that the suggestion is not merely that faith-based official justifications for state decisions are acceptable so long as they are chaperoned by public justice reasoning. On my argument they are inappropriate in principle, as breaches of the principle of state impartiality towards faith.

Negotiating discursive diversity

What will happen if we go further down the road of 'confessional candour'? Will there be a reckless free-for-all in which absolutely anything can be said in political debate? Three factors will militate against this possibility. First, I have already argued that at 'declaratory' moments, a principle of restraint does indeed come into play when state officials present public justifications for the state's actions. By itself, that will set a public example of the high importance attached by the state to respect for all faiths.

Second, political deliberation would continue to operate fully within the law, ruling out any political reasoning that slanders opponents, incites hatred, violence or terrorism, or indulges in xenophobic or racist rhetoric. Laws against such types of speech exist and must be rigorously enforced. The prosecution in 2006 of radical Islamist 'Sheikh' Abu Hamza al-Masri, who between 1997 and 2003 had come to dominate Finsbury Park Mosque, for breaching laws against incitement to murder and racism, was wholly justifiable. Such legal constraints may need tightening or loosening from time to time.[18]

Third, in addition to legal restraints on political speech, the main formal deliberative settings of most constitutional democracies have rules in place constraining unseemly political language, such as those governing election campaigns or parliamentary debates. The Revd Dr Ian Paisley could call the Pope the Antichrist in his Free Presbyterian churches but not in public places, such as in the House of Commons, or in the European Parliament, from the chamber of which he was ejected in October 2008 for just such an offence.

Within such institutional and legal boundaries, however, there should be no discouragement or disparagement of the free articulation of faith-inspired political views in democratic deliberative contexts. Rowan Williams describes the likely outcome of such an approach as 'a crowded and argumentative public square which acknowledges the authority of a legal mediator or broker whose job it is to balance and manage real difference'.[19] In the same vein, Gordon Brown (after leaving office) called for 'a strong faith politics which is part of an open and teeming public square, part of a deliberative politics that allows each citizen to bring the richest account of themselves to the public square and thus break the hold of ... sterile versions of secular liberalism'.[20]

Some might worry that this could feed an already turbulent identity politics, and fracture the political community into hostile and self-enclosed tribes. That is a risk, as contexts as diverse as Northern Ireland until the Belfast Agreement or contemporary India under Modi show. But, first, current regimes of 'secularism' have failed to stop it. Second, whether such speech is destructive depends entirely on how an argumentative public square is 'framed' and how its participants comport themselves within it. Baggini, for one, does not think exclusivist secularism is the solution:

> Traditional secularism ... has to go. In its place must be a public domain in which religion is allowed back in. The idea is not to create conflicts of belief, but to allow disagreements to be resolved openly, without people feeling the need to deny the differences in the fundamental convictions that shape their views. The secret of a harmonious society in which different religious and non-religious beliefs are held is not for everyone to remain silent on the things that divide us, but to discuss differences openly in a spirit of mutual respect and understanding.[21]

He adds: 'For atheists this is not an appealing prospect' – his worry being the familiar and legitimate fear of 'sectarianism'. But the aim of 'allowing disagreements to be resolved openly rather than remaining silent on what divides us' is at the heart of the democratic pluralism I am commending. Conflicts of faith-based conviction are increasingly shaping many areas of public policy, not only in bioethics but in economics, healthcare, technology, education, international order and more. In economics, for example, neo-liberal economic theory – still remarkably resilient among Western political classes and leading business schools in spite of the ongoing fallout of the 2008 financial crash – is now ranged against an array of other faith-influenced paradigms, such as social economics, postcolonialism, feminism and radical ecology. There is simply no getting away from the fact that public policy debates on these issues will, at times, be wracked with deep divisions. While we must seize with alacrity whatever opportunities for consensus-building or co-belligerence come our way, an adequate conception of democratic deliberation must accommodate the difficult cases of democratic disagreement, not only the easy cases of convergence.

Attempts to impose a consensus of core policy principles risk foreclosing valuable, perhaps 'prophetic', critique, some of which will come from the margins. Platitudinous appeals to 'the common good' – or 'for the nation to come together' – risk settling for a hasty 'consensus' that excludes, rather than a difficult, perhaps less stable consensus that at least has striven to attend to all voices. A quick and easy consensus might turn out to have been a cosy agreement among established elites, or merely the prejudices of the majority culture, silencing legitimate, if unorthodox, interventions. This could occur over matters as diverse as the ethics of healthcare (where the hospice movement might have something unexpected to say), immigration reform (where voices such as the 'Windrush generation' must now be heeded), or the regulation of abortion (where the testimony of disabled people must be attended to). Whatever policy consensus is produced from democratic processes will be more stable if it is preceded by a protracted, vigorous exchange of justifying reasons. This may make for potentially turbulent, even temporarily destabilizing forms of public discourse. But in a political culture characterized by deep diversity, democratic debate risks being eviscerated if we disparage the expression of the most powerful springs of political ideas and actions. We need to leave space for innovative, critical and radical interventions that can challenge the tendency for liberal democracy to slide into politically correct conformism, condescending elitism, even veiled oppression.[22] Indeed, a willingness to countenance adversarial stances within democratic debate actually fulfils the liberal norm of mutual respect far better than an adherence to the cramping 'doctrine of restraint'. As theologian Timothy Jackson puts it: 'It is an irony of civility that at times more sincere respect is shown to others by confronting them with revolutionary possibilities and transformative vocabularies than by assuming the status quo.'[23]

Conclusion

This chapter has outlined a constructive case for 'faithful speech' – public reasoning in democratic forums on matters of law and policy that is grounded in and may be expressive of faith-based political convictions. I have argued that we must distinguish between what is appropriate for citizens and their representatives in 'the representative sphere' and what is permissible for state officials when justifying policy to the public at 'declaratory moments'. The representative sphere includes both the realm of civil society and the deliberative phases of policymaking. In those phases, elected representatives, even government ministers, may, if they choose, allude to the faith-based groundings of their policy arguments. In the representative sphere, participants may practise 'confessional candour' without breaching any norm of constitutional democracy. Denying the legitimacy of such candour is one of the 'wrongs of secularism'. But while participants enjoy democratic permission to practise such candour, it is normally not contextually intelligent to do so. But that is a matter of discursive prudence, not constitutional principle. When policy decisions are justified to the public by state officials, however, those officials should exercise 'declaratory restraint'. Because the state has no authority to 'assess the legitimacy' of faith-based convictions, such officials should not present them in public explanations of the policy being adopted. Speaking as they do on behalf of the whole political community, they must aspire to avoid reasons that will knowingly and publicly divide the people at the level of their deepest commitments (they may not always succeed in that goal).

The challenge of negotiating deep differences politically in a way that enables constructive deliberation rather than discursive deadlock is both sobering and urgent, as Paul Vallely notes:

> The key question is can we now find a way of creating something positive and healthy from this crucible, or are we sleepwalking into an age of confrontation and blind defensiveness ... We need to do something more than contain or translate that which we fear and do not understand. We need to find a balance which maintains the secularist separation of church and state but which allows the thinking and acting of religions to play their part in shaping the post-atheist culture which is forming all round us. It is the search for a new political language, and it is a massive and vital task.[24]

My account of Christian democratic pluralism seeks such a balance.

Notes

1 John Locke, *A Letter on Toleration* (1689), ed. James H. Tully (Indianapolis, IN: Hackett Publishing Company, 1983), 36, 39.

2 John Rawls, *Political Liberalism* (New York: Columbia University Press, 1996), 220.

3 John Inazu proposes a set of deliberative practices aspiring to 'tolerance, humility and patience' in *Confident Pluralism: Surviving and Thriving Through Deep Difference* (Chicago, IL: University of Chicago Press, 2016), 83–103.

4 Quoted in Elizabeth Wicks, 'Religion, Law and Medicine: Legislating on Birth and Death in a Christian State', *Medical Law Review* 17.3 (2009), 429.

5 Julian Baggini, 'The Rise, Fall, and Rise Again of Secularism', *Public Policy Research* 12.4 (2006), 211.

6 Jürgen Habermas, 'Religion in the Public Sphere', *European Journal of Philosophy* 14.1 (2006), 10. Emphasis added.

7 See Bryan McGraw, *Faith in Politics: Religion and Liberal Democracy* (Cambridge: Cambridge University Press, 2010), chapter 6.

8 The following paragraphs draw on my article at http://ukscblog.com/religious-influence-on-law-a-response-to-lord-justice-laws/.

9 The statement was given in his judgment on an application for leave to appeal, *McFarlane v Relate Avon Ltd* [2010] EWCA Civ 880 (2010) 29 BHRC 249. Paragraph references in the text in this section are to this case.

10 Sir John also holds to a deeply problematic religious epistemology, arguing

that 'in the eye of everyone save the believer religious faith is necessarily subjective, being incommunicable by any kind of proof or evidence' (para. 21). To found a law on such a basis would be 'irrational, divisive, capricious and arbitrary' (para. 22). Indeed it would, if religious belief were actually like that. But the idea that religious belief is mere private, subjective opinion has long been rebutted by philosophers of religion.

11 For an instructive account of the complexities surrounding this possibility, see Wicks, 'Religion, Law and Medicine'.

12 I am not suggesting that judges declare their faith convictions during overt legal reasoning. But greater attention to the influence of diverse jurisprudential philosophies on law during processes of legal education would be of great benefit.

13 See the chapters by Sam Norton and Brian Griffiths in Jonathan Chaplin and Andrew Bradstock, eds, *The Future of Brexit Britain: Anglican Reflections on National Identity and European Solidarity* (London: SPCK, 2020).

14 This will parallel statement D about the rule of law, discussed in Chapter 4 (p. 91).

15 This term is coined by Oliver O'Donovan in Craig Bartholomew et al., eds, *A Royal Priesthood? The Use of the Bible Ethically and Politically. A Dialogue with Oliver O'Donovan* (Milton Keynes: Paternoster Press, 2002), 313, in a response to my chapter in that book. For him, however, it is a criticism.

16 The suggestion to call this a 'declaratory' moment was put to me by Rex Ahdar.

17 In fact it already does, as Nick Spencer documents in *The Political Samaritan: How Power Hijacked a Parable* (London: Bloomsbury, 2017).

18 On free speech, see Anshuman A. Mondal, *Islam and Controversy: The Politics of Free Speech After Rushdie* (Basingstoke: Palgrave Macmillan, 2014).

19 Rowan Williams, 'Secularism, Faith and Freedom', in *Faith in the Public Square* (London: Bloomsbury, 2012), 27.

20 Gordon Brown, 'Faith in Politics', lecture hosted by the Archbishop of Canterbury, 16 February 2011.

21 Baggini, 'The Rise, Fall, and Rise Again of Secularism', 210.

22 See Abdal Hakim Murad [Tim Winter], 'Can Liberalism Tolerate Islam?', *ABC Religion and Ethics* (20 April 2012), www.abc.net.au/religion/can-liberalism-tolerate-islam/10100608 (accessed 10/12/20).

23 Timothy Jackson, 'The Return of the Prodigal', in Paul Weithman, ed., *Religion and Contemporary Liberalism* (Notre Dame, IN: University of Notre Dame Press, 1997), 197.

24 Paul Vallely, 'Private Spheres, Public Squares', *Third Way* 31.5 (June 2008), 17.

6

Faithful Conscience

Introduction

In July 2008, Tim Nicholson was made redundant from his job as head of sustainability for Grainger plc, a large build-to-rent housing company. Launching an employment discrimination claim, he alleged that the real reason for his removal was that Grainger disapproved of his environmental beliefs. He claimed these were 'philosophical beliefs' protected under employment discrimination law on the same basis as religious beliefs. Nicholson won his case at first instance and on appeal.[1] His beliefs were summarized in the case thus: 'mankind is heading towards catastrophic climate change and therefore we are all under a moral duty to lead our lives in a manner which mitigates or avoids this catastrophe for the benefit of future generations, and to persuade others to do the same.'[2]

The case was interesting because it was a significant test of how widely the courts would interpret the term 'belief' in the emerging language of 'religion or belief' in UK equality law. The answer in this and subsequent cases seems to be 'quite generously', although courts have continued to wrestle with delimiting the precise scope of 'philosophical belief'.[3] There is now a legal consensus that law should protect non-religious as well as religious convictions. Also emerging is a broader public sense that we want to live in a society in which someone holding a world view motivated by care for our fragile ecological future should be free to participate fully in a major business sector like the housing industry. This is a way of honouring 'faithful conscience'.

Defending public space for the Tim Nicholsons of this world is a central concern for the model of Christian democratic pluralism I am proposing. Such pluralism requires ample legal space for 'faithful conscience' – for environmentalists and for adherents to many other religious or secular 'faiths', as I call them (or 'beliefs', as the law calls the latter). The goal of such a model is that 'governments should make it neither harder nor easier to follow the dictates of conscience; they should neither burden nor favor persons or groups whose consciences have been shaped by a particular faith tradition or by a secular belief structure.'[4] It also requires ample cultural sympathy, not for the content of any particular faiths but for the possibility that many diverse faiths can flourish and be thought of as 'worthy of respect in a democratic society' (to use the language of the European Convention on Human Rights). My model of democratic pluralism encourages participation by faith-based citizens and associations in as many parts of the public realm as they can make a credible contribution.

The previous two chapters defended the legitimacy, and outlined the character, of constructive faith-motivated speech in democratic debates about law and policy. This chapter and the next defend the possibility of faith-motivated participation in other areas of public life, notably employment and the provision of public services. Democratic pluralism favours wide public space for faith-based individuals and associations to engage in public action pursuant to the common good. It argues that they should be generally free to do so without having to mute their conscientious convictions or to merge their aspirations wholly with what they see as the cultural mainstream – aspects of which they, like Tim Nicholson, may regard as damaging to the common good.

Faith-motivated individuals and associations already contribute substantially to British public life under a religious remit in numerous areas of social life: business, education, healthcare, youth and social services, drug rehabilitation, community development, the arts and many more, often without any perceived difficulty. Of course, much of what religious individuals and groups contribute is not presented under any 'religious remit' at all but is offered 'anonymously' via secular organizations, in ways that defy precise mapping and often display few if any distinctive characteristics. There may be veiled questions of religious conscience in such settings but the principles by which such questions should be resolved become clearer in settings where the religious motivation is explicit and contested.

Accordingly, in this chapter and the next I focus on issues arising from self-conscious religious participation in public life in which controversial normative questions of democratic pluralism come to the fore. In this chapter I explore 'faithful conscience' – specifically, the question whether individual believers should be granted 'exemptions' from generally applicable laws on grounds of religious conscience, such as that granted in 1989 to turbaned Sikhs releasing them from safety regulations mandating the wearing of helmets or hard hats on construction sites.[5] In the next chapter I consider 'faithful association' – in particular, what degree of 'autonomy' from uniform state regulation faith-based associations should enjoy when partnering in the provision of public services like education, health or social welfare,[6] such as was denied to a maintained Orthodox Jewish school, JFS, in 2009 when its religiously determined admissions policy was deemed to breach the Race Relations Act 1976.[7] In both chapters I focus on *religious* conscience and association because – notwithstanding the case of Tim Nicholson – these have found themselves in collision with the law more often than have their secular equivalents (not that environmentalism is exclusively 'secular'). British democracy seems to have more problems accommodating religious faiths than it does secular ones.

It is important to note that the legal controversies occasioned by 'faithful conscience' concern only one cluster of issues arising within a quite limited area of faith-based participation in British public life. The highest-profile cases have tended to fall into two categories. One is clashes between the claimed freedom rights of (mostly) Christian believers and the claimed equality rights of women or sexual minorities[8] – as in the so-called 'gay cake' case in Northern Ireland pitting a bakery run by two conservative Christians (the Ashers) against a gay couple wanting them to place on the cake a message supporting gay marriage.[9] The other is requests from (mostly) Muslims to express 'faithful conscience' in matters such as distinctive clothing – as in the 2007 case of Shabina Begum from Luton, who sought an exemption from her maintained school's uniform policy in order to wear a fuller form of Islamic dress;[10] or gender relations – as in the 2018 case of the Al-Hijrah Muslim school that wished to continue a policy of segregating boys and girls within the school.[11] Both claimants lost their case.

This category of cases may seem insignificant or irksome to onlookers (secular or religious) who cannot identify with the conscientious stances represented in them. But they are worth exploring precisely as 'canaries in the mine' for how tolerant the 'secular mainstream' is willing to be towards minority religious viewpoints that it may regard as disagreeable or even reactionary. Advocates of Christian democratic pluralism will wish to press their secular-minded fellow citizens to be as tolerant of such unpopular viewpoints as possible. As I note below, such advocates should adopt a similar stance where a majority religion, including Christianity, is the mainstream. Thus, for example, they will vigorously defend the rights of atheists in a country like Pakistan (whose lives, like those of Christians, are under threat from extremist Islamists) or gays and lesbians in a country like Uganda (where some conservative Christians have supported criminalizing homosexual sex).

Faithful conscience and religious freedom

Issues of individual exemptions and associational autonomy typically surface as concerns over the degree of protection offered by the law for 'religious freedom'.[12] Robust protection of religious freedom should be a fundamental component of any political community wishing to defend convictional pluralism.[13] Such protection is crucial both for respecting individual rights and also for eliciting as many faith-motivated contributors to public life as possible. Religious freedom should not, however, be treated as an isolated, still less absolute, claim-right but construed against a background of other important public goals conducive to the common good. Such a contextual approach aligns well with an emphasis, deep in Christian political theology, that freedom as such should be understood not first as defence against intrusion (as if the default assumption is that other people are threats) or as an end in itself (as if pure choosing had any inherent moral value). Rather, freedom is a necessary prerequisite for citizens to pursue worthwhile personal and social goals.[14] For people of religious faith to be able to contribute to economic life or public services effectively and with integrity, they must be no less free than are secular citizens to bring their distinctive visions of the common good to bear, and should not be put under explicit or tacit pressure to 'sing from a secularist script' as a condition of public acceptance. Questions of exemptions and autonomy are, then, not only about 'defending rights' but also about how to support the practice of equal conscientious citizenship.

Both individual and associational religious freedoms are robustly protected in the UK. They are guaranteed especially in the European Convention on Human Rights (ECHR), which was incorporated into British law in the Human Rights Act 1998. Article 9.1, on 'freedom of thought, conscience and religion', affirms:

> 1. Everyone has the right to freedom of thought, conscience and religion; this right includes freedom to change his religion or belief, and freedom, either alone or in community with others and in public or private, to manifest his religion or belief, in worship, teaching, practice and observance.

The freedoms guaranteed by that clause, are, like all legal rights, subject to limitation, as specified in clause 2:

> 2. Freedom to manifest one's religion or beliefs shall be subject only to such limitations as are prescribed by law and are necessary in a democratic society in the interests of public safety, for the protection of

public order, health or morals, or for the protection of the rights and freedoms of others.[15]

The valid purpose of the second clause is to allow for the proper and necessary 'balancing' of the right to 'manifest' religion or belief against other legitimate rights and public purposes. The difficult demands of such balancing are sometimes downplayed by champions of religious liberty when they treat religious liberty in abstraction from the wider nexus of rights, duties and public goods for which the political community – including all citizens – is responsible. However, the inherent ambiguity of phrases like 'necessary in a democratic society', 'public order, health or morals' and 'the rights and freedoms of others' has unleashed ongoing controversy over what these 'limitations' on religious manifestation practically mean. It has often been left to courts to specify their exact implications, sometimes with very variable and highly controversial outcomes (as illustrated in the two European cases I cited in Chapter 3).

Three distinctions arising from Article 9.1 are important to my case for democratic pluralism. Two are explicit in the wording. The first is between the 'right to believe' and the 'right to manifest'. The 'right to believe' means the negative freedom (the absence of legal restraint on the ability) to choose, hold to, change, or not reveal, one's religion. It refers to the inner life (the *forum internum*) of the believer. The 'right to manifest' means the positive ability to practise religion outwardly (the *forum externum*), not only in private life, homes and religious institutions but also in public settings. The second distinction is between individual and communal (or what I will mostly call 'associational') religious freedom. I explain in the next chapter that this is no less vital than individual religious freedom because, in most faith traditions, much of what is valuable about religious life is constitutively communal.

A third distinction, between religious and non-religious belief, emerged in subsequent ECHR jurisprudence and is what lay behind the Tim Nicholson case. In a landmark 1993 case, the European Court of Human Rights (ECtHR) defined 'freedom of religion or belief' as including both religious and non-religious convictions: 'freedom of thought, conscience and religion is one of the foundations of a democratic society' both for religious people and for 'atheists, agnostics, and sceptics'.[16] Many commentators now propose that religious and secular convictions be treated under a wider category of 'freedom of conscience' – such as Tim Nicholson's 'philosophical belief' in the need to resist climate change. As far as this goes, this is congenial to my model of democratic pluralism. It places adherents to all faiths, religious or secular, on an equal legal footing. (Below I enter an important qualification about the scope of 'conscience'.)[17] Some have expressed the worry that such a broadening will open the floodgates to all kinds of spurious exemption claims – for Jedi Knights, for example (who were actually cited in *Grainger*). The law, however, now operates with a reasonably precise definition of 'belief' that at least mitigates this danger. For example, the employment tribunal in *Grainger* stipulated that for legal purposes, 'belief' must:

> be genuinely held; be a belief and not an opinion or viewpoint, based on the present state of information available; be a belief as to a weighty and substantial aspect of human life and behaviour; attain a certain level of cogency, seriousness, cohesion and importance; and be worthy of respect in a democratic society, compatible with human dignity and conflict with the fundamental rights of others.[18]

The notion of the 'right to manifest' merits further elaboration. A right to believe without a robust right to manifest such belief, especially beyond merely personal life or within religious communities, would substantially diminish the practical worth of such a right, reducing religion to a private preoccupation and curtailing legitimate public expressions of pluralism. Three considerations can be adduced in defence of this claim: integrity, diversity and scrutiny.

First, a robust right to manifest protects *integrity*. It is central to human integrity to be able, as far as possible, to order one's life on the basis of one's deepest convictions, whether religious or secular.[19] As Ian Leigh puts it:

> In seeking relief from legal obligation, the person making the appeal is seeking to avert the moral harm that would follow from being compelled to act against their conscience ... State recognition of conscience claims allows the individual ... to integrate their beliefs and their actions, so avoiding the need to partition the two or ... to closet expressions of the core of their personhood.[20]

This is not special pleading on the part of religious citizens but a universal appeal that the state show proper respect for one of the deepest sources of human motivation. As Roger Trigg puts it: 'Stopping the manifestation of any religion is itself a challenge to the dignity of human beings. It throttles an important part of their nature.'[21]

The status of such an appeal has sometimes been given short shrift by secularist thinkers. Oxford bioethicist John Savulescu, for example, holds that: 'A doctor's conscience has little place in the delivery of modern medical care ... If people are not prepared to offer legally permitted, efficient, and beneficial care to a patient because it conflicts with their values, they should not be doctors.'[22] By contrast, liberal political theorist Cécile Laborde argues that a potentially wide range of claims might arise from what she terms 'identity-protecting commitments' (IPCs). An IPC is 'a commitment, manifested in a practice, ritual, or action (or refusal to act), that allows an individual to live in accordance with how she thinks she ought to live'. Anything that qualifies as an IPC can be considered as eligible for protection: it can enjoy prima facie 'exemption candidacy'.[23] Liberals, fearing special treatment for religion in breach of the liberal principle of neutrality, have often been sceptical of exemptions. But Laborde argues that liberalism values integrity as 'an ideal of congruence between one's ethical commitments and one's actions'.[24] Integrity requires that 'persons act out of their own convictions ... out of commitments with which they deeply identify'.[25]

It is important to affirm that religious obligations – indeed, any conscientious commitments – experienced by citizens as binding are to be defined subjectively by the individual not according to some objective test such as conformity to traditional religious orthodoxy decided by 'religious experts'. For example, while there may be no clear textual or traditional requirement that Muslim women must be veiled in public, the integrity of those who deem it to be required for religious reasons must be respected. Some religious critics might counter that we cannot do full justice to religion if it is only subjectively defined – that this is a concession to a secular humanist understanding of religion. But we are here asking how *the state* should identify those 'identity-protecting commitments' it may have a duty to protect, not how *believers* should view the epistemological status of those claims. I do not view true religion as capable of purely subjective determination but as definable only in relation to the object of belief, namely God as understood in the Christian Scriptures. But the principle of the religious impartiality of the state means that I must not look to the state to endorse my, or my faith community's, account of ultimate truth, including truth about the nature of religion itself. If the state is not competent to 'assess the legitimacy' of religious belief (as the ECtHR puts it), it is also not competent to resolve whether religion (or other faiths) can be properly defined objectively or subjectively.

Second, a robust right to manifest protects *diversity*. It creates public space for minority views that challenge mainstream assumptions – a possibility of immense importance for a healthily responsive democracy. As I noted in the previous chapter, while democracies rightly seek consensus around laws and public policies, this can only be approached by rigorously safeguarding the possibility of dissensus. Protecting space for dissent is the only way to ensure that some citizens might eventually support an emerging consensus freely rather than under compulsion or, at best, resentfully.

They will at least have had a say in the process. This means protecting the 'right to manifest' especially for viewpoints we may find irrational or even dehumanizing. For example, I find the view that financial investments may be moved at will even at the risk of destroying the livelihood of workers dependent on them – a view resting on a deeper libertarian faith in the efficacy of markets – to be guilty on both counts. I do not seek to restrict the public manifestation of such a view, although I will work democratically to curtail what I regard as its publicly damaging effects.

This has particular significance for religious or cultural minorities.[26] Many members of such minorities experience their 'identity-protecting commitments' as impeded by the continuing predominance in public culture and institutions of Christian and/or secular conventions that do not comprehend them well. This is so for two reasons. One is that for many religions, commitment involves not just mental assent to doctrines but also participation in concrete communal rituals or customary practices, as seen, for example, in Catholicism, Judaism, Islam or Hinduism. We do not want the legal protection of 'conscience' to favour an intellectualist, individualist or 'Protestant' notion that fails to capture much of what is important to other faiths. The contrast can be overblown, for some of these elements are also present in mainstream Protestantism (as I noted in Chapter 3 in relation to the demanding ecclesiology of the Dissenters). But it is true that for many faiths, religious duties often arise from the requirements not so much of individual conscience as of community, tradition, ritual or identity. This is what was at stake in the case of *Ghai v Newcastle City Council*. Davender Kumar Ghai, a devout Hindu, sought permission to be cremated on an open-air funeral pyre, contrary to the statutory requirement that cremations take place in a regulated crematorium. Hindu 'doctrine' imposes no such obligation but for Ghai it was a powerful cultural expectation. Ghai lost at first instance when the court ruled that such an event would cause public offence, but won on appeal (rightly in my view) subject to the cremation taking place within a suitable structure that could be construed as a 'building'.[27]

This leads us to the other reason why the case for diversity is important to minority faiths. Assessments of how well a state is doing in treating its diverse citizens equitably do not start from a blank slate. They must reckon with the enduring effects of historically acquired advantages enjoyed by what have been its dominant faith(s) – with what Laborde terms 'majority bias'.[28] These advantages will often be least visible to those enjoying them. Not all of them are unjustifiable. Where they are rooted, like Sunday rest, deeply in a nation's most formative historic faith and now also offer relief to a majority of citizens (societies justifiably preserve one privileged day for such a purpose as a matter of employment justice), they may arguably be maintained, while allowing exemption claims, where feasible, for those preferring different days. And not all of them are remediable: European nations like the UK find themselves with, for example, a massive historical endowment of visible testaments to the predominance of Christianity, such as churches, cathedrals, colleges, inscriptions or symbols in public places (not to speak of dominant thought-forms and types of language). These will remain rooted to the spot for a while yet. Moreover, they are an important part of the cultural identity of the majority of citizens and so have a valid prima facie claim to be preserved for that reason as well.

But the persistence of these advantages explains why it is important for states in such societies to be particularly solicitous of reports from minority faiths (religious or secular) that their 'identity-protecting commitments' are disproportionately burdened by them.[29] Claims to alternatives to Sunday rest, or to accommodation of non-Christian religious holidays, clothing, dietary practices (halal food), symbols or ethical duties should thus be entertained seriously. For example, the Islamic ban on usury is partly accommodated by making available 'shari'a compliant' mortgages and bonds.[30] The UK should resist the illiberal French route of restricting distinctively Islamic head coverings in public places or the Swiss route of restricting the building of new minarets. While no one can have all aspects of their identity-protecting commitments fully and equally protected, states in historically majoritarian religious cultures can usually do more to remove the more egregious examples of majority bias. Laborde thus rightly argues that where these impact adversely on religious or cultural minorities, 'rectificatory accommodations' may be required in order to level the playing field.[31]

While I have suggested that the ECtHR has not always upheld religious freedom rights adequately, it has sometimes grasped the importance, for democratic pluralism, of protecting the unconventional viewpoints of minority religions. As its Grand Chamber once put it:

Although individual interest must on occasion be subordinated to those of a group, democracy does not simply mean that the views of a majority must always prevail: a balance must be achieved which ensures the fair and proper treatment of people from minorities and avoids any abuse of a dominant position ... Thus respect on the part of the State towards the beliefs of a minority religious group ... by providing them with the opportunity to serve society as dictated by their conscience might, far from creating unjust inequalities or discrimination ... rather ensure cohesive and stable pluralism and promote religious harmony and tolerance in society.[32]

To Christians concerned that such an approach would erode the foundations of Britain as a 'Christian nation' – and thus even imperil the space for tolerance of minorities that already exists – I would reply as follows. Christianity was born as a misunderstood, powerless and often despised minority, has endured such circumstances in many non-Western settings and now begins to do so again even in post-Christian societies. It should therefore be the first to grasp the importance of minorities gaining protection and respect from a hitherto indifferent or hostile majority culture. Openness to greater inclusion of minority faiths in public life is not a pragmatic 'concession' to the fact of pluralism – one that might be reversed if the majority faith regained dominance – but a mandate of public justice. It fulfils the political imperatives of the gospel far better than mounting last-ditch defences of inherited public privileges that have the effect, however unintended, of sustaining the marginalization of minority faiths.

A robust right to manifest protects people's integrity and permits a diversity of convictions to be expressed in public. Its third advantage is that it also ensures *scrutiny*. As noted, democratic pluralism is not a complete free-for-all. It encourages maximum democratic participation by all who can make a reasonable case that they seek to advance the core purpose of the political community (however they precisely define it). By allowing faith-based beliefs to be expressed or enacted in public settings and not just entertained in private, we expose them to the test of public debate. Their proponents are thereby invited to be made accountable for the consequences of their convictions in open democratic forums. This is not to suggest that faith convictions themselves must be subjected to tests of public acceptability, or even revealed in public. Conscientious freedom also includes the right not to have to disclose one's deepest convictions. But when such convictions ground a claim to public manifestation (not only exemptions), it is reasonable to expect some kind of public explanation to be offered. While democratic pluralism will be open to a wide range of such explanations, a degree of public scrutiny is appropriate in order to mitigate the possibility that faith-based convictions (religious or secular) might feed socially destructive practices.

Religious freedom versus equality?

Controversies issuing from the ECHR's ambiguous wording and contested jurisprudence are only part of the background to current tensions in the UK. Here many voices are levelling the broader critique that the UK is experiencing the effects of a legal and policy trend occurring across several liberal democracies, in which the freedom to manifest religion is being needlessly curtailed by an expanding regime of equality law. This has come to the fore in a succession of much publicized legal cases where religious freedom rights appeared to clash directly with such laws, and where claimants to the former have mostly lost. Existing statutory provisions for conscientious religious objection, such as for medical practitioners in the case of abortion, have not proved effective as precedents governing the reception of new exemption claims. In a 2015 survey of the religious freedom of Christians across Europe, the rapporteur to the Parliamentary Assembly of the Council of Europe expressed concern about religious liberty in the UK in the light of such developments.[33]

These particular clashes have arisen mostly as a result of the substantial expansion of equality law in the UK since 2000, coupled with the rising prominence of human rights law following the Human Rights Act 1998. Equality laws were already in place to protect, for example, against race discrimination and to equalize the status of women, but a notable push towards expansion and systematization emerged during the 2000s, culminating in the Equality Act 2010.[34] This has brought about a substantial change in the way law protects equality in the UK, described as an embrace of 'transformative equality'[35] – the pursuit of an agenda of social and cultural change going well beyond formal equality before the law. The Equality Act 2010 requires public bodies actively to promote substantive equality of treatment and oppose discrimination across nine 'protected characteristics', one of which is 'religion or belief', and via many different means.[36]

While this is not the place for an analysis of the Equality Act 2010 as a whole, I judge that many of the *objectives* of the Act are justifiable in terms of what I am calling 'public justice'. This principle does indeed mandate the state to oppose arbitrary discrimination and promote equality of treatment, especially among historically disadvantaged groups such as people of disability, BAME citizens or sexual minorities. Public justice will certainly at times require 'transformative' state action, including and going beyond the terms of the Equality Act 2010. As I have noted, Christian political theology supports not only equal human dignity as a spiritual principle but also many kinds of concrete equal treatment in public life, apart from which the proclamation of equal dignity rings hollow. The Act promises to secure better protection of the nine characteristics than had hitherto been available under law, and it has often done so. How far it has done so in the case of 'religion or belief' is what is at issue here. I am entertaining, then, no indictment of the Equality Act 2010 as such but only one kind of (perhaps unintended) consequence of one element of it – albeit a telling one.

A fundamental argument for a generous approach to religious conscience is that while formal equality before the law secures identical
treatment, substantive equality sometimes demands differential treatment.
It is often asserted, rightly, that in a state committed to treating all citizens equally there should be 'one law for all'. Some then argue that those
opting for unconventional or idiosyncratic convictions (religious or secular) should simply accept that a regime of uniform legal rules is necessary
for society and conform to it without complaint. There is a prima facie
plausibility to this: citizens should indeed be prepared at times to 'bear
the consequences of belief' by paying the higher price of such belief, perhaps, for example, in reduced employment opportunities.[37] Pacifists, for
example, are already willing to bear such costs. They acknowledge that
their convictions prevent them from working in the arms industry. They
do not seek employment in this industry, only then to launch claims to
exemption from actions that contribute to producing lethal weapons.

But such an argument overlooks the point that where general laws have
the effect of imposing *substantial* and *disproportionate* burdens on an
individual's ability to practise their faith in settings they legitimately seek
to contribute to, a prima facie case exists for modifying such laws. One
way to do this is to grant legal 'exemptions' to the believers concerned (as
pacifists enjoy under the right of 'conscientious objection' from, at least,
serving in the armed forces). This does not involve any compromise of
'one law for all' but is an attempt to specify *what that one law requires*
of differently situated people. Thus, the Equality Act 2010 itself contains
many exemptions from its general requirements on grounds of religion
or belief. All citizens of the UK are subject to that *one law*, and all are
equally entitled to avail themselves of the exemptions it provides.

Demands for a capacious exemptions policy have, however, been
growing in intensity because the equality and non-discrimination provisions systematized in the Equality Act 2010 have increasingly been
colliding with claims to individual and associational religious manifestation. The issue is not whether there is one law for all but what the law
as a whole actually requires in cases of prima facie conflicting rights.
Critics claim to discern the influence of an 'exclusivist secularist' view
among lawmakers and courts of the scope and seriousness of religion
in the life of the believer and of its value for public life. They claim that
this testifies to a broader cultural problem of 'religious illiteracy'.[38] As
regards individual freedom, they charge that the law is failing to grant
justified conscience-based exemptions in employment or the provision of
services. Religious citizens may be free to contribute to the public sector,
but increasingly only on terms set by a 'secularist' equality rights paradigm. Such critics do not (or should not) imply that religious citizens are

generally legally obstructed in other areas of public life; and most of such citizens' contributions to public life fall in such areas. As noted, we are considering here a fairly limited area of public action.

Such a critique is not an eccentric grievance. It received ample airing in a report of the All-Party Parliamentary Group Christians in Parliament, *Clearing the Ground: Parliamentary Report into the Freedom of Christians in the UK*. The report concluded that 'there is a problem with how Christianity is understood and handled in Britain today.' The problem is both legal and cultural, and 'plays out on a national, local and personal level through laws, policies and regulations that restrict the freedoms of Christians to articulate and live out their beliefs'.[39] The charge could equally apply to other religious faiths. It requires careful analysis.

Exemptions: special pleading or substantive equality?

Over the last two decades, a wide range of requests have been made for individual and associational exemptions from laws that constrain specific kinds of religious manifestation.[40] *Individual exemption claims* have arisen in several contexts: the wearing of religious symbols (Christian crosses, Sikh turbans) or clothing (Muslim head coverings) ruled out by employers' dress codes;[41] requests to engage in prayers during working hours, to celebrate special religious holidays, to express beliefs at work, or to be exempted from the serving of alcohol; or the provision of services by private or public bodies such as the refusal by Gary McFarlane (the Relate counsellor whose case was discussed in the previous chapter) to offer sex therapy to same-sex couples.[42] *Associational exemption claims* have included, in addition to Ashers and JFS, a commercial hotel run by Hazelmary and Peter Bull that declined to rent a double-bedded room to a same-sex couple,[43] and Catholic Care, an adoption agency that declined to place children with same-sex couples (discussed in the next chapter).

The territory is highly complex and no blanket solutions for all claims would be available even if the law were crystal clear and the courts fully consistent.[44] We are not, in such cases, engaged in a gladiatorial contest between good and evil (and narratives of 'persecution' of the religious seriously distort the facts and debase the currency of that term). It is also worth registering that the method of granting exemptions from generally applicable laws that impact different citizens differently is not an ideal way for societies to respond to convictional pluralism. It assumes the essential propriety of the original law but then entertains exemption claims as a form of 'concession' to supplicants with supposedly tender consciences. This feeds the perception that exemptions are 'second-rate solutions to problems of moral conflict'.[45] Far better to address convictional diversity 'at source', so to speak, when law and public policy are first drafted (as was partly done in the Equality Act 2010).

Several of the most heated controversies have centred on claims of *indirect discrimination* on grounds of religion and belief. Indirect discrimination is defined as 'the equal application of a provision, criterion or practice which puts the individual concerned and others like him or her at a particular disadvantage and which cannot be shown to be a proportionate means of achieving a legitimate aim'.[46] One widely debated case, *Ladele v London Borough of Islington*,[47] reveals the genuine difficulties of addressing such complaints but also points to a promising way forward that is eminently fitting for a pluralist society.

Lillian Ladele was a marriage registrar working for Islington Council who declined, on grounds of her belief in traditional Christian sexual ethics, to preside over same-sex civil partnerships introduced under the Civil Partnerships Act 2004 (CPA).[48] She had signed a contract in 2002 on the basis of a job description that made no mention of civil partnerships. But she was expected to preside at such ceremonies because Islington Council had decided in light of the CPA to 'designate' all its registrars as civil partnership registrars. The CPA did not require them to do so, and some councils had not, although it did require councils to ensure there were sufficient registrars to meet local demand. Ladele was initially offered a temporary arrangement whereby she would only preside at the signing process. During this time she was able to arrange informal rota swaps with colleagues so as to avoid even having to do this. Eventually she concluded that the arrangement was unacceptable because it still involved her participating in a civil partnership to which she in conscience objected; she would still be 'condoning' a sexual practice (not a sexual identity) incompatible with her biblical faith. But two gay colleagues had lodged a complaint with the council on the basis that they found her stance 'homophobic' and in breach of the council's Dignity for All policy. This policy required freedom from discrimination on grounds of (inter alia) sexual orientation, and all staff and members of the public to be treated with dignity and respect. Following a disciplinary hearing commenced by the council in which she was threatened with dismissal, she launched an Employment Tribunal (ET) claim. The council then appealed against the ET's finding in her favour.[49]

The Employment Appeal Tribunal and the Court of Appeal (CA) subsequently found that she had indeed suffered 'disadvantage' but that this was justified because of the lawfulness of the council's Dignity for All policy, which was deemed (in my view, plausibly) to be a 'legitimate aim'.[50] They also found that the council was *entitled* to adopt universal designation (applying to all registrars), even though they were not *obliged* by the CPA to do so.[51] But they concluded that, once Dignity for All had been adopted, accommodating Ladele's request for an exemption 'would necessarily undermine' the council's 'non-discriminatory objectives'.[52]

I suggest that here we have a compelling example of where an entirely workable 'reasonable accommodation' was available to an employer but unjustifiably refused. Reasonable accommodation is an adjustment in working conditions to permit an employee to remain in post while retaining conscientious integrity. The council could simply have declined to designate all registrars as registrars of civil partnerships, making room for freedom of conscience for the very small number of staff with concerns. Dignity for All did not itself mandate universal designation; and nor did existing equality legislation. Here, the 'public sector equality duty' was being read more expansively than the law required.[53] But the courts found that universal designation was a 'proportionate means' of achieving the council's legitimate aim. This meant that any disadvantage suffered by Ladele was deemed justifiable in the cause of the greater good of the policy. The CA, for example, asserted that Dignity for All had 'overarching policy significance' for the council and had 'fundamental human rights, equality and diversity implications', so that the impact on Ladele could thus be overridden.[54]

It is far from clear that this follows. One crucial step in the courts' reasoning was that while the council's policy caused her 'disadvantage' it did *not*, after all, impair her religious freedom. It did not 'impinge upon her religious beliefs: she remained free to hold those beliefs, and free to worship as she wished'.[55] This is because Ladele was being required to perform 'a purely secular task'; and her objection 'was based upon her view of marriage, which was not a core part of her religion; and Islington's requirement in no way prevented her from worshipping as she wished'.[56] Citing ECtHR jurisprudence, the CA concluded that Article 9 provisions primarily protect 'personal convictions' or 'acts that are closely linked to those matters such as acts of worship or devotion'.[57] They protect the *forum internum* but do not always 'guarantee the right to behave in the public sphere in a way which is dictated by such a belief'.[58]

The court was here reading the right to manifest in a minimalist and distorting way, reducing religion to 'personal convictions' with no compelling implications for public action and thus imposing upon Ladele a construction of her faith that was false to her own understanding of its scope and seriousness. Only thus could it conclude that a theology of marriage is 'not a core part' of her faith. But as I argued in Chapter 3, it is not within the competence of any organ of state to rule on what counts as a 'core part' of anyone's faith.[59] To do so is a straightforward breach of the principle of jurisdictional secularism and the effect was a significant downgrading of Ladele's Article 9 rights to religious freedom.

Fortunately, courts have subsequently retreated from using the criterion of the 'core' of a religion in assessing whether an infringement of religious freedom was 'justified'. This will not, of course, guarantee success for future claims since they will still need to be weighed against other factors in the necessary balancing, or 'proportionality', exercise that accompanies indirect discrimination cases. In such exercises, judges will always have to take a view of the scope and seriousness of religion, on which there remains cause for concern. But when it came to consider the case, the ECtHR issued a judgment that should have the effect of boosting the individual right to manifest under Article 9. It is a welcome, if modest, retreat from judicial overreach in this area.[60]

What, then, of the 'offence' claimed by Ladele's gay colleagues? Human rights lawyer Robert Wintemute holds that although accommodating Ladele would have removed the risk of direct harm caused by a public official refusing to serve a gay couple to their faces, it would still have amounted to indirect harm, namely 'exclusion from part of the service offered by the employer'.[61] This is the case irrespective of whether the customer knows about a restriction of service: customers are entitled to '100 per cent of the employer's capacity to serve, whether they know about it or not'. And colleagues would also 'have good reason to be offended' if they did come to know of it, which they likely would have.[62] Accommodating Ladele would thus have amounted to direct discrimination on grounds of sexual orientation. Ladele was thus 'not a case of sexual orientation trumping religion, but rather the greater harm of potential direct discrimination trumping the lesser harm of potential indirect discrimination'.[63]

Wintemute is right to say that 'Islington Council did not post a "no Christians need apply" sign.' But he misleads in suggesting that 'It was Ms Ladele who wished to post a "no same-sex couples need apply to me" sign.'[64] Couples do not apply to individual employees for the service but to the employer. In claiming that Ladele was in effect seeking to 'impose' her religion on others,[65] Wintemute also implausibly stretches the meaning of this term. His proposal for how such conflicts could be avoided is that people in Ladele's situation could 'consider revising their belief' that participating in 'sinful' acts is to condone such acts.[66] Now if I, as a fellow Christian, were in a personal conversation with Ladele, that is a line I might well pursue. But to set the law in such a way that those sincerely unconvinced by such an argument are effectively excluded from certain forms of public service is a troubling direction to take for a society that values pluralism.

But there was, first, no 'exclusion from part of the service': given the availability of other colleagues, no gay couples would be hindered in accessing a civil partnership.[67] The legal duty to provide the service should be seen as falling on Islington Council not on particular employees. Second, to assert that offence is caused merely by *knowing* that certain employees have declined to offer you a service on grounds of religious conscience, or that a colleague has been accommodated by your employer on such grounds, worryingly lowers the bar on what counts as an 'offence'. It is entirely understandable that gay couples or colleagues might have felt offended by this accommodation. But is this really a case of an offence that is harmful enough to merit legal proscription? Isn't part of living with deep diversity just being willing to bear many (unintended) 'offences' occasioned by convictional divergences from one's fellow citizens or colleagues? As I have noted, to participate in a democracy is to be prepared to live with a degree of loss. This is one such case. But the loss was all on Ladele's side.

We see here two problems in the way equality law has been operating. First, under equality law, the 'group disadvantage' criterion involves courts making comparative judgments regarding the impact of a law on a group defined in terms of a shared protected characteristic. The question, then, is whether the law treats an individual less favourably than others in the relevant group. But since individuals' attitudes to their religion or belief can differ so widely within a group – so that what may be 'core' for one is a matter of indifference for another – there is a risk that one individual's particular conscientious claims may be lost to view when seen only as a member of a group. 'Group disadvantage' can be too nebulous a concept to do the work that needs to be done in assessing conscientious burdens on very diverse individuals.[68] Second, equality rights are tending to be read by public authorities or employers in an overly expansive way, sometimes going beyond the demands of law itself. This means that what counts as 'harm' or as a 'legitimate aim' will also correspondingly be inflated beyond what is necessary for the protection of others' essential rights or the pursuit of necessary public policies. Such misconceptions are here converging so as to accord higher general priority to equality rights than to religious liberty rights. The outcome is that the scope and seriousness of the conscientious claims of individuals is, to put it mildly, imperfectly grasped.

My model of democratic pluralism calls for a different balance between the legitimate demands of religious liberty and equal treatment seen in this case. On the one hand – and unlike some religious critics of equality law – Julian Rivers rightly observes that tensions between the two are inevitable in a morally and religiously plural society, and that reconciling them is often far from straightforward:

It is undoubtedly a restriction of my liberty when I am told that I cannot exercise discretion over who I allow to stay in my Bed & Breakfast. But it is also a restriction of my liberty when I am asked intrusive questions about my personal life and turned away when I turn up. It is undoubtedly a restriction of my equality when I cannot live openly with my same-sex partner because of social disapproval of my relationship. But it is also a restriction on equality when I cannot live openly with my religious belief because of legal restrictions on the contexts in which I can live consistently with its precepts.[69]

On the other hand, in resolving such conflicts, both perspectives must be accorded equal initial weight. A 'liberty-perspective' and an 'equality-perspective' should not be viewed as alternatives but as 'complementary normative perspectives'.[70] But the way liberty and equality rights have come to be specified in British law 'creates a structural imbalance in favour of equality-perspectives'.[71]

My affirmation of 'maximum' freedom for faithful conscience might seem to put me straightforwardly on the side of 'liberty-based' accounts. My view does indeed assume a robust commitment to religious liberty as a default state duty, which then might turn out to need restricting as the state discharges other elements of its public justice task. But those other aspects are *also* a 'default state duty'. I have tried to show how public justice is a capacious and internally coherent conception of the task of the state. Now I am specifying that, among many other things, it includes norms of both individual religious liberty and equal treatment. Such an approach does not imply a one-sided liberty-based approach but mandates a maximum realization of *public justice in its entirety*.

For example, a just state must be committed to 'distributive justice'. This is certainly embraced within my conception of public justice, which, as noted, could include elements of 'transformative equality'. This could imply, for instance, imposing new wealth taxes, constraining destabilizing capital flows or restricting the freedom of industrial polluters. Equally, public justice might at times call for constraints on certain religious freedom rights in the interests of certain equality rights of others.[72]

My approach also helps clarify the question of the *onus of justification*. Is the onus on claimants to religious liberty to justify exemptions from general statutes, or on the state to justify limitations on religious liberty? That will depend in part on how high a ranking one accords to religious liberty among the array of rights (and other interests) that a state needs to balance. A higher ranking will tend to place the onus on the state (or employer) to justify limitations, while a lower ranking will tend to place it on religious exemption claimants. But, again, are we really forced to choose between the onus being on one side or the other? This is surely another false binary. If the goal is a maximal realization of public justice in all its dimensions, all legitimate rights-claims enter equally at the outset. We should not assert expansive religious rights with no consideration of one's duties to wider public goods, only then to have to rein in those rights in the light of the demands of equal justice. But nor should we rush ahead with laws designed to promote such equality without due regard to the rights, religious or otherwise, that might get limited in the process, only then ending up having to make corrective exemptions.

Can we be more accommodating?

In any event, in the UK today there are two potentially promising routes by which a better balance between religious liberty and equality rights might emerge. One is to work for a significant boosting of the existing route under equality law of claiming 'indirect discrimination' on grounds of religion or belief.[73] This would involve making more effective use of the balancing or 'proportionality' exercise in indirect discrimination cases.[74] Leigh points out the potential advantages of this route. Noting that religious conscience claims are often 'portrayed and felt by the adversaries to be part of a continuing "Culture War"', he proposes that:

> proportionality reasoning can help to defuse the aura of excessive symbolism and partisanship that often surrounds what in reality are relatively localized disputes that could be amendable to practical solutions in which neither side need lose excessively ... [This] can help to move away from a winner takes all mentality in which every legal decision is played out against a larger narrative about secularism or religious exceptionalism.[75]

If such a route were successful, that would be a considerable gain.

Others, however, argue that there is a strong case for the UK formally to adopt 'reasonable accommodation' as a legal principle.[76] Many cite the Canadian model, where there is a legal duty on employers to offer accommodation to a conscientiously burdened employee subject to certain specified conditions.[77] Reasonable accommodation seeks to create more secure space in the employment context for such employees while recognizing the necessary costs and constraints employers face in designing an effective working context that does not unduly burden them or other employees. The principle is, in fact, already implicit in the Equality Act 2010 (ss. 20–22), which imposes a duty on employers to ensure that a person with a disability is not disadvantaged in doing a job where 'reasonable adjustment' is possible. The principle of reasonable accommodation is no blank cheque for employees. Employers may be permitted to adopt a practice that bears disproportionately on burdened employees. In Canada, to do this they must be able to show that the practice is pursuant to a 'purpose rationally connected' to the performance of the role, has been introduced in good faith and is 'reasonably necessary' to that purpose. Alistair Henderson explains how the principle seeks a judicious balance of employee and employer interests:

> In order to show a standard is reasonably necessary the employer must demonstrate that it is impossible to accommodate the employees sharing the protected characteristic of the claimant without imposing undue hardship on the employer. Undue hardship might arise as a result of a wide range of factors such as financial cost, disruption of collective agreements, morale problems for other employees, interchangeability of workforce and facilities, the size of the employer or safety. However, crucially, this test requires an employer to make every effort to accommodate an employee before it will be found that a discriminatory standard or practice is lawful.[78]

Three considerations incline me to favour serious consideration of the reasonable accommodation route. One is that, on the Canadian model, following a request, the onus is on the employer to show that the requested accommodation would not meet the necessary conditions, rather than on the claimant to demonstrate that it does. Given that the individual employee is always going to be in the weaker position in such a contest (due to the high costs of legal representation and the fear of alienating colleagues), a duty of reasonable accommodation could serve to empower potentially vulnerable individuals or minorities. If this brings into the open a host of new claimants currently lacking the resources to proceed, that is something a society committed to democratic pluralism should want to know and seek to redress.

Over time, adopting reasonable accommodation might also further incentivize employers to explore informal accommodations long before either side felt the need to resort to law. Such informal resolutions are manifestly preferable to litigation.[79] In a 2011 report, the Institute for Business Ethics found that while most large employers lacked formal policies on religion in the workplace, a majority were already practising some form of accommodation regarding special time off, space for religious observance, religious dress codes or dietary requirements. A few were also voluntarily incorporating a commitment to reasonable accommodation of religion in their corporate codes of ethics.[80] A statutory duty of reasonable accommodation might find that it is pushing at an open door.

A second consideration concerns the substance of such cases. Some suggest that the outcomes of a reasonable accommodation route would not differ much from those already or potentially available under the indirect discrimination route. They point out that a notion of accommodation is already implicit in the requirement on employers to offer a 'justification' for restricting manifestation.[81] It has thus been claimed that the idea of reasonable accommodation is already 'penetrating UK anti-discrimination jurisprudence'.[82] However, some observers would think that at least some of the lost religious liberty claims were plausible candidates for exemptions. Henderson suggests that the outcome in cases such as Ladele might have turned out differently if employers were obliged to pursue reasonable accommodation:

> If instead of the broad question 'was this requirement a proportionate means of achieving a legitimate aim?', the question had instead been 'could her conscientious objection have been accommodated without imposing undue hardship on the Council?' the court may well have come to a different decision.[83]

Reasonable accommodation 'would require more precise reasoning and thus greater transparency in setting out why a discriminatory standard was considered to be justifiable'.[84] By contrast, those who find most of these cases to have been rightly decided are likely to favour the status quo. For example, following a review of the law in 2016, the Equality and Human Rights Commission called for no changes at all to existing law (except, however, for a possible *narrowing* of the scope of the exemption for faith schools in staffing decisions).[85] Moreover, for the indirect discrimination route to start to yield better outcomes for religious liberty claimants, a significant evolution in legal attitudes towards the scope and seriousness of religion would seem to be required. I do not yet see sufficient receptivity to such a shift.

A third consideration is that a formal adoption of a statutory duty of reasonable accommodation would, irrespective of particular outcomes, send a powerful signal by the state of its commitment to respecting convictional pluralism. It would be a notable statement of 'symbolic inclusion', sending a message to individuals wrestling with issues of conscience that the law is solicitous of their concerns and does not regard them as eccentric but as normal, indeed in principle honourable. Elevating public respect for conscience through statutory respect is precisely the sort of instrument that a society committed to democratic pluralism should embrace. There is, then, a case for a more thorough official exploration of the possibilities of a legal duty of reasonable accommodation of religion and belief.

Conclusion

This chapter has explored one facet of how to create sufficient public and legal space for 'faithful conscience'. It has approached the question through the emerging conflicts between religious liberty rights and equality rights and has sought to bring to the fore how resolutions to such conflicts are not mere matters of legal procedure or even contending legal principle. Behind such tensions lie substantive and contested questions of what the just treatment of convictionally diverse citizens requires, which in turn are shaped by rival construals of the scope and seriousness of religion. Any balancing exercise (whether legislative or judicial) will be influenced, even if indirectly, by larger, substantive conceptions of justice, whether liberal egalitarian, libertarian, radical feminist, postmodern or Christian (for example). These will tend to generate at least partially divergent proposals on how to integrate the many demands of (what I am calling) public justice. In a democracy marked by deep diversity, there will be no final resolution to this discursive plurality, only ongoing political and legal contestation issuing in a series of shifting, partial settlements of different duration.

There will often be convergences on the ingredients, and sometimes the outcomes, of such a balancing process. Some of these might come to be constitutionally entrenched, taking them off the democratic political agenda for the foreseeable future. But significant points of disagreement should also be expected. Every conception of justice faces genuine challenges in striking proper balances among such claims and none can pre-emptively claim to be above the convictional fray – to be impassive guarantors of substantive 'neutrality'. This is why I stated in Chapter 3 that jurisdictional secularism amounts to the *intent* of states to deal with plural faiths impartially, rather than the *guarantee*. Because what 'justice' demands is so contested, one person's or group's perception that 'just integration' has occurred will be another's occasion for a complaint of 'bias'.[86] I have presented an approach to just integration reflecting 'Christian democratic pluralism', inviting others to offer their own alternative accounts with a view to a multi-sided negotiation in which charges of 'bias' might at least be mitigated.

This chapter has argued that, when citizens of faith (religious or secular) enjoy capacious convictional freedom to manifest their faith in public and are thus enabled to make their (sometimes distinctive) contributions to the provision of public goods and services with convictional integrity, faithful conscience is honoured. This is an essential ingredient of a political community that seeks to elicit maximum participation in the shared but multi-pronged and always contentious pursuit of the common good. Seeking 'exemptions' via courts from generally applicable laws is only one way in which such goals might be advanced. As noted, it is far from an ideal way to proceed. Rather than having to correct laws that turn out to be indifferent to or disproportionately burdensome on minority individual consciences (Christian, non-Christian, secular), it would be far better to build respect for conscientious plurality into law and policy *from the start*, and in areas going well beyond the field of exemptions. This would enhance respect for conscience in the public mind and avoid putting fellow citizens into the posture of supplicants for exceptional treatment. Equality has been 'mainstreamed' in UK law. Conscientious plurality should now be mainstreamed. In the next chapter I show how this proposal is equally relevant to the question of the public role of religious associations. We turn, then, to 'faithful association'.

Notes

(Websites accessed 12/10/20)

1 *Grainger Plc v Nicholson* [2009] UKEAT 0219/09/0311, [2010] 2 All ER 253.

2 *Grainger*, para. 12.

3 Subsequently, 'humanism' has been recognized as a protected philosophical belief. Broad political philosophies have been recognized but not support for a political party, or 'English nationalism', or traditional views of gender identity. See Paul Weller et al., *Religion or Belief, Discrimination or Equality: Britain in Global Contexts* (London: Bloomsbury Academic, 2013), 58–9. 'Stoicism' was recognized in 2020: Russell Sandberg, 'Stoicism Protected as a Belief under the Equality Act: *Jackson v Lidl*', *Law and Religion UK* (25 September 2020), https://lawandreligionuk.com/2020/09/25/stoicism-protected-as-a-belief-under-the-equality-act-jackson-v-lidl/.

4 Steven V. Monsma and J. Christopher Soper, 'Conclusion: The Implications of Equal Treatment', in Steven V. Monsma and J. Christopher Soper, eds, *Equal Treatment of Religion in a Pluralistic Society* (Grand Rapids, MI: Eerdmans, 1998), 206.

5 See Weller et al., *Religion or Belief*, 23.

6 The distinction is not quite so clear, since claims to institutional autonomy are sometimes described as claims to 'exemptions'.

7 *R (E) v Governing Body of JFS* [2009] UKSC 1; [2009] 1 WLR 2353.

8 See Maleiha Malik, 'Religion and Sexual Orientation: Conflict or Cohesion?', in Gavin D'Costa et al., eds, *Religion in a Liberal State* (Cambridge: Cambridge University Press, 2013), 67–9; Julian Rivers, 'Law, Religion and Gender Equality', *Ecclesiastical Law Journal* 9.1 (2009), 24–52.

9 *Lee v Ashers Baking Company Ltd and others* [2018] UKSC 49. [2018] 3

WLR 1294. The bakery's argument was supported by prominent gay rights campaigner Peter Tatchell.

10 *R (Begum) v Denbigh High School Governors* [2006] UKHL 15, [2007] 1 AC 100.

11 *HM Chief Inspector v Interim Executive of Al-Hijrah School* [2017] EWCA Civ 1426, [2018] IRLR 334. This is a voluntary aided faith school. At the time, 25 other mixed-sex faith schools (including Jewish and Christian ones) had similar policies. Single-sex schools are not deemed discriminatory under the Equality Act 2010.

12 On UK developments up to 2015, see Peter Edge and Lucy Vickers, *Review of Equality and Human Rights Law Relating to Religion or Belief*, Equality and Human Rights Commission Research Report 97 (London: EHRC, 2015).

13 See Nick Spencer, *How to Think About Religious Freedom* (London: Theos, 2014); Rex Ahdar and Ian Leigh, *Religion Freedom in the Liberal State*, 2nd edn (Oxford: Oxford University Press, 2013), chapters 2 and 3.

14 See Joel Harrison, *Post-Liberal Religious Freedom: Forming Communities of Charity* (Cambridge: Cambridge University Press, 2020). This is not, of course, a uniquely religious perspective: see Joseph Raz, *The Morality of Freedom* (Oxford: Oxford University Press, 1986).

15 The European Convention on Human Rights 1950, as adopted by the Council of Europe.

16 *Kokkinakis v Greece* (1993) 17 EHRR 397 para. 31. On the difficulties of defining 'religion' and 'belief', see Edge and Vickers, *Review of Equality and Human Rights Law*, chapter 2.

17 For a defence of an inclusive notion of freedom of conscience, see Jocelyn Maclure and Charles Taylor, *Secularism and Freedom of Conscience* (Cambridge, MA: Harvard University Press, 2011).

18 *Grainger*, para. 24.

19 See Cardus Religious Freedom Institute, *The Imperative of Conscience Rights* (Hamilton, ON: Cardus, 2018).

20 Ian Leigh, 'The Courts and Conscience Claims', paper given at Cambridge Conscience Conference, 3 June 2017, 9. A revised version of the paper under the same title appears in John Adenitire, ed., *Religious Beliefs and Conscientious Exemptions in a Liberal State* (Oxford: Hart, 2019), 89–109.

21 Roger Trigg, *Equality, Freedom and Religion* (Oxford: Oxford University Press, 2012), 43.

22 John Savulescu, 'Conscientious Objection in Medicine', *British Medical Journal* 332 (2006), 297. Quoted in Trigg, *Equality, Freedom and Religion*, 106–7.

23 Cécile Laborde, *Liberalism's Religion* (Cambridge, MA: Harvard University Press, 2017), 203–4. It might not survive further scrutiny, however.

24 Laborde, *Liberalism's Religion*, 203.

25 Laborde, *Liberalism's Religion*, 204.

26 Using the term 'minorities' to refer to non-Christian faiths is less and less apt given that in the UK the number of regularly worshipping Muslims now matches that of Christians.

27 *R. (Ghai) v Newcastle upon Tyne City Council* [2010] EWCA Civ 59, [2011] QB 591.

28 Laborde, *Liberalism's Religion*, 229–38.

29 This is a key concern of *Living with Difference: Community, Diversity and*

the Common Good: Report of the Commission on Religion and Belief in British Public Life (Cambridge: Woolf Institute, 2015).

30 As provided in the Finance Act 2007.

31 Laborde, *Liberalism's Religion*, 230.

32 *Bayatyan v Armenia (2012)* 54 EHRR 15, para. 126.

33 Parliamentary Assembly of the Council of Europe, Committee on Equality and Non-Discrimination, *Tackling Intolerance and Discrimination in Europe with a Special Focus on Christians*, Report, Doc. 13660 (7 January 2015), http://assembly.coe.int/nw/xml/XRef/Xref-DocDetails-EN.asp?FileID=21340&lang=EN. It noted much more serious threats to religious freedom elsewhere in Europe.

34 For background on legal developments in the 2000s, see Weller et al., *Religion or Belief*, chapter 4.

35 Bob Hepple, 'The New Single Equality Act in Britain', *The Equal Rights Review* 5 (2010), 21.

36 Julian Rivers, 'Is Religious Freedom Under Threat from British Equality Laws?', *Studies in Christian Ethics* 33.2 (2020), 180–1.

37 See Peter Jones, 'Bearing the Consequences of Belief', *Journal of Political Philosophy* 2.1 (1994), 24–43.

38 See, for example, *Clearing the Ground: Parliamentary Report into the Freedom of Christians in the UK* (London: Christians in Parliament, 2012), which found a 'deep and widespread level of religious illiteracy in public life' (14), http://2019.christiansinparliament.org.uk/wp-content/uploads/2019/02/Clearing-the-ground.pdf. See also All-Party Parliamentary Group on Religious Education, *Improving Religious Literacy: A Contribution to the Debate* (London: House of Commons, 2016), which reported 'growing concerns among academics, politicians, faith leaders and teachers that too many people lack the relevant skills to understand and discuss issues about religion precisely at the time when they are most needed' (3).

39 *Clearing the Ground*, 9. Martin H. M. Steven, *Christianity and Party Politics: Keeping the Faith* (Abingdon: Routledge, 2011) indirectly confirms this by titling chapter 7 of his book as 'Still Fighting a Losing Battle? Equalities and the Weaknesses of the Christian Lobby'.

40 For an overview until 2015, see Edge and Vickers, *Review of Equality and Human Rights Law*. For European cases, see Silvio Ferrari and Sabrina Pastorelli, eds, *Religion in Public Space: A European Perspective* (Farnham: Ashgate, 2012); W. Cole Durham, Jr et al., eds, *Islam, Europe and Emerging Legal Issues* (Farnham: Ashgate, 2012).

41 Generally, UK law allows more latitude than, for example, France, Belgium, the Netherlands and Switzerland on clothing and symbols in the workplace and in public spaces. See Daniel J. Hill and Daniel Whistler, 'Religious Symbols and the European Court of Human Rights', *Law and Justice* 171 (2013), 52–69.

42 *McFarlane v Relate Avon Ltd* [2010] EWCA Civ 880, (2010) 29 BHRC 249.

43 *Bull and Bull v Hall and Preddy* [2012] EWCA Civ 83, [2012] 1 WLR 2514.

44 See Paul Billingham, 'How Should Claims for Religious Exemptions be Weighed?', *Oxford Journal of Law and Religion* 6.1 (2017), 1–23.

45 Julian Rivers, 'Outline of a General Right to Freedom of Conscience', paper presented at Cambridge Conscience Conference, 13 June 2017, 5.

46 Julian Rivers, *The Law of Organized Religions: Between Establishment and Secularism* (Oxford: Oxford University Press, 2010), 126. *Direct* discrimination occurs when one person treats another less favourably than other similarly situ-

ated persons on grounds of their protected characteristic, the logic being that the characteristic is irrelevant to their just treatment.

47 *Ladele v The London Borough of Islington* [2009] EWCA Civ 1357, [2010] 1 WLR 955.

48 See Matthew Gibson, 'The "God Dilution"? Religion, Discrimination and the Case for Reasonable Accommodation', *Cambridge Law Journal* 72.3 (2013), 578–616.

49 Having been refused leave to appeal to the Supreme Court, Ladele appealed to the ECtHR. Unusually, the ECtHR considered her case alongside three other prominent UK religious liberty cases (MacFarlane, Shirley Chaplin and Nadia Eweida) (*Eweida and others v UK* (2013) 57 EHRR 8). Eweida won her case. The ECtHR did not so much reject the substantive claims of the other three as deem them to fall within the 'margin of appreciation' allowed to domestic courts by the ECHR. It was thus permitted but not required under the Convention for the UK to deny their claims.

50 *Ladele*, paras 43, 48, 49.

51 *Ladele*, para. 75.

52 *Ladele*, para. 49.

53 Rivers, 'Is Religious Freedom Under Threat', 187.

54 *Ladele*, para. 51.

55 *Ladele*, para. 51.

56 *Ladele*, para. 52.

57 *Ladele*, para. 56.

58 *Ladele*, para. 57.

59 This has long been recognized as a legal principle. As Lord Reid put it in a 1949 case: 'No temporal court of law can determine the truth of any religious belief: it is not competent to investigate any such matter and it ought not to attempt to do so.' Quoted in Robert Meakin, 'Taking the Queen's Shilling: The Implications for Religious Freedom for Religions Being Registered as Charities', *Law and Justice* 178 (2017), 62.

60 See Michael Bartlett, 'Conscience in the Courts – another view of *Eweida*', *Law and Justice* 171 (2013), 70–8; Mark Campbell, 'Strasbourg, Conscience and Religious Belief', *Ethics in Brief* 18.5 (Cambridge: KLICE, 2013).

61 Robert Wintemute, 'Accommodating Religious Beliefs: Harm, Clothing or Symbols, and Refusals to Serve Others', *Modern Law Review* 77.2 (2014), 242.

62 Wintemute, 'Accommodating Religious Beliefs', 242.

63 Wintemute, 'Accommodating Religious Beliefs', 249.

64 Wintemute, 'Accommodating Religious Beliefs', 249.

65 Wintemute, 'Accommodating Religious Beliefs', 250.

66 Wintemute, 'Accommodating Religious Beliefs', 253.

67 The CA itself acknowledged the point: *Ladele*, para. 44.

68 Peter Smith notes that a later case (*Mba v Mayor and Burgesses of the London Borough of Merton* [2013] EWCA Civ 1562, [2014] 1 WLR 1501) has had the effect of considerably weakening the 'group disadvantage' test of discrimination, thus strengthening individual religious rights (even though the claimant here lost her case). 'Towards the Reasonable Accommodation of Religion', *Law and Justice* 174 (2015), 77–95.

69 Rivers, 'Is Religious Freedom Under Threat', 185.

70 Rivers, 'Is Religious Freedom Under Threat', 185. By contrast, Wintemute

explicitly favours an 'equality perspective' ('Accommodating Religious Beliefs', 226–7). So does Laborde (*Liberalism's Religion*, 218).

71 Rivers, 'Is Religious Freedom Under Threat', 197. Rivers claims that equality is almost becoming a 'state-sanctioned ideology' ('Is Religious Freedom Under Threat', 188).

72 For example, a Christian employed by a local authority who used her work email account to criticize same-sex relationships to the head of the Lesbian and Gay Christian Movement was found to have acted unlawfully – rightly, in my view, because here an employee is using an employer's resource, without permission, to advance a controversial personal position. See *Haye v London Borough of Lewisham* [2010] ET 2301852/09.

73 See Lucy Vickers, *Religious Freedom, Discrimination and the Workplace*, 2nd edn (London: Hart, 2016), chapters 6 and 7.

74 See Neil Foster, 'Freedom of Religion and Balancing Clauses in Discrimination Legislation', *Oxford Journal of Law and Religion* 5.3 (2016), 385–430.

75 Leigh, 'The Courts and Conscience Claims', 11.

76 Lady Hale, then Vice-President of the Supreme Court, entertained the idea in 'Religion and Sexual Orientation: The Clash of Equality Rights', Comparative and Administrative Law Conference, Yale Law School, 7 March 2014. The Equalities and Human Rights Commission seemed favourable to the idea in 2014 but retreated from it in 2016 ('Religion or Belief: Is the Law Working?' (London: EHRC, 2016)). See also James Orr, *Beyond Belief: Defending Religious Liberty Through the British Bill of Rights* (London: ResPublica, 2016).

77 See Laura Barnett, Julia Nicol and Julian Walker, *An Examination of the Duty to Accommodate in the Canadian Human Rights Context* (Ottawa: Library of Parliament Publication No. 2012-01-E, 10 January 2012); Alistair Henderson, 'Reasonable Accommodation and Religious Liberty', *Ethics in Brief* 22.4 (Cambridge: KLICE, 2017).

78 Henderson, 'Reasonable Accommodation', 2.

79 See EHRC, 'Religion or Belief in the Workplace: A Guide for Employers following recent European Court of Human Rights Judgments' (February 2013).

80 Simon Webley, 'Religious Practices in the Workplace', IBE Occasional Paper 3 (London: Institute for Business Ethics, 2011). Accommodating disability is already obligatory under the Equality Act 2010. See also ACAS, *Religion or Belief Discrimination: Key Points for the Workplace* (London: ACAS, 2018).

81 As Peter Edge and Lucy Vickers put it: 'A failure to accommodate a request by religious employees for different treatment may amount to indirect discrimination, unless the refusal to accommodate can be justified' (*Review of Equality and Human Rights Law*, 51).

82 Smith, 'Towards the Reasonable Accommodation of Religion', 87.

83 Henderson, 'Reasonable Accommodation', 3.

84 Henderson, 'Reasonable Accommodation', 3.

85 The EHRC has intervened in several indirect discrimination cases, mostly against the religious liberty claimants.

86 See Jonathan Chaplin, 'Rejecting Neutrality, Respecting Diversity: From "Liberal Pluralism" to "Christian Pluralism"', *Christian Scholar's Review* 35.2 (2006), 143–75.

7

Faithful Association

Introduction

In 2008, the CEO of a Christian organization keen to partner with the government complained to an interviewer that the government's indifference to the religious motivations of the organization's work was 'disrespectful, discriminatory and shortsighted'. This was one of several similar charges recorded in a report commissioned by the Church of England on government–Church relations in the welfare sector, published in 2008.[1] The report, entitled *Moral But No Compass: Government, Church and the Future of Welfare*, concluded that 'Government's decision to ignore theology as a governance criterion means that the state has delineated what constituted "good" religion and asserted that faith did not impact on organisational behaviour … this privatised the public consequences of religious ideas.'[2] It also found that the Charity Commission construed 'the advancement of religion' in a way that 'has little or no relation to the way that many people of faith actually understand their way of life'. For example, the work of cathedrals 'is self-defined by a deep understanding of the idea of "hospitality" … to subdivide [a cathedral's] charitable activities … into the "religious" as opposed to the educational, charitable and others would be to rewrite its theology.' This would involve the Commission in making 'judgements as to what constitutes good religion despite protestations to the contrary'.[3]

Such official attitudes are evidently an obstacle to the practice of 'faithful association' in the public realm.[4] Fast-forward, however, to the Library of Birmingham in December 2014, for the launch of a new 'Faith Covenant' between local authorities and faith bodies, commissioned by the All-Party Parliamentary Group on Faith and Society, with support from FaithAction (a network of faith-based and community organizations).[5] The first commitment in the covenant affirms that 'Faith communities are free to practise their beliefs and religious observances without restriction, and to raise their voice in public debate and to be respected, within the framework of UK law.' At the event Cllr James McKay, cabinet member for social cohesion, equalities and community safety on Birmingham City Council, said:

Faith communities have always been called upon to tackle hardship and need in our communities. It is the absolute bedrock of what it means to have faith, and people of faith were serving their communities long before the state ever woke up to the fact that it had responsibilities, too ... The Faith Covenant provides a set of working principles that help us all get the biggest social benefit out of this partnership ... Organisations and services can only become stronger by working together in an open and generous way, with a shared set of values and principles to guide their activities on a daily basis.[6]

By the end of 2020, 13 local authorities had signed the covenant. In 2017 the Local Government Association, in association with FaithAction, published *Working with Faith Groups to Promote Health and Wellbeing*, a guidance document based on the covenant, explaining how faith groups can contribute to better health outcomes in local communities.[7]

This is a developing story. In September 2020, Danny Kruger MP submitted a report commissioned by the prime minister, *Levelling Up Our Communities: Proposals for a New Social Covenant*. In it he called for a 'big, open and comprehensive' offer by government to faith communities to form a coalition to address serious social problems faith communities are best placed to tackle.[8] Government enthusiasm to enlist the resources of faith communities for public purposes seems undimmed (although Kruger's own proposals involved no new funding commitments from government).

This chapter makes a case for 'faithful association' in the provision of public services. It recognizes that faith-based contributions operate within a policy framework that brings with it certain necessary constraints. But it argues for as much latitude as possible for faith-based providers to offer their services in ways consistent with their core mission and values, so as to make a distinctive contribution to the common good rather than merely replicating secular provision.

Faith in public services

The appearance of the Faith Covenant signals real progress towards better mutual understanding on both sides of the faith–government debate. But it does not represent a radical break in government attitudes. It is hardly new for governments in the UK to seek to enlist the 'faith sector' behind their policy objectives. Religious associations in Britain have, in any case, long been involved in the delivery of social welfare of numerous kinds, often independently but sometimes in partnership with the state.[9] Many, of course, deliberately keep their distance from the state in order to retain greater freedom to define and implement this mission. But since the early twentieth century, Britain has not followed either the French model of exclusive secularism (*laïcité*) or the American model of strict church–state separation, but has tacked closer to the structured cooperation approach seen in countries such as Germany, Austria, Italy, Belgium and the Netherlands.[10] In those countries, faith-based organizations routinely participate in the public as well as the private sector by running schools, universities, hospitals or social service organizations, within the framework of an integrated and regulated service funded partly or fully by the state. In the UK, as elsewhere, it is sometimes not the case that the state *invited* such bodies to become public service providers within a system it had created, but that – as Cllr McKay observed – such bodies were providing these services long before the state entered the fray, and the state subsequently *integrated* them into its own systems. This is pre-eminently the case in education, where church provision of schools and colleges long predates state provision, even the modern state itself, sometimes by several centuries.[11] Awareness of this history already suggests that the question should not be, 'On what terms should the state *admit* religion to the public sector?' but rather, 'How can the state *support* traditional and newer faith-based providers of public services by justly integrating them into the wider regimes of public service for which it now takes ultimate responsibility?'

New Philanthropy Capital estimated that by 2016, of the 188,000 registered charities in the UK, 55,000 were faith-based, accounting for nearly a quarter of the sector's income in England and Wales.[12] Much of this charitable effort has been provided by Christian churches and organizations operating at all levels, often independently of government.[13] Some have also participated in the supply of public services, received public funding and thus come under greater state oversight.[14] Especially since 1997, governments have positively encouraged partnerships with civil society bodies generally, including faith-based ones. The new era of partnership was launched under New Labour as one strand of its commitments to empowering communities, strengthening 'cohesion' and embracing 'multi-culturalism' (for example by funding Muslim, Hindu and Sikh schools). Faith-based organizations were recognized as key collaborators with central and local governments towards such goals.[15] As one report put it, 'Religious congregations were increasingly seen as reservoirs of under-tapped and responsible voluntarism that could be channelled into the government's initiatives for civil renewal.'[16] For example, the Home Office created a Faith Communities Unit in 2003; the Department of Communities and Local Government (DCLG) set up a Faith Communities

Consultative Council in 2006; a Faith Communities Capacity Building Fund invested £20 million in the sector in the years after 2006. John Battle MP was appointed the prime minister's faith envoy.

The new partnership was not universally welcomed. So extensive had it become that even religious critics began to talk of an emerging 'new establishment' between state and religion,[17] with one warning that unlike the establishment of the Church of England, the new one was taking on an increasingly 'Erastian' form, 'one in which the state monopolizes jurisdiction over the ordering of society and ... religious institutions and initiatives are rendered wholly subordinate to the state'.[18] Secularist critics attacked it for compromising state neutrality, permitting discrimination against employees and service users and lowering standards.[19]

A different form of partnership, linked to a wider 'localism' strategy, was launched in the early years of the 2010 Cameron government under the short-lived Big Society programme – short-lived chiefly because the government's austerity programme substantially limited the funding available for social projects, while simultaneously making them more necessary.[20] Baroness Sayeeda Warsi was appointed minister for Faith and Communities at the DCLG from 2012 to 2014. The coalition government rejected Labour's multiculturalist language and embraced a new 'Christian heritage' approach in which Christianity, and especially the Church of England, would serve as a favoured channel for funded projects. This was seen, for example, in the decision of the DCLG to invest £5 million in the Near Neighbours programme launched in 2011, centred on Anglican parishes, administered by the Church Urban Fund, but intentionally multifaith.[21]

Notwithstanding major policy and funding shifts and a continuous soundtrack of dissent over one or other aspect of governmental strategies, these successive initiatives have facilitated important new expressions of 'faithful association' in the public realm. To mention one of the more visible, the Oasis chain of faith-based charities, launched in 1985 as a private homelessness project, now operates 47 academies and a range of housing, youth, advice, health, community and anti-trafficking projects, using a 'community hub' model. In 2020 it was invited to manage a secure children's prison in Medway, Kent.[22] A less well-known one is Kainos Community, a Christian ministry working with offenders both within prisons (six since 1999) and in the community. Its Challenge to Change programme offered inside prisons is accredited by the Correctional Services Accreditation and Advisory Panel.[23] There are many more cases of 'faithful association' active across a wide range of public service areas and highly diverse in size, mode of operation and relation to government. Since the 1990s, governments have most certainly 'done God'.[24]

A flourishing and respectful partnership between faith-based providers and government in the delivery of welfare and other public services is exactly what my model of Christian democratic pluralism would favour. In its 2016 report, *Faith in Public Services*, Oasis presented constructive proposals on how this might be better realized. But the conflicts reported in *Moral But No Compass* have not gone away and law and public policy continue inadvertently to hamper some manifestations of 'faithful association'. Notwithstanding progress indicated by initiatives such as the Faith Covenant, in his 2020 report to government Danny Kruger reported similar concerns:

> ... the estrangement of faith-based social action and the public sector is a very bad thing. Faith groups have an enormous amount to offer society, but too often public servants are reluctant to partner with them, still less to formally contract with faith-based organisations to deliver publicly-funded services. This reluctance can arise from ignorance about religion and about the contribution these organisations can make, especially in poor and immigrant communities – what we might call 'faith illiteracy' – but too often it arises from 'faith phobia': an active objection to the principle of faith communities working in partnership with government.[25]

Critics from other places on the political spectrum raise a very different concern: that faith-based organizations involved in public service provision risk becoming complicit in a damaging project to legitimate 'neo-liberalism' and shrink the state. Chris Baker, from the William Temple Foundation, responding to the launch of Oasis's report *Faith in Public Services*, warns: 'In its eager willingness to mop up the tragedy of wasted and downtrodden lives, the omnicompetent church plays into the hands of the neo-liberal agenda of the marketisation of our compassion and moral duty to care for the vulnerable and the weak.'[26] 'Faithful association' is a highly contested concept.

In this chapter I focus on selected points of tension – especially legal ones – between faith-based organizations and the state in the delivery of public services. As with the previous chapter, the aim is not to offer a survey of the landscape but to bring to the fore key normative questions these tensions pose to my model of Christian democratic pluralism. Again it is worth noting the asymmetry of standing between faith-based and secular organizations. Secular organizations are typically not thought to need to justify the perspective from which they deliver public services – if they think they operate with a 'secular perspective' at all. No one thinks we need a 'covenant' between government and organizations motivated by secular faiths. Such bodies benefit from the widespread assumption that 'secular' services are convictionally 'neutral' and so by definition 'public' in a way that religious groups are not. Religiously motivated organizations seem to confront an onus of justification not generally faced by secular ones.

The assumption that secular services are convictionally neutral is hard to sustain. It is difficult to see how any significant public good like education or healthcare or gender equality could be delivered in a way that is not implicated in deep and contested convictions about the nature of personhood (does it consist primarily in rationality or embodiment?), the conditions for human flourishing (should these maximize individual liberty or social solidarity?) and the human good (is it given, constructed or just illusory?).[27] Kruger echoes the point forthrightly:

> Public servants frequently assume that religious belief belongs in the private sphere: that the public square is somehow a values-free zone. This is to forget the religious foundations of our politics, and to overlook the fact that there are no values-free zones anywhere. Secular public servants bring their philosophy to work, too. Like religious people they have a moral vision, strive for personal righteousness, and wish that everyone thought like they did; unlike religious people they don't always recognise their own religiosity. The exclusion of faith, in all but its ceremonial aspects, from our public life means that the orthodoxies of technocratic secular liberalism have total sway. The public square should be more plural than this.[28]

Nothing essential to the argument of this chapter hangs on the success of that particular claim (Kruger perhaps overstates the 'sway' of 'technocratic secular liberalism'). My aim here is only to argue that Christian democratic pluralism calls for, wherever possible, a level playing field on which putative religious providers can, if they wish, be considered fully equal partners in the public realm.

Defending associational autonomy

I noted in the last chapter that religious freedom for institutions is as important as religious freedom for individuals because much of religious life is inherently communal. The communality of religious life includes, for example, corporate *practice* (worship and other rituals; other religiously motivated acts such as offering a social service, creating a social, or indeed a commercial, enterprise; disseminating a faith);[29] corporate *identity* (the experience of being a member of an enduring supra-individual body with authority to define and uphold that identity; the ability to determine membership and doctrine); and corporate *memory* (an awareness of participating in an enduring historical tradition; the capacity for intergenerational transmission). These and other communal dimensions of religion require, in turn, the legal possibility of corporate *self-governance* so that such dimensions can be both sustained internally and protected externally against improper interventions from the state or other social bodies.[30] Such self-governance is not merely an aggregation of individual members' liberties but is the 'power of a community for self-government under its own law'.[31] This applies as much to faith-based associations offering public services as to institutions of worship.

In legal discourse the right to associational self-governance is termed 'autonomy'. Since the 1980s, notably under the jurisprudence of the European Court of Human Rights (ECtHR), rights to the autonomy of religious associations have in fact been strengthened.[32] This reflects a growing recognition by the court both of the 'organized' nature of religious life and of the fact that, as the court has put it, 'the autonomous existence of religious communities is indispensable for pluralism in a democratic society'.[33] Securing such associational autonomy affirms the fundamental right to associate for lawful, freely chosen purposes and the desirability of an institutionally rich society offering multiple outlets for human flourishing and diverse contributions to the public good. As noted in Chapter 2, the health and vitality of such a realm of independent, self-governing associations – 'civil society' – is vital to the successful functioning of a representative and participatory democracy.[34]

The 'autonomy' of religious associations is closely linked to the religious 'neutrality' of the state – its commitment to impartial or even-handed engagement with all faiths. Neutrality does not mean 'blindness' to religions (equally ignoring them all) or 'sameness' of treatment (regulating them all uniformly). As with differently situated individuals, so with associations, equality can require differential treatment. There are, however, signs of a legal and political move in the UK and Europe away from even-handedness and towards sameness. The gradual imposition of a regime of uniform equality and non-discrimination regulations inadvertently risks compromising the proper autonomy of religious associations.

UK law – of which ECtHR jurisprudence is only one layer – defines and protects the autonomy of religious associations in a multitude of ways. Autonomy is in the first instance protected via generic individual rights to freedom of association and associational rights to freedom of speech or expression, to hold property, to enter into contracts and so forth. Notwithstanding a wide variety of types of legal status enjoyed by religious bodies,[35] courts today often treat them as 'contracted associations'. Their internal rules will thus generally be seen as matters of private law to which the state will normally defer.[36] This obviously does not mean that religious associations are outside the remit of the state. It means, first, that the state will respect a core of autonomous jurisdiction that it does not create – a point of profound importance for democratic pluralism. As Julian Rivers observes, 'the existence of organizations which rival the State provides … a social location of legitimacy and coordination that has a real chance of resisting excessive State power.'[37] Second, it means that the state will nevertheless engage with such bodies in various ways. These include protecting the religious body's public legal rights (such as to speech, property); balancing the body's own rights with the wider public good (as in planning or health and safety regulations); and defending the public rights of individual members against such bodies (such as non-discrimination rights). Maintaining such an integrated arrangement of individual, associational and state rights is essential for a society seeking to affirm convictional pluralism within a larger framework of public justice.

Law does recognize certain rights of individual members of associations, for example the right to be treated by one's association according to 'natural justice'.[38] But such rights should be seen as defensive not aggressive: they should protect members against associational injustice but not allow members to act against an association so as to undermine its core beliefs or internal order. Thus, for example, members of a religious association do not have 'religious freedom' *against* the association. The law assumes that when someone joins a religious body they give up their individual religious freedom against that body – just as a member of a political party, upon joining it, renounces her freedom to express whatever political opinions she wishes.

Contrary to the rhetoric of some religious critics, the Equality Act 2010 partly reaffirms this arrangement. It does not represent a deliberate or systematic assault on the autonomy of religious associations. Indeed, some local authorities see equality law as a positive ground for working with diverse faith groups. Many of the Act's provisions, for example its protections against racial or sexual or disability discrimination, have proved unproblematic and are supported by religious associations' own beliefs. It protects not only institutions of worship ('organized religions') but also organizations 'with an ethos based on religion or belief' ('religious organizations') and those 'related to religion or belief'. It offers different kinds and degrees of exemption from various non-discrimination norms to associations in each category.[39] These include those linked to sex, marital status and sexual orientation.[40] For example, sexual orientation discrimination in employment is allowed in some cases where it is necessary (1) 'to comply with the doctrine of the organisation' or (2) 'to avoid conflicting with the strongly held religious convictions of a significant number of the religion's followers'.[41]

The Act thus seems to allow considerable autonomy to religious associations to govern themselves in keeping with their faith or ethos. It allows them to take religion into account in their hiring policies where there is a 'genuine occupational requirement' that an employee support the organization's beliefs. This would be inadmissible in the state, which long ago abolished 'religious tests', but is an essential component of religious autonomy. 'Schools with a religious designation' in the maintained sector may, for example, restrict some of their staff positions to those adhering to their faith. Voluntary aided schools, which are partially funded, have considerable leeway on the matter (they may select teaching staff on the basis of religion), while fully funded voluntary controlled and foundation schools may reserve up to a fifth of positions for those in sympathy with their faith basis. In addition, many religious associations may control who is entitled to become a member, restrict who may participate in their activities and restrict to whom they offer goods, facilities and services.

Such zones of autonomy are democratically justifiable as means whereby religious associations may enjoy the goods of corporate life, preserve their integrity and identity over time and be free to make a distinctive contribution to public life if they wish, rather than replicating secular provision. They secure what American liberal pluralist William A. Galston calls 'expressive associational liberty': 'the absence of constraints ... that make it impossible or significantly more difficult for ... groups to live their lives in ways that express their deepest beliefs about what gives meaning and value to life'.[42] Those who speak pejoratively of such zones as allowing the 'right to discriminate' need only be reminded that non-religious institutions enjoy many analogous rights. Humanists UK is not obliged to hire senior staff who do not meet an occupational requirement that they support secular humanism; a political party is entitled to restrict membership to those affirming its core principles and to expel those who vote for another party; a trade union is not obliged to offer health insurance to non-members; a women's refuge is entitled to decline to serve men who may be fleeing domestic abuse.

Yet notwithstanding the exemptions enjoyed by religious associations, the autonomy of such bodies has begun to suffer from a creeping, if unintended, process whereby non-state associations are made subservient to the public purposes of the state. Luke Bretherton thus critiques what he terms 'institutional isomorphism', a 'process where religious organizations reshape themselves to fit government policy and thereby lose their distinctiveness, while taking on the same institutional shape and processes [such as professionalization or bureaucratization] as state agencies'.[43] Harnessing faith groups for state purposes 'risks closing down the free, non-instrumental space that religious belief and practice holds open and which ... is central for the formation of society as a space of free deliberation'.[44]

Similarly, Nancy L. Rosenblum identifies an imperious 'logic of congruence' at work in the relation between the state and associations:

> ... in its capacity as sovereign, government attempts to enforce conformity with public principles should stop far short of the censorious position that looks on associations, including religious groups, as private boot camps for citizenship. This stern pedagogical perspective dictates that the internal lives of associations be made to conform to public norms. The logic of congruence is inevitable.[45]

At the extreme, the logic of congruence could, as William Galston warns, result in a system in which 'constitutional uniformity crushes social pluralism'.[46]

I suggest that elements of equality law inadvertently tend towards such 'congruence' insofar as they unduly constrains areas of discretion essential to the identity and ethos of religious associations. The Equality Act 2010 represents a wider (if unwitting) legal trend in liberal societies in which the balance is increasingly tilting away from associational rights and towards individual and state rights, eroding the autonomy and vitality of civil society.[47] The legal detail is forbidding so I will attempt to clarify key points of principle relevant to my larger argument by way of three examples: two from areas where religious bodies have made long-standing and widely appreciated, albeit at times controversial, contributions – welfare and schools; and a third concerning an activity less familiar and more controversial – Islamic shari'a councils.

Faith-based welfare

One controversial case involved a collision between equality laws and private Catholic adoption agencies. It is important to note, first, that head-on collisions between the state and Catholic social organizations are rather exceptional.[48] As Ben Ryan reports in a recent study, many Catholic welfare charities have long operated without coming into conflict with the state. Mostly this is because they are private entities retaining extensive autonomy, but several have collaborated in the delivery of public services without particular difficulty. Ryan cites examples such as Father Hudson's Care, the social care agency of the archdiocese of Birmingham, founded in 1902 and now offering a wide range of social services in cooperation with local government.[49] He reports that some Catholic charities echo the experience of other Christian charities, of being under an additional burden to justify themselves to public bodies and 'expected to jump through quite a few hoops to meet public criteria', but that this was not regarded as exceptionally burdensome.[50]

The conflict involving Catholic adoption agencies, however, was of a different order.[51] In a long-running dispute triggered by new sexual orientation regulations, several Catholic adoption agencies wished to continue to offer adoption services in line with Catholic moral doctrine, according to which same-sex couples were ineligible for the agency's services. These agencies had, as it happens, acquired a reputation for successfully finding homes for 'hard to place' children – one of their distinctive contributions to the common good. In the key legal case, one such agency, Catholic Care, unsuccessfully sought permission from the Charity Commissioners (and then, on appeal, the Charity Tribunal) to amend its charitable objects so as to allow it to claim the relevant exemption. The High Court declined to uphold Catholic Care's appeal, sending the decision back to the Commissioners, which refused to change its decision.

While the legal reasoning was complex, two particular and problematic arguments played a key role in the outcome. One (echoing *Ladele v London Borough of Islington*) was that Catholic Care's denial of services to same-sex couples did not unjustifiably restrict its religious freedom since it only involved a manifestation of 'non-core beliefs'. Fortunately, as noted in the previous chapter, this argument is no longer available to courts. The other, however, was that the self-governance rights of the organization could be overridden by non-discrimination law in the case of an agency performing a 'public function'. Whatever one makes of the ruling, and irrespective of one's stance on the agency's policy, it cannot be denied that this is a very burdensome constraint on the 'conscience' of a religious welfare provider.[52] Indeed, following the ruling, all the Catholic agencies concerned felt bound either to close or to sever their ties to the Church. This effectively sends a message to putative faith-based partners: 'You are welcome to contribute to society's care for vulnerable children but only on the condition that you abandon your distinctive theology of care and adopt a majority secular view.' As Rivers puts it, while the law allows for '*religious* pluralism' in welfare services, it does not allow for '*sexual-ethical* pluralism'; 'Catholic adoption agencies can be Catholic ... but they cannot act on the basis of a Catholic sexual ethics'.[53]

This is actually only one instance of the potentially adverse consequences of a long-term shift in the charity sector from a model of self-regulation to one of expanding government oversight, now increasingly shaped by equality law. The trend is also evident in other challenges facing religious charities generally. These arise from the fact that, since the Charities Act 2006, charities must prove to the Charity Commission that they are offering a 'public benefit'. The long-standing presumption that religion (of pretty much any variety) meets that expectation has been abandoned.[54] For bodies qualifying as 'religious', the public benefit criterion had long been thought to be met if a religious charity could show either 'public access' (meaning that a sufficiently broad section of the public – not necessarily a large number – has access to its services);[55] or, where services were confined to members, that it could show 'public impact' (which could be met even if only indirect social benefit could be adduced). But in 2011 the Commission introduced the more demanding requirement that a qualifying religious body should have 'an identifiable, positive, beneficial moral or ethical framework that is promoted by religion which demonstrates that the religion is capable of impacting on society in a beneficial way'.[56] Needless to say, the vague criterion of 'beneficial impact' is open to much contestation, allowing the possibility that mainstream, majoritarian (mis)perceptions about the supposed benefits and harms of various religiously motivated activities will override minority conceptions of the good. The risk of a logic of congruence is evident.

Such a logic has been evident in service contracts offered to religious associations by, for example, local authorities with whom they seek to partner in delivering a public service.[57] Governmental bodies enjoy wide discretion in shaping such contracts, creating the risk of unduly constraining an association's proper autonomy (not just that of religious ones). Local authorities may not breach the equality rights of providers, such as by pre-emptively excluding religious providers (which would be direct discrimination). But if they impose undue contractual demands on the manifestation of any association's religious beliefs in the performance of the service, it could be argued that they are in effect practising indirect discrimination. A closely related factor is the funding model employed by some local authorities. In 2008, *Moral But No Compass* reported the frustrations of faith-based organizations keen to pursue goals such as the 'Christian idea of unconditional solidarity' as a response to 'multidimensional poverty'. They found themselves confronted with 'simplistic' price and performance targets imposing narrow quantitative measures of success.[58] In an age of austerity, local governments also often lack the resources of money and imagination to enter into creative partnerships with faith providers and are forced to opt merely for best market price.

Mitigating the remaining force of the logic of congruence in the welfare sector will likely require a range of legislative, judicial and attitudinal changes. For example, one would be for the Charity Commission to redefine 'public benefit' so that it does not unduly burden or exclude associations that pose no harm to the rights of others but that adopt counter-cultural stances – whether 'the Christian idea of unconditional solidarity' or a commitment to married heterosexual parenting. Insofar as a 'logic of congruence' remains at work, some religious charities will ask themselves whether the regulatory burden being imposed on them is any longer worth the advantages of charitable registration. As noted, many already refrain from partnering with government for just this reason. That may well be the right course for them. But a policy that, albeit inadvertently, has the effect of diminishing legitimate expressions of pluralism in the public sector would both undermine stated government policy and risk atrophying a valuable source of social good.[59]

Another desirable change would be to attempt wherever possible to mitigate the impact of what Rivers calls 'horizontal effect'. This assumes that rights initially framed as rights against the state 'can double up as rights against everyone', including individuals and associations:

> The effect has been to create the presumption that non-State actors should respect these rights as well … the assumption is that the preservation of religious identity on the part of the civil society group needs justification *against* the individual who does not share that identity. The logic of many human rights cases has been to force the parties into a grid of State-versus-individual which is potentially destructive of the identity of non-State collectivities.[60]

Democratic pluralism certainly champions human rights, but not at the expense of damaging the rich associational pluralism necessary for a healthy civil society that facilitates productive and protective relationships between the state and individual citizens.

Faith schools

A wide range of issues has arisen in recent years concerning the proper autonomy of faith schools. One particularly controversial flashpoint has been the issue of admissions policy, the focus of the JFS case cited in the last chapter. An Orthodox Jewish school (formerly known as Jewish Free School) had declined to admit a child not recognized to be Jewish by the Office of the Chief Rabbi on account of the manner of his mother's conversion.[61] This was pursuant to its (lawful) policy of favouring Jewish applicants when places were oversubscribed. Because the child of a Jewish mother is automatically Jewish, it is essential for Jews to be able to decide if a mother is indeed Jewish, which can be the case either through descent or conversion. Equality law permits faith schools to be exempt from the non-discrimination requirements of the provision of service regulations, in matters such as curriculum, worship and admissions.[62] However, in a 5:4 ruling the Supreme Court 'determined that JFS's refusal to admit a child who was not recognized as Jewish by the Office of the Chief Rabbi constituted an exclusion based on racial rather than theological grounds, and therefore the pupil had to be admitted'.[63] The court asserted (correctly) that the Race Relations Act 1976 (RRA) required that 'No school ... is permitted to discriminate in its admissions policy on racial grounds.' But, it said, JFS's admission policy depended on 'birth link criteria' that led to the boy being treated less favourably on racial grounds.[64] This trumped any consideration of associational autonomy. The fact that the 'motivation' for the policy was 'religious' was deemed irrelevant, since the RRA only permits a consideration of the 'ground' of the decision; and that, the court ruled, was 'racial'. Concurring, Lord Brown nevertheless registered his discomfort with a judgment that:

> insists on a non-Jewish definition of who is Jewish ... the imposition of a test for admission to an Orthodox Jewish school which is not Judaism's own test and which requires a focus (as Christianity does) on outward acts of religious practice and declarations of faith, ignoring whether the child is or is not Jewish as defined by Orthodox Jewish law.[65]

On the larger question of autonomy, Lord Hope's opinion prevailed:

> It has long been understood that it is not the business of the courts to intervene in matters of religion ... the court must inevitably be wary of entering so self-evidently sensitive an area, straying across the well-recognised divide between church and state ... It is just as well understood, however, that the divide is crossed when the parties to the dispute have deliberately left the sphere of matters spiritual over which the religious body has exclusive jurisdiction and engaged matters which that are regulated by the civil courts.[66]

This, however, does not *justify* the court's decision so much as *redescribe* it as one about the long-contested boundary between the 'spiritual' and the 'civil'. To assume that as soon as civil law is 'engaged' we have left the realm of 'the spiritual' is itself a contestable view of the scope of religion, assuming there will not be matters that could truly be both. In such cases, one might equally conclude not that a religious body has 'left the sphere of matters spiritual' but that civil law has improperly intruded into this sphere. Moreover, to interpret JFS's admissions policy in terms of a clear distinction between 'motivation' and 'grounds' is already to read it through a distorting lens: its criterion of Jewishness is necessarily both.

Lord Rodger pointed out the damaging effects of the ruling on associational pluralism, asserting that it meant that 'there can in future be no Jewish faith schools which give preference to children because they are Jewish according to Jewish religious law and belief' and that this amounts to 'manifest discrimination against Jewish schools in comparison with other faith schools'.[67] The appropriate response to such an outcome, I submit, is not to acquiesce in this squelching of educational pluralism but to amend the Race Relations Act 1976 and any other equality laws accordingly.[68]

Many critics of faith schools argue generally that the use of any religious criterion in admissions is inherently objectionable. Some hold this view because they oppose faith schools in principle, however much they might conform to state expectations. Others, however, support the idea of faith schools offering a distinctive ethos within a mixed economy of schools, while simultaneously opposing the use of faith-based criterion in staff or student selection. Trevor Cooling points to the tension in this position, while also exposing the vulnerability of faith schools that themselves fail to grasp it:

> It is unclear how the distinctive ethos of a faith school is created if none of the students or staff is recruited on the basis that they hold that faith. This seems to suggest that religious belief is irrelevant 'clutter' when it comes to creating a school's distinctive religious ethos. There is the ring of absurdity to a position which maintains that faith is integral to the school's ethos and then insisting that the community cannot recruit the people who understand and can create that ethos. Lack of attention to this aspect of faith-based institutions is what leads them to losing their distinctive ethos ... The danger is that the faith label to a school actually means very little in identifiable distinctiveness, but becomes an excuse for the selection of more motivated and upwardly-mobile families who are prepared to attend church to gain access to the school, creating a successful school (in results terms) but not a distinctive school (in faith terms). That *would* be unfair discrimination and would certainly not reflect a Christian aspiration for running schools.[69]

Maintained faith schools also face other constraints on their freedom to operate according to a distinctive ethos. They are required to teach the national curriculum, which is framed according to wholly secular tests of what counts as important and valid knowledge (RE is compulsory in most schools but is not part of the national curriculum). Voluntary controlled and foundation schools are not permitted to require all teaching staff (never mind ancillary staff) to share the faith of the school, even though this could restrict some schools' ability to cultivate a distinctive ethos across the whole of its life.

It is nevertheless important to take note of the concerns of critics of faith schools' autonomy. A key objection is that in areas such as rural villages where a faith school is the only available choice, this amounts to a significant constraint on the freedom of conscience of parents not sympathetic to the faith of the school.[70] This is a powerful argument and it is one to which major providers of faith schools like the Church of England (which often runs the only primary school in a village) are not sufficiently attentive. One solution would be that policy should permit voluntary aided faith schools (which enjoy more freedom to set a religious ethos) only where an adequate alternative provider is reasonably available. This could be achieved either by permitting an increase in the number of smaller schools or in confining voluntary aided status to towns or cities where a genuine choice of schools exists. It could be argued that this is a reasonable 'cost' to religious parents in a society that affirms both religious liberty and educational equality. It would, admittedly, amount to a significant policy shift.

Additional challenges may confront minority faith schools (e.g. Muslim, Jewish, Hindu, Sikh) on account of prevailing Christian and secular assumptions of how faith relates to education. This is one reason why most of them opt for voluntary aided status, where they enjoy a wider margin of discretion.[71] In 2007, the Muslim Council of Britain issued a call for a wide range of needs of Muslim pupils to be met in schools, going well beyond those that Christian schools would seek.[72] While these are routinely catered for in Muslim schools within the maintained sector, the great majority of Muslim families do not have (or choose) access to such schools and some needs (such as religious dress or provision for prayers) are surely legitimate expectations within any community school, not just faith schools. While policy is now more inclusive of religious minorities, law, Rivers argues, has had the effect of 'narrow[ing] down the significance that religion is allowed to have. From the perspective of minority faiths, law shapes the significance of religion in education in a more or less distorting fashion.'[73]

But, as noted, nor do Christian schools occupy an entirely happy place.

Notwithstanding the enduring predominance of Christianity, and especially the Church of England, in the faith school sector – the cause of much secularist criticism – it is unarguable that Christianity too is now a minority faith (even though its schools are popular with parents). Like others, Christian faith schools increasingly find themselves needing to justify their existence within a system that certainly wants to retain their considerable resources but on terms set more and more by the state.[74] Tough choices may lie ahead for Christian schools currently enjoying full state funding, at least if they wish to (and know how to) embody a distinctive ethos across the board. They may find themselves increasingly drawn to the voluntary aided option in order to maintain sufficient control over curriculum, staffing or admissions. That may be the best choice for Christian schools that are committed to maintaining a cohesive ethos. Schools would then have to decide if their desire for greater autonomy was sufficient to meet the challenge of making up the ensuing financial shortfall.

What is 'public'?

I now want to step back from the details of the examples considered above and pick up a fundamental question underlying much of the debates surrounding them. This is the question of the nature and scope of the 'public realm'. This will allow me to put in place further building blocks of the larger view I am developing.

The meaning of 'public' in debates over cases like those I have discussed above is often either ambiguous or problematic. In the Human Rights Act 1998 a body is a 'public authority' if it is, first, part of the state, as with a government department, an NHS hospital or the police – these are deemed 'pure' public authorities.[75] But, second, a body is also 'public' if and insofar as it discharges a 'public function'. Such a body could be *private* (for example, G4S providing prison security); or *voluntary* (such as Barnardo's providing a children's home). When and insofar as it fulfils a public function, it is treated as a body under the direction of a 'public authority'. In the Equality Act 2010, the 'public sector equality duty' is also specified as applying both to any 'public authority' and to persons (or bodies) exercising 'public functions', including private commercial enterprises offering employment or services to the general public. Such public authorities and persons are obliged to 'have due regard' to all the anti-discrimination and equality-promoting provisions of the Act.[76]

These legal definitions raise important questions about the meanings of 'public' and 'private', and 'state' and 'civil society'. Let me suggest, in three propositions, why the term 'public' needs more precision. First, the 'public realm' is much wider than the political community. In Chapter 1, I defined 'public' as the space 'between' the many individuals and associations of society, as 'an arena of reciprocal interaction, communication or exchange among these particular agents that is open to all and not owned by anyone (not even the state)'. Most of the associations that operate in public space are not the creation of or under the direct control of the state – civil society groups, family life, arts organizations and many more. Second, as a result, 'the public realm' is much wider than 'the public sector', the zone of public service provision that is owned, delivered or managed by the state. Third, neither is the public sector coterminous with the *state sector*, since it includes a swathe of practices that remain private (not owned, delivered or directly managed by the state), even while contributing to 'public' services (that is, those that the state has undertaken to guarantee).[77]

On the basis of these distinctions, I propose a conception of the state in which, pursuant to its mandate for public justice, it identifies a range of specific public resources (education, welfare, health and so forth), and commits itself to seeing them secured – *by some means*. It can do so either by direct state provision (the construction, funding and managing of a new hospital or school which it owns and funds) or by supporting and regulating the 'private' (preferably non-profit)[78] supply of the service by a range of providers who might stand in a variety of funding and supervisory relationships to the state.

This understanding of 'public' differs from two influential contemporary alternatives. On a classical liberal conception, the state should play only a minimal role in securing services like education, health or welfare, undertaking to offer only a basic floor of provision (a 'safety net') for impoverished or low-income citizens who otherwise would lack access to them. Beyond that, such services should be supplied by private providers under conditions of market competition. This model is committed to resisting absolute poverty but not to promoting equality of opportunity. The chief objections to it are that it does not reckon with the reality of widespread 'market failure' in the provision of such services and that it denies to the state the responsibility to promote 'social justice'. It is worth noting that religious citizens who may see in the libertarian view robust support for religious liberty should choose their allies carefully, for libertarians will not be sympathetic to their likely commitments to social justice.

By contrast, on a social democratic conception it is assumed that plenary authority to provide what are deemed to be essential public services lies with the state as sole organ of democratic sovereignty. On this view, a small sector of private providers (such as independent fee-paying schools, private hospices or care homes) might, perhaps, be reluctantly tolerated for political reasons. They might, perhaps, have weaker regulatory supervision imposed on them than would apply to the public sector itself. But if such providers desired to participate in the public sector (a private faith school becoming a community school, or a private care home seeking state funding), most or all of the regulatory conditions applying to state providers would then apply. The key assumption is that the state alone can guarantee equal access for all citizens to the provision of such services and that permitting a broad plurality of providers might place such access at risk – such as by weakening accountability, compromising non-discrimination rights or allowing a 'postcode lottery' of provision.

The principal flaw in this model is its tendency to conflate the state not only with the public sector but with the entire public realm. This conflation explains why, for many who hold such a view, non-state institutions immediately become subject to the full range of regulatory constraints the moment they receive registration or funding (full or partial) from the state. It is as if state recognition or funding exercises a kind of 'Midas touch', converting all that is private into public 'gold'. As one liberal political theorist puts it, religious organizations contributing to public services such as education or health 'are not entitled to exempt themselves from norms designed to protect the freedom, equality, and solidarity of citizens, *when they act on behalf of the state*'.[79]

However well intentioned – protection of citizens is certainly a necessary part of the state's role – this again shows the 'logic of congruence' at work. Irrespective of the merits of any particular exemption claim, why should we deem a faith-based health provider to be acting 'on behalf of' the state at all, as distinct from contributing to a public purpose 'with the support of and under the supervision' of the state? Why assume that a 'public' service necessarily is one for which the state has *plenary* authority, which it may then conditionally 'delegate' to another provider? I would argue, rather, that such a provider acts as a non-state partner in the joint provision of a societally recognized public service, for the provision of which the state has resolved to act as final guarantor. Thus, we should say that when the state supports the public contribution that non-state bodies voluntarily offer, *the state is acting on their behalf*. We should positively affirm the value of a plurality of conscientious commitments and practices within areas such as education, health, social care and welfare, rather than seeing plurality as a (perhaps grudging) concession that must be closely policed.[80]

This account of the 'public' realm allows us to assess two common criticisms of recent faith-based provision of public services. Both criticisms alleged that the state has been co-opting faith-based providers into policy goals that might distort the very mission that called them into being and that supplies their energy. Critics of faith-based public services under Labour since 1997 were particularly concerned that such missions were being subordinated to inchoate and distorting policy goals such as 'cohesion', 'security' or the generation of 'social capital'.[81] Similar criticisms were echoed in a 2020 British Academy/Faith and Belief Forum report, which found that 'often cohesion policy is generally dominated by narrower concerns for national identity, security and loyalty.' The report claimed that 'faith is reduced to a concerning "other" and a risk factor for crisis, and has commonly been subtly racialised as the preserve of ethnic minorities in a broadly secular mainstream.'[82] Critics of arrangements initiated by Conservative-led governments since 2010 have been concerned rather with the compromises risked as faith-based providers are used as cover to minimize the damage done by an ideological project of 'austerity'.[83]

I offer two remarks on these criticisms. One is that the fact of significant reductions in funding available for public services, while undoubtedly damaging in most cases, does not in itself question the legitimacy of independent associations (faith-based or otherwise) partnering with government in order to make their distinctive offerings to the common good. Such offerings have validity irrespective of whatever else the state does. The fact that faith-based providers are doing what formerly the state might have done is not in itself problematic. There is no fixed range or quantity of services that must be supplied directly by the state sector; and there is no reason why that sector should dominate the provision of services anyway. So long as faith-based providers retain their freedom to critique a policy regime they find objectionable, there is no reason why they should not continue to make their particular offerings. My other remark is that whatever the funding arrangements and larger policy climate with which faith-based providers find themselves confronted, they must consistently guard the integrity of their mission and be prepared to withdraw from offering a public service if that mission is substantially compromised by such a partnership. As noted, many have concluded, and many more might conclude, that the price of partnering with the state is just too high to risk such a compromising 'mission drift'.

On the model of a thickly plural public sector that I am proposing, an important shift in the *burden of justification* also follows: from seeing the state as the pre-emptive legislator imposing uniformity for the sake of just public ends, but then conceding (or not) minority supplications for restricted 'exemption' or 'autonomy', to asking how the state can, from the start, intentionally harness the strengths of plural providers, imposing uniformity only where necessary. Such a default assumption would signal the state's strong commitment to upholding the autonomy of religious associations not only for negative, protective purposes but also as an acknowledgement that in conditions of deep diversity the state needs the moral and social energies of many different communities of faith in a shared pursuit of public goods. My proposal is that such a thickly plural public realm should become the desired direction of travel in the future evolution of public services.[84]

Yet we must acknowledge that for such an idea to win traction it would be enormously helpful if faith-based institutions could articulate not only a case for negative protection of associational freedom but also a positive case that their public offerings are sufficiently distinctive and valuable to justify a capacious sphere of legal autonomy. Catholic Care was unable to make that case on behalf of Catholic adoption policies; JFS (narrowly) failed to do so over their admissions policy; Al-Hijrah School could not do it over gender segregation. I leave open the question whether and how each of them might have succeeded. But here a significant challenge arises. In a telling comment on a case involving faith schools' hiring policies, Lucy Vickers suggests that 'it will usually be difficult to convince a[n employment] tribunal that being of a particular religion or belief is an occupational requirement even in faith schools, as it is rare (apart from where religious instruction is given) for religion to be a defining element of such a role.'[85] To the extent that this is so, it shows that faith schools generally are not, do not seek to be or do know how to be, or at least are not perceived to be, distinctive in areas other than religious instruction, worship and general ethos.[86] If they cannot, for example, show how their faith makes a difference to other core school purposes, they risk becoming defined in the public mind mainly by what they are against (or, as Cooling notes, only in terms of academic success).

To address this challenge, faith schools might, for example, seek to articulate a distinctive faith perspective in their curricular content. They might approach economics in terms of justice, solidarity and ecological responsibility rather than 'rational utility maximization', as in the still-dominant neo-classical paradigm. In history they might question secular modernist views of historical progress (such as those behind the secularization thesis), and thus be more attentive to the stories of the victims of that 'progress', such as minority racial, ethnic, indigenous and faith communities. In sociology, they might present a positive, evidence-based view of the stable two-parent family (including same-sex parented ones where the school could endorse this theologically). In modern languages, they might teach to prepare students to be more than consumerist tourists and 'to be a blessing as strangers in a foreign land and ... hospitable to strangers in their own homeland'.[87] Schools might also more openly encourage an ethos supporting sexual restraint and confident body image as wholesome alternatives to the emotionally destructive sexual permissiveness and body-shaming often seen among children of school age. And they might embody a form of education inspiring students to think in terms of vocation or public service rather than one narrowly preoccupied with competition in the job market. Of course, some faith (and secular) schools already attempt to meet some such goals, but a state seriously committed to the flourishing of a plurality of educational visions could do much more to support them in doing so.

The same proposal in principle applies to any case of 'faithful association'. For example, an intriguing debate is emerging over whether commercial entities, generally regarded as wholly 'secular', might wish to embody a religious ethos.[88] Because they are deemed to perform 'public functions', they are excluded from the exemptions granted in the Equality Act 2010.[89] But the stark opposition between 'religious' and 'commercial' activities is false to the actual motivations of some faith-based businesses. Such for-profit entities should, I suggest, also be allowed to claim religious autonomy on similar terms to churches and non-profits.[90] Only a pre-emptive assumption that business practices cannot be infused by principles of faith would exclude the idea from the start.[91]

Paul Marshall cites compelling examples of such infusion.[92] The American supermarket chain Wegmans, for example, 'seeks to reflect Catholic social teachings on solidarity, subsidiarity, the dignity of the human person, and the care of the common good'. It has been deemed by *Fortune* magazine to be 'the second-best place to work in America'. Similarly, 'Nucor Steel, the second-largest steel company in the U.S., makes compensation for both the CEO and the company's employees rise or fall together depending on the company's success.' In another Catholic-inspired business, The Wine Group, the second-biggest wine company in America, 'senior executives are only rewarded with stock bonuses for their work 20 years down the road, so that planning for the company is based on a "20-year time horizon".'

These examples show that even though a commercial enterprise must generate a profit in order to stay afloat, this 'does not preclude it from integrating other guiding principles, including religiously based ones, into its ethos and operations ... even for-profit corporations can have religious duties and embody religious convictions.' Marshall's conclusion is that 'for-profit entities that are authentically shaped by religious ground-motives deserve religious freedom protections along with their non-profit, NGO, and congregational counterparts. In other words, they are due the rights and protections of institutional religious freedom.'[93] Non-discrimination (and other types of) law might thus need to be amended if it impedes faith-based commercial enterprises from living out their distinctive vision for business. Indeed, law ought to be not only permissive in this regard but positively encouraging of new business models promoting meaningful and socially useful jobs, shared ownership, workplace justice and solidarity, community service and ecological responsibility.[94]

Articulating a positive case for the autonomy of a faith-based school, charity, business or any other association will be challenging for many existing or putative public service providers (although they should seek to make such a case irrespective of any relation to the state). Even if it cannot be made, there is still a prima facie argument for such autonomy on negative religious freedom grounds. But foregrounding the way an association makes a distinctive, if sometimes counter-cultural, contribution to the common good is likely to win it more friends than one that appears to appeal only to identity defence. As law and policy steadily put more pressure on religious associations to articulate their distinctiveness in order to shore up whatever differential treatment they currently enjoy, making such a case will become ever more necessary. Faith communities need to redouble their efforts to inspire their members with a confident vision of 'faithful association' as a means to contribute to the common good and then to equip them to be articulate spokespeople for such a prospect.

A complex case of associational autonomy: shari'a councils

In the previous chapter, I alluded to a case of an individual exemption involving an evangelical Christian (Lillian Ladele) and in this chapter, to leading cases of associational autonomy involving Catholics (Catholic Care) and Jews (JFS). I now consider a special case of associational autonomy involving Muslims: 'shari'a councils'. This has so far involved relatively few legal cases but it has occasioned an intense policy debate in which a different sort of clash between religious freedom and equality rights is playing out. We encounter here three questions taking us beyond the parameters of the issues considered so far. First, given that in this case elite and public opinion is currently overwhelmingly on the side of 'equality rights' over 'religious freedom', where should the balance actually lie? Second, does this attitude after all reflect a 'majority bias' against an unfamiliar religious minority in a society dominated by secular and Christian perceptions of what counts as 'acceptable religion'? Third, are members of this minority themselves – especially women – being subjected to injustice by their own faith-based associations?[95] The case yields important insights on the parameters of democratic pluralism and merits extended analysis.

Shari'a councils (sometimes called 'tribunals') have occasioned exceptional levels of media anxiety, hostility and misinformation, so it is important to be clear about what they are.[96] Such councils offer an informal, private forum in which Muslims can receive advice and rulings from Islamic religious scholars, mostly on matters concerning Islamic marriage and divorce and sometimes on related issues. From one perspective, they can be seen as a form of communal religious self-governance, permitting Muslims to resolve interpersonal disputes within the religious community itself according to religious law, without having to incur the cost and publicity (and thus 'shame') of civil courts. They have been emerging in areas with large Muslim populations since at least the 1980s.

Separately, a national body, the Muslim Arbitration Tribunal (MAT), was created in 2007 to provide formal 'arbitration' services, mostly on commercial matters (but sometimes on domestic ones) in accordance with shari'a law but within the constraints of UK law.[97] Private arbitration is widely used in the UK for many purposes, mostly non-religious, and operates under the Arbitration Act 1996, whereby agreements reached through arbitration can be enforced as contracts in civil courts, but set aside if they can be shown to be unfree or unfair under national law. In cases of conflict, national law will always prevail. MAT operates under this Act. The freedom to enter into private arbitration – to resolve disputes without turning to the state – is a fundamental civil right and it is difficult to deny that it should in principle be equally available to all citizens, including those who wish to have their disputes heard under limited aspects of religious law.[98]

The growth of such private bodies has generated impassioned public debate over questions such as whether Muslim women are choosing such services freely or under (patriarchal) community pressure; whether the councils' rulings are undermining the equal civil rights and protections of women and children, even condoning illegal acts such as wife-beating or forced marriage;[99] whether they serve to reinforce tendencies towards religious and ethnic 'segregation'; and whether the very existence of such bodies is creating a 'parallel legal system', thereby undermining the principle of 'one law for all'.

On the last of these concerns, it is vital to note that shari'a councils (and the MAT) are fundamentally different from officially recognized religious courts under formal systems of 'legal pluralism'. These exist in multi-religious states such as India, Malaysia, Lebanon and Israel and can include Islamic, Christian, Jewish and Hindu courts. Such courts do indeed function as 'parallel legal systems'. The state assigns an official religious group identity to some or all citizens and requires (or at least permits) them to have matters such as marriage, divorce, child custody or inheritance adjudicated under the relevant religious courts.[100] Contrary to many media portrayals, shari'a councils and the MAT are not examples of this kind of 'legal pluralism'. They are not 'courts' but private bodies having no officially recognized status (although, as noted, some of the decisions of the MAT can be enforced by civil courts).

While much of the public rhetoric around such bodies has been ill-informed, inflammatory and often frankly Islamophobic, the concerns noted above are serious. A growing body of evidence of discriminatory practices towards women has been gathered, especially by women's organizations. As a result, two official inquiries were recently instituted. The Home Affairs Select Committee initiated one in 2016, and although this closed when parliament was dissolved in 2017, it had by then accumulated a large body of evidence, from calls for modest or radical reform,[101] to outright denunciations of councils as inherently oppressive and unreformable. Also in 2016, the then Home Secretary Theresa May commissioned an independent review of their operation, chaired by Professor Mona Siddiqui, which reported in 2018.[102] The review (*Review*) merits attention as the most recent officially commissioned consultation.

The inquiry's terms of reference were to ascertain 'whether sharia law is being misused or applied in a way that is incompatible with the domestic law in England and Wales, and in particular whether there were discriminatory practices against women who use sharia councils' (3). Rejecting the suggestion that such councils amount to a parallel legal system (10), the *Review* found justifications under human rights law for their existence based on the rights to a private life, to freedom of religion and to freedom of association. It thus declined to propose banning them. It defined a council as 'a voluntary local association of scholars who see themselves or are seen by their communities as authorised to offer advice to Muslims principally in the field of religious marriage and divorce' (while noting that some are registered as charities, others as businesses, while others lack any legal status) (10).[103] It reported that the vast majority of users were women seeking an Islamic divorce, especially where a husband (who has a right of unilateral divorce) was reluctant to grant one (12–13). It noted that a key reason why Muslim women used such councils was that, lacking a civil marriage (for a variety of reasons), this was the only way they could obtain a divorce that would be recognized in their own community. The report noted that 'it is clear from all the evidence that sharia councils are fulfilling a need in some Muslim communities' (23).

It also noted that the state has a mandate to intervene in such councils if there is evidence of the infringement of the rights and freedoms of participants (9) (as it does, of course, in the case of any voluntary body). While noting evidence of 'good practice', the *Review* also disclosed a litany of reported problems. One is that many councils consulted had experienced no 'mainstream training' and lacked an understanding of the distinctions between 'arbitration' (which is regulated by statute), 'mediation' (which is not) and 'reconciliation counselling' (which is purely informal) (11). These three processes can, however, yield very different material outcomes.[104] The *Review* called for more evidence on whether what was often called 'mediation' was intruding into areas that properly belong in a civil law context (for example asset distribution, custody disputes), thus placing women's rights at risk (11–12). It cited evidence of inappropriate questioning of women, insistence on mediation (with women sometimes being asked to make financial concessions in return for a divorce), delay, misinformation about women's rights under civil law, and lack of women on panels (although it offered no quantitative analysis of the extent of such practices) (16).[105]

In the light of these findings, the *Review* made three main recommendations. First, in order to give Muslim women the full protection of civil law, marriage and divorce law should be changed to require a civil marriage to take place prior to or simultaneously with an Islamic marriage. Second, a range of educational initiatives should be launched via advice centres, NGOs and women's groups to raise awareness of women's rights under civil law and their vulnerability in the absence of civil registration of their marriages. Third, a scheme of regulation of shari'a councils should be introduced in order to protect women's rights (a proposal apparently not opposed in principle by the councils consulted). Three options are entertained: councils adopt a scheme themselves ('self-regulation'); a scheme is devised by the state and then adopted by councils; a scheme is imposed by the state and enforced along the lines of OFSTED. The *Review* rules out the first both because of the Sunni tradition that each mosque (and thus council) is independent and also because of the likely lack of capacity to achieve national coordination. It rules the third out because this might be seen as conferring legitimacy on councils, which it does not do in the case of parallel bodies such as Jewish batei din or Catholic tribunals. Instead it favours the second, proposing that the state establish a body with a code of practice – covering all the concerns raised in the report – for shari'a councils to accept and implement by self-regulation. Such a body would include both council members and family lawyers, have a suitable gender balance, and ensure effective monitoring mechanisms (19–20).

Given the incendiary nature of the issues in the public mind, it was always unlikely that the *Review* would elicit a speedy consensus on the way forward. Russell Sandberg, an expert in religious family law, charges that its terms of reference operated with a 'loaded' question, which it then failed to answer.[106] The inquiry had already been boycotted by a large number of British and overseas women's organizations, and a highly critical open letter explaining why was appended to the report itself (27–34). Predictably, responses to its publication diverged widely.[107] The government itself responded on three occasions during 2018 and 2019.[108] It affirmed religious freedom as the basis for shari'a councils' right to exist, asserted the primacy of national over religious law, committed itself to exploring legal routes to registering Islamic marriages and supported the recommended educational initiatives. But it declined to establish any kind of state-endorsed regulatory body for councils at all, on account of the fear of 'conferring legitimacy on them as alternative forms of dispute resolution' and feeding the perception of 'parallel systems'. The *Review* included a 'dissenting view of regulation' from one panel member, which claimed that *any* system of regulation would give 'quasi-legal status' to councils, reinforce the perception of a 'parallel legal system' and 'perpetuate the myth of separateness' (21).

While more research is evidently required – the core of the report is a mere 15 pages[109] – the thrust of a democratic pluralist response is clear.[110] First, calls for the kind of official 'legal pluralism' cited above should be resisted. As noted, shari'a courts under that system are not examples of the associational *pluralism* I have argued for – which champions associational independence from the state – but are a form of religious *corporatism* whereby the state delegates part of its own legal jurisdiction to a non-state body, thereby entrusting (at least in the first instance) some of the fundamental rights of its citizens to a non-state entity. Shari'a councils or tribunals should retain the status of voluntary associations. Second, the right of Muslims to utilize religiously informed mediation or arbitration should be maintained as an affirmation of Britain's commitment to equal religious freedom and freedom of association. Simply banning shari'a councils would be unfair and draconian. It would be a clear case of 'majority bias' and might well be overturned in courts on either religious freedom or equality grounds or both. Third, concerted awareness programmes along the lines suggested in the report should certainly be promoted, but for these to win legitimacy and thus be effective, they must be led primarily by those within Muslim communities, especially women, the principal users. Fourth, cumulative evidence of violations of the equal legal rights of Muslim women by shari'a councils has now reached a threshold that does require state intervention: such rights are among the 'baseline constitutional norms' any version of pluralism must respect. But steps in this direction should proceed through extensive community consultation and seek wherever possible to facilitate internal reform, rather than risk subjecting shari'a councils to a pre-emptive 'logic of congruence'.[111] Fifth, decisions on legislation should in any case await a much broader-based official review, both of the place of religious mediation and arbitration among all faith communities, and of the state of family and marriage law in general. Sandberg warns against proceeding hastily and in an ad hoc fashion towards making marriage registration compulsory, because there are sometimes valid reasons why Muslims do not currently register their marriages, making a nuanced approach necessary.[112] In 2020, the Law Commission published a major review of weddings in England and Wales, and the government has promised to take its work into account as it responds to the *Review*.[113]

Given that policy is in flux on the matter, the fivefold 'democratic pluralist' response I have suggested must be tentative.[114] Its goal should be to affirm both public space for religious diversity and the rigorous protection of equal individual rights, especially for women – if necessary against the religious communities of which they are a part.

Conclusion

In the previous chapter, I argued that religious individuals should as far as possible enjoy exemptions from laws that substantially and disproportionately impede their 'identity-protecting commitments'. In this chapter, I argued that religious associations should enjoy autonomy from such laws where necessary to defend their corporate integrity. Autonomy, or self-governance, is vital for associations (religious or secular) to secure the distinctive goods of corporate life, as well as to promote a vigorous civil society that allows multiple conduits of human creativity and blocks overweening state power. Government policy since the 1990s has eagerly embraced the resources that faith-based associations are thought to bring to the delivery of public services. While the autonomy of religious associations is reasonably well protected in the UK, legal and policy trends are, however, currently serving to restrict associational freedom unnecessarily.

We need a broad public reassessment of the distinction between areas in which associational autonomy take precedence and those in which the state must lay down basic constitutional protections for all citizens, such as non-discrimination rights. A political community committed to the aspirations of democratic pluralism will respond to claims to associational autonomy generously, but not uncritically. It will accord high regard to its citizens' fundamental convictions, expressed individually or associatively, acknowledging that these may imply public manifestations that in the eyes of a secular mainstream (or other religious communities) may seem eccentric or objectionable. It will strive by various means to accommodate those manifestations where they do not impair other people's rights, cause them other kinds of harm or demonstrably impair the public good. Such a political community will do this, first, out of respect for citizens' deep interest in moral integrity; second, to keep the forum of public practice and deliberation open to challenging, counter-cultural visions of the common good that might offer unexpected wisdom; and third, to enhance the participation of minority voices that would otherwise be denied the opportunity to contribute to public ends and so be tempted to retreat into potentially dangerous isolation.

In this and the previous chapter, I have addressed this question with an eye on how 'faithful conscience' and 'faithful association' are *impacted by the state*. In the next chapter, I address the no less controversial question of how, and how far, faith-motivated citizens and associations might legitimately *shape state policies* that all must live under – the question of 'faithful power'.

Notes

(Websites accessed 14/12/20)

1 Francis Davis, Elizabeth Paulhus and Andrew Bradstock, *Moral But No Compass: Government, Church and the Future of Welfare: A Report to the Church of England and to the Nation* (Chelmsford: Matthew James Publishing, 2008), 53.

2 Davis et al., *Moral But No Compass*, 53.

3 Davis et al., *Moral But No Compass*, 55.

4 In this chapter, 'association', 'institution' and 'organization' are used inter-changeably.

5 See www.faithandsociety.org/covenant/full/. FaithAction is the APPG's secretariat. www.faithaction.net/. Government continues to engage with FaithAction, most recently on the impact of COVID-19 on faiths.

6 See www.faithandsociety.org/covenant/launch/.

7 See www.local.gov.uk/sites/default/files/documents/working-faith-groups-prom-6ff.pdf. For other outcomes, see All-Party Parliamentary Group on Faith and Society, 'The Faith Covenant: Update 2016'.

8 *Levelling Up Our Communities: Proposals for a New Social Covenant*, a report to Government by Danny Kruger MP (2020), 37. Available from www.dannykruger.org.uk/sites/www.dannykruger.org.uk/files/2020-09/Levelling%20Up%20Our%20Communities-Danny%20Kruger.pdf.

9 For historical surveys since the nineteenth century, see Frank Prochaska, *Christianity and Social Service in Modern Britain: The Disinherited Spirit* (Oxford: Oxford University Press, 2006); Lesley Husselbee and Paul Ballard, eds, *Free Churches and Society: The Nonconformist Contribution to Social Welfare 1800–*

2010 (London: Continuum, 2012); John Wolffe, ed., *Evangelical Faith and Public Zeal: Evangelicals and Society in Britain 1780–1980* (London: SPCK, 1995).

10 See Steven Monsma and Christopher J. Soper, *The Challenge of Pluralism: Church and State in Five Democracies* (Lanham, MD: Rowman & Littlefield, 2009); Kees van Kersbergen, *Social Capitalism: A Study of Christian Democracy and the Welfare State* (London: Routledge 1995).

11 See, for example, *Faith in the System: The Role of Schools with a Religious Character in English Education and Society* (London: Department for Children, Schools and Families, 2007).

12 Cited in Nick Spencer, *Doing Good: A Future for Christianity in the 21st Century* (London: Theos, 2016), 44.

13 On 'Christian social action', see, for example: The National Churches Trust, *House of Good: The Economic and Social Values of Church Buildings to the UK* (London: National Churches Trust, 2020); *Cinnamon Faith Action Audit National Report* (London: Cinnamon Network, 2016); Samuel Wells, Russell Rook and David Barclay, *For Good: The Church and the Future of Welfare* (Norwich: Canterbury Press, 2017); Paul Bickley, *Doing Good Better: The Case for Faith-based Social Innovation* (London: Theos, 2017); Spencer, *Doing Good*; Ben Ryan, *Catholic Social Thought and Catholic Charities in Britain Today: Need and Opportunity* (London: Theos, 2015); Tim Thorlby and Alison Gelder, *Our Common Heritage: Housing Associations and Churches Working Together* (London: Centre for Theology and Community/Housing Justice, 2015).

14 Private welfare associations retain extensive but not total autonomy. See Julian Rivers, *The Law of Organized Religions: Between Establishment and Secularism* (Oxford: Oxford University Press, 2010), 276–9.

15 See Home Office, *Working Together: Cooperation Between Government and Faith Communities* (London: Home Office, 2004); DCLG, *Face to Face and Side by Side: A Framework for Partnership in our Multi Faith Society* (London: DCLG, 2008).

16 Therese O'Toole et al., *Taking Part: Muslim Participation in Contemporary Governance* (Bristol: Centre for the Study of Ethnicity and Citizenship, University of Bristol, 2013), 41.

17 Jenny Taylor, 'There's Life in Establishment – But Not As We Know It', *Political Theology* 5.3 (2004), 329–49; Luke Bretherton, *Christianity and Contemporary Politics: The Conditions and Possibilities of Faithful Witness* (Chichester: Wiley-Blackwell, 2010), 36.

18 Bretherton, *Christianity and Contemporary Politics*, 45.

19 British Humanist Association, *Quality and Equality: Human Rights, Public Services and Religious Organisations* (London: British Humanist Association, 2007). The National Secular Society (NSS) renewed the 'discrimination' critique in *Faith-Shaped Holes: How Religious Privilege is Undermining Equality Law* (London: National Secular Society, 2020).

20 For assessments of Big Society, see Ian Sansbury, Ben Cowdery and Lea Kauffmann-de Vries, *Faith in Public Services: The Role of the Church in Public Service Delivery* (London: Oasis Foundation, 2016); Guy Brandon, *The Big Society in Context: A Means to What End?* (Cambridge: Jubilee Centre, 2011).

21 See www.near-neighbours.org.uk/. See also O'Toole et al., *Taking Part*, 47–8.

22 See www.oasisuk.org/. Oasis and other faith-based providers have come in

for critique from the National Secular Society: www.secularism.org.uk/opinion/ 2016/06/faith-in-public-services.

23 See https://kainoscommunity.org/.

24 See also the report of the All-Party Parliamentary Group Christians in Parliament, *Faith in the Community: Strengthening Ties between Faith Groups and Local Authorities* (London: Christians in Parliament, 2013).

25 *Levelling Up Our Communities.*

26 Chris Baker, 'Propping up the State? Omnicompetent Faith in a Disorganised World', *William Temple Foundation Blog* (4 May 2016), https://williamtemple foundation.org.uk/propping-up-the-state-omnicompetent-faith-in-a-disorganised-world/.

27 See, for example, Raymond Plant, *Politics, Theology and History* (Cambridge: Cambridge University Press, 2001).

28 *Levelling Up Our Communities.*

29 Paul Bickley reports that when delivering public services the vast majority of churches and religious charities 'decry activities which might be described as "proselytising"'. *The Problem of Proselytism* (London: Theos, 2015), 9. Demos reports the same in Jonathan Birdwell, ed., *The Faith Collection* (London: Demos, 2013).

30 Jane Calderwood Norton, *Freedom of Religious Organizations* (Oxford: Oxford University Press, 2016), offers a contrasting liberal defence of associational autonomy deriving from the overriding value of personal autonomy (12–28), which, however, often yields comparable legal conclusions to my own.

31 Rivers, *Law of Organized Religions*, 334. See also Calderwood Norton, *Freedom of Religious Organizations*; Rex Ahdar and Ian Leigh, *Religious Freedom in the Liberal State*, 2nd edn (Oxford: Oxford University Press, 2013), chapter 11.

32 Rivers, *Law of Organized Religions*, 55–71.

33 *Hasan and Chaush v Bulgaria* (2002) 34 EHRR 55, para. 62.

34 Jeanne Heffernan Schindler, ed., *Christianity and Civil Society: Catholic and Neo-Calvinist Perspectives* (Lanham, MD: Lexington, 2008); Simone Chambers and Will Kymlicka, eds, *Alternative Conceptions of Civil Society* (Princeton, NJ: Princeton University Press, 2002).

35 Rivers, *Law of Organized Religions*, 74, 107.

36 Rivers, *Law of Organized Religions*, 73–4, 107. The Church of England is exceptional in this regard because its laws are part of the law of the land.

37 Rivers, *Law of Organized Religions*, 336.

38 Rivers, *Law of Organized Religions*, 88–96. He terms this natural justice a 'universal floor of procedural fairness' (112). See also Calderwood Norton, *Freedom of Religious Organizations*, chapter 2.

39 No exemptions are allowed in relation to disability, but some are allowed in relation to age and race.

40 See Peter Edge and Lucy Vickers, *Review of Equality and Human Rights Law Relating to Religion or Belief*, Equality and Human Rights Commission Research Report 97 (London: EHRC, 2015), 45–6.

41 These are known as the 'compliance' and 'non-conflict' principles. On the effects of equality law on religious employers generally, see Calderwood Norton, *Freedom of Religious Organizations*, chapter 3.

42 William A. Galston, *Liberal Pluralism: The Implications of Value Pluralism for Political Theory and Practice* (Cambridge: Cambridge University Press, 2002), 101.

43 Bretherton, *Christianity and Contemporary Politics*, 45.

44 Bretherton, *Christianity and Contemporary Politics*, 43–4.

45 Nancy L. Rosenblum, '*Amos*: Religious Autonomy and the Moral Uses of Pluralism', in Nancy L. Rosenblum, ed., *Obligations of Citizenship and Demands of Faith: Religious Accommodation in Pluralist Democracies* (Princeton, NJ: Princeton University Press, 2000), 187–8. For a defence of 'congruence', see Stephen Macedo, 'Transformative Constitutionalism and the Case of Religion: Defending the Moderate Hegemony of Liberalism', *Political Theory* 26.1 (1998), 56–80. For a critique, see Paul Billingham, 'Shaping Religion: The Limits of Transformative Liberalism', in Jonathan Seglow and Andrew Shorten, eds, *Religion and Political Theory: Secularism, Accommodation and the New Challenges of Religious Diversity* (London: Rowman & Littlefield International, 2019), 57–77.

46 Galston, *Liberal Pluralism*, 20.

47 Patrick J. Deneen, *Why Liberalism Failed* (New Haven, CT: Yale University Press, 2018), chapter 2; Adrian Pabst, *The Demons of Liberal Democracy* (Cambridge: Polity, 2019), chapters 4, 5; Paul Hirst, *From Statism to Pluralism: Democracy, Civil Society and Global Politics* (London: UCL Press, 1997).

48 See Caritas Social Action Network, which has nearly 50 affiliates: www.csan.org.uk/.

49 Ryan, *Catholic Social Thought and Catholic Charities*, 19–20.

50 Ryan, *Catholic Charities*, 65.

51 *Catholic Care (Diocese of Leeds) v Charity Commission for England and Wales* [2010] EWHC 520 (Ch), [2010] 4 All ER 1041. See Frank Cranmer, 'Catholic Care: Can an Adoption Agency restrict its Services to Heterosexual Adoptive Parents?', *Law and Religion UK* (3 November 2012), www.lawandreligionuk.com/2012/11/03/catholic-care-can-an-adoption-agency-restrict-its-services-to-heterosexual-adoptive-parents/; Calderwood Norton, *Freedom of Religious Organizations*, 169–78.

52 The decision was reaffirmed in 2020 in a similar case. See Frank Cranmer, 'May a Christian Fostering Agency discriminate on Grounds of Sexuality? *Cornerstone*', *Law and Religion UK (12 August 2020)*, www.lawandreligionuk.com/2020/08/12/may-a-christian-fostering-agency-discriminate-on-grounds-of-sexuality-cornerstone/.

53 Rivers, *Law of Organized Religions*, 285.

54 Robert Meakin, 'Taking the Queen's Shilling: The Implications for Religious Freedom for Religions Being Registered as Charities', *Law and Justice* 178 (2017), 57–79.

55 See Meakin, 'Taking the Queen's Shilling', 61–2.

56 Quoted in Meakin, 'Taking the Queen's Shilling', 64.

57 See Davis et al., *Moral But No Compass*, 85–94; Rivers, *Law of Organized Religions*, 279–82.

58 See Davis et al., *Moral But No Compass*, 85. Rivers argues that 'law and Government policy ... has drifted towards the subordination of religion to Governmental ends and the combining of public financial privilege [e.g. tax-exempt status] with Governmental regulation' (*Law of Organized Religions*, 179).

59 This point is endorsed in the Cabinet Office's policy document, *Civil Society Strategy: Building a Future that Works for Everyone* (London: Cabinet Office, 2018). Although it lacks a dedicated chapter on faith-based organizations, it reaffirms the government's commitment to recognizing 'collaborative commissioning' in which

'social value' (given statutory recognition in the Social Value Act 2012) is counted as an independent criterion for public sector commissioning purposes (115).

60 Rivers, *Law of Organized Religions*, 321–2; see also 36.

61 *R (E) v JFS* [2009] UKSC 15, [2010] 2 AC 728. See Calderwood Norton, *Freedom of Religious Organizations*, 38–45; Frank Cranmer, 'Who is a Jew? Jewish Faith Schools and the Race Relations Act 1976', *Law and Justice* 164 (2010), 75–83; Bernard S. Jackson, 'Jewish Approaches to Law (Religious and Secular)', *Law and Justice* 164 (2010), 63–74.

62 See Paul Weller et al., *Religion or Belief, Discrimination or Equality: Britain in Global Contexts* (London: Bloomsbury Academic, 2013), 52.

63 Weller et al., *Religion or Belief*, 52.

64 *R (E) v JFS*, para. 103.

65 *R (E) v JFS*, para. 258.

66 *R (E) v JFS*, paras 157, 158.

67 *R (E) v JFS* paras 225, 226. All Jewish schools (not only Orthodox ones) subsequently have had to amend their admissions policies.

68 Lady Hale conceded that had parliament drafted the RRA differently, a different outcome could have been possible.

69 Trevor Cooling, *Doing God in Education* (London: Theos, 2010), 65.

70 National Secular Society (NSS), *The Choice Delusion: How Faith Schools Restrict Primary School Choice in England* (London: National Secular Society, 2020), estimates that 'Almost three in ten families across England live in areas where most or all of the closest primary schools are faith schools.' See also NSS, *Faith-Shaped Holes: How Religious Privilege is Undermining Equality Law* (London: National Secular Society, 2020).

71 On concerns over private ('supplementary') Muslim schools, see Philip Lewis and Sadek Hamid, *British Muslims: New Directions in Islamic Thought, Creativity and Activism* (Edinburgh: Edinburgh University Press, 2018), chapter 2; Myriam Cherti and Laura Bradley, *Inside Madrassas: Understanding and Engaging with British Muslim Faith Supplementary Schools* (London: IPPR, 2011).

72 These include modest dress, permission for beards, halal food, provision for prayers, segregated sports, teaching of Arabic. *Towards Greater Understanding: Meeting the Needs of Muslim Pupils in State Schools* (London: MCB, 2007).

73 Rivers, *Law of Organized Religions*, 267.

74 See Ian Mansfield and Tim Clark, *The Watchmen Revisited: Curriculum and Faith in Ofsted's New Inspection Framework* (London: Policy Exchange, 2020), 9–12. See also www.christian.org.uk/news/secular-ofsted-is-fuelling-division-says-influential-think-tank/.

75 See Weller at al., *Religion or Belief*, 50–5.

76 For further complexities, see Calderwood Norton, *Freedom of Religious Organizations*, 181–5.

77 By 'private' here I mean either 'for profit' (commercial entities, which could include workers' cooperatives or community interest companies) or 'non-profit' (e.g. voluntary bodies, some social enterprises, cooperatives or public service mutuals). Mutuals are championed by Mutuo: www.mutuo.coop/.

78 See Caroline Julian, *Making it Mutual: The Ownership Revolution that Britain Needs* (London: ResPublica, 2012).

79 Annabelle Lever, 'Equality and Conscience: Ethics and the Provision of Public Services', in Cécile Laborde and Aurélia Bardon, eds, *Religion in Liberal Political*

Philosophy (Oxford: Oxford University Press, 2017), 245 (emphasis added). Calderwood Norton agrees: 'Positively supporting or enabling ... discrimination through a contractual relationship whereby the [religious] organization provides the goods or services *on behalf of a public authority* ... sanctions the discrimination. It throws the moral weight of the state's sanction behind it [and] tells the person discriminated against that it is also the state's view that discriminating against persons like them is justifiable' (*Freedom of Religious Organizations*, 188) (emphasis original). But only if the organization is, as she erroneously puts it, 'operating as an arm of the state' (188).

80 James Noyes and Phillip Blond, *Holistic Mission: Social Action and the Church of England* (London: ResPublica/Resurgo Social Ventures, 2013), makes a powerful case for such an approach, with a focus on churches as providers.

81 See Bretherton, *Christianity and Contemporary Politics*, 36–45. Bretherton argues (writing in 2010) that when government enlists faith groups in the delivery of funded services, instead of bringing them together for purpose of 'cohesion' it actually risks dividing them by luring them into a game of competitive bidding for contracts (42–3). For a critique of the distortion of religious priorities that occurs when the state construes faith in terms of a neo-liberal idea of 'social capital', see Adam Dinham, *Faith and Social Capital After the Debt Crisis* (Basingstoke: Palgrave Macmillan, 2012).

82 Madeleine Pennington, *Cohesive Societies: Faith and Belief* (London: British Academy/Faith and Belief Forum, 2020), 61.

83 This was Chris Baker's critique, cited above ('Propping up the State?').

84 This aligns with the associationist model of the state proposed by Paul Hirst: *Associative Democracy: New Forms of Economic and Social Governance* (Cambridge: Polity, 1994); *From Statism to Pluralism.*

85 Lucy Vickers, *Religious Freedom, Religious Discrimination and the Workplace* (Oxford: Hart, 2016), 215. Quoted in EHRC, *Religion or Belief: Is the Law Working?* (London: EHRC, 2016), 28.

86 Charles Clarke and Linda Woodhead, *A New Settlement Revised: Religion and Belief in Schools* (London: Westminster Faith Debates, 2018) contains many worthwhile proposals congenial to my model of democratic pluralism, but does not address the distinctiveness of faith schools beyond worship, ethos and RE.

87 David I. Smith and Barbara Carvill, *The Gift of the Stranger: Faith, Hospitality and Language Learning* (Grand Rapids, MI: Eerdmans, 2000), 57–8. See Cooling, *Doing God in Education*, 39–48.

88 Frank Cranmer, 'Can a Commercial Company Have "Beliefs"? *Exmoor Coast Boat Cruises Ltd v Revenue & Customs*', *Law and Religion UK* (22 December 2014), https://lawandreligionuk.com/2014/12/22/can-a-commercial-company-have-beliefs-exmoor-coast-boat-cruises-ltd-v-revenue-customs/.

89 Thus Hazelmary and Peter Bull were not permitted to restrict access to double-bedded rooms in their hotel to heterosexual couples (*Bull and Bull v Hall and Preddy* [2012] EWCA Civ 83, [2012] 1 WLR 2514).

90 See Rex Ahdar, 'Companies as Religious Liberty Claimants', *Oxford Journal of Law and Religion* 5.1 (2016), 1–27; Calderwood Norton, *Freedom of Religious Organizations*, 178–81.

91 Equally, of course, a secular business should be free to adopt a distinctive ethos, including, for example, commitments to solidarity, equality, justice, competitiveness and so forth, understood in secularist terms.

92 Paul Marshall, 'Can For-Profit Corporations be Religious?', Religious Free-

dom Institute (25 July 2020), www.religiousfreedominstitute.org/cornerstone/can-for-profit-corporations-be-religious.

93 Marshall, 'Can For-Profit Corporations be Religious?'.

94 I would add one caution: given the significantly greater power that medium to large businesses can exercise compared to smaller ones, such an enhanced conscientious freedom would need to be subject to certain conditions designed to protect the legitimate rights of others. These could include, for example, a duty to declare their convictions in advance to prospective customers and employees (to avoid the indignity of being turned away), and the absence of local monopoly (to avoid depriving people of scarce employment opportunities or of an important service).

95 This is the chief concern of Baroness Cox, *A Parallel World: Confronting the Abuse of many Muslim Women in Britain today* (Bow Group/Austrian Society for Policy Analysis, 2015).

96 See Calderwood Norton, *Freedom of Religious Organizations*, chapter 5, which also discusses Jewish tribunals (batei din).

97 See www.matribunal.com/. Criminal law, child welfare and personal status (e.g. paternity, legitimacy, marriage and divorce) are excluded.

98 For a comparison between the MAT and Jewish batei din, see Gillian Douglas et al., *Social Cohesion and Civil Law: Marriage, Divorce and Religious Courts* (Cardiff: Cardiff Law School, 2011).

99 MAT has produced a statement declaring forced marriages to be against Islamic law: 'Liberation from Forced Marriages' (MAT, 2008). www.matribunal.com/.

100 See Ayelet Shachar, *Multicultural Jurisdictions: Cultural Differences and Women's Rights* (Cambridge: Cambridge University Press, 2001).

101 See, for example, 'Written evidence submitted by Nazia Rashid'; Muslim Women's Network UK, 'Written Evidence to the Home Affairs Select Committee Inquiry on Shariah Councils', November 2016, both available at www.parliament.uk/business/committees/committees-a-z/commons-select/home-affairs-committee/inquiries/parliament-2015/inquiry6/publications/.

102 Mona Siddiqui (Chair), *The Independent Review into the Application of Sharia Law in England and Wales* (London: Home Office, February 2018). Page references in the text in this section refer to this document.

103 As to how many exist, the review took evidence from eight councils, identified another ten offering online services, and added that 'academic and anecdotal estimates vary from 30 to 85'. No sources are cited but the figure of 85 probably comes from Denis MacEoin, *Sharia Law or 'One Law for All'?* (London: Civitas, 2009), which, however, only names 19 identifiable ones, estimating 'dozens' more (many seeming to operate online).

104 For example, under family law, courts may encourage informal mediation and approve its outcome so long as not unreasonable. See Rivers, *Law of Organized Religions*, 102; and Annex E of the *Review*, 39–40.

105 See also Calderwood Norton, *Freedom of Religious Organizations*, 147–53.

106 Russell Sandberg, 'A Fear of *Sharia*: Why the Independent Report is a wasted Opportunity', *Law and Religion UK* (7 February 2018).

107 For example, there was a trenchantly critical one from 'One Law for All', https://onelawforall.org.uk/sharia-laws-are-part-of-the-extremist-threat-and-not-a-

solution/. See also *Sharia in Britain: A Threat to One Law for All and Equal Rights* (London: One Law for All, 2010).

108 These were: a written ministerial statement from the Home Secretary in February 2018 (www.parliament.uk/written-questions-answers-statements/written-statement/Commons/2018-02-01/HCWS442); *Integrated Communities Strategy Green Paper: Building Stronger, More United Communities* (London: Ministry of Housing, Communities and Local Government, March 2018); a ministerial contribution to a Westminster Hall debate in 2019 (https://hansard.parliament.uk/Commons/2019-05-02/debates/201F2DB0-FCE5-412F-AAB8-83CAA66F308A/ShariaLawCourts). In 2019 it drew up an *Integrated Communities Action Plan* setting out further steps on the question: https://assets.publishing.service.gov.uk/government/uploads/system/uploads/attachment_data/file/778045/Integrated_Communities_Strategy_Govt_Action_Plan.pdf. For an overview of developments up to 2019, see Catherine Fairbairn, *Islamic Marriage and Divorce in England and Wales*. House of Commons Library Briefing Paper No. 08747 (18 February 2019).

109 Compare this to the 192-page report produced for the Ontario government on the question in 2004: Marion Boyd, *Dispute Resolution in Family Law: Protecting Choice, Promoting Inclusion* (Ministry of the Attorney General, Ontario, 2004), www.attorneygeneral.jus.gov.on.ca/english/about/pubs/boyd/fullreport.pdf.

110 Existing work includes Russell Sandberg, ed., *Religion and Legal Pluralism* (Abingdon: Routledge, 2017); Elham Manea, *Women and Shari'a Law: The Impact of Legal Pluralism* (London: I. B. Tauris, 2016).

111 This is also Calderwood Norton's view (*Freedom of Religious Organizations*, 153–62).

112 Sandberg, 'A Fear of *Sharia*'. See also Russell Sandberg and Sharon Thompson, 'The Sharia Law Debate: The Missing Family Law Context', *Law and Justice* 177 (2016), 180–92; 'Written evidence submitted by Dr Tim Winter, Lecturer in Islamic Studies, University of Cambridge to Home Affairs Select Committee Inquiry on Shariah Councils', available at https://old.parliament.uk/business/committees/committees-a-z/commons-select/home-affairs-committee/inquiries/parliament-2015/inquiry6/publications/. Julian Rivers shows why separating marriage entirely from the state would be no solution: 'Could Marriage Be Disestablished?', *Tyndale Bulletin* 68.1 (2017), 121–51.

113 See www.lawcom.gov.uk/project/weddings/.

114 My approach is a combination of what Maleiha Malik calls 'cultural voluntarism' and 'mainstreaming', as distinct from 'prohibition', 'non-interference', 'recognition' or 'transformative accommodation' (*Minority Legal Orders in the UK: Minorities, Pluralism and the Law* (London: British Academy Policy Centre, 2012)).

8

Faithful Power

Introduction

In September 2015, the Muslim Women's Network UK (MWNUK) issued a statement urging the government to live up to 'British values' in its response to the refugee crisis breaking across Europe. 'Horrified' by the crisis, MWNUK urged Britain 'to do more and live up to our legacy of compassion towards refugees':

> [We] advocate the use of the word 'refugee' in the way it was first used in 1685 when 50,000 French Huguenots were given refuge in England after escaping persecution. It was also used in the 1930s and 1940s when thousands of European Jews were given sanctuary in Britain from persecution at the hands of Nazism; and was used in the 1970s when over 30,000 Ugandan Asians escaped ethnic cleansing and settled in Britain ... [W]e insist that the UK must uphold its legal obligations as a founding signatory to the Geneva Convention of 1951 which protects refugees, and under the Universal Declaration of Human Rights 1948. In 2014, David Cameron outlined British Values as '... a belief in freedom, tolerance of others, accepting personal and social responsibility, respecting and upholding the rule of law ...' To not support these refugees is to deny the very essence of what makes us British.[1]

Muslim women urging 'British values' on a Conservative government? However one assesses the government's refugee policies since 2015, this is a striking manifestation of the use of 'faithful power' in a just cause. It is one that disrupts our stereotypes about how religion, especially Islam, acts politically, and points to intriguing possibilities of faith-motivated democratic engagement.

Not all cases of the deployment of faithful power are as obviously commendable as this. In 2015, Lutfur Rahman, the recently re-elected mayor of the London Borough of Tower Hamlets, was removed from office by an election commissioner (a judge) on multiple counts of corrupt and illegal practice contrary to the Representation of the People Act 1983. One of them was exerting 'undue spiritual influence' on the Muslim Bangladeshi voters of east London.[2] At the likely instigation of the local chairman of the Council of Mosques, a close ally of Rahman, 100 local imams had signed a letter to a local Bangladeshi paper urging voters to support Rahman in the 2014 mayoral elections, which he narrowly won. Giles Fraser, an Anglican priest who had recently chaired the Fairness Commission in Tower Hamlets, observed that the relevant clause actually dates back to the Corrupt and Illegal Practices Act 1883. He noted that this was introduced in a climate of intense English anti-Catholicism and anti-Irish racism to prevent newly enfranchised Irish voters from being subjected to illicit pressure by Roman Catholic clergy. The judge, he observed, had actually drawn a direct comparison between the susceptibility to religious manipulation of Irish voters in the 1880s and what he supposed was that of the Muslim Bangladeshi voters of 2014.[3]

Yet troubling though that comparison is, an analysis of the case must also reckon with the factor of the very powerful kinship (*biraderi*) loyalties that remain operative among the east London Bangladeshi community (and other South Asian Muslim communities).[4] While *biraderi* perform important social functions and have often opened up new routes to political participation for Muslims,[5] they have also facilitated a 'clan politics' based on 'a close community with strong patriarchal structures that allows for non-political party ties and networks to be exploited by politicians of all backgrounds'. Such a system 'stifles challenges and innovation from within some of the UK's Muslim communities, and is particularly felt by women and young people as a barrier to participation'.[6] The judgment made clear that Rahman had come to power (and, earlier, wielded power) by cynically and ruthlessly exploiting such clan loyalties.[7]

This dismal episode feeds the widely held assumption that religious interventions in democracy are generally damaging. This chapter argues, however, that in spite of such cases, there are many eminently legitimate examples of 'faithful power' where citizens deploy the resources of faith both to defend their and others' rights, and to influence the deployment of state power so as to reshape public policy generally. Faithful power is the democratic steering of state power, through multiple means, towards objectives influenced by faith.[8] As with the previous two chapters, I focus on religious rather than secular faiths.

What might faithful power look like? Participation in political speech is already one such form of democratic power. In Chapter 5, I argued that faith-based political reasoning, suitably defined and circumscribed, is a legitimate use of democratic power, while also cautioning that it was improper on the lips of state officials justifying laws to the public. In this chapter, I have in mind more tangible forms of democratic power, such as mobilizing supporters, organizing, campaigning, lobbying and protesting or other democratic means to steer the use of state power towards (or away from) particular laws or policies – of which the MWNUK statement on refugees is one instance. I will argue that the right use of faithful power is good for democracy.[9] To bring the features of constructive faithful power into sharper relief, however, I begin with a more extended account of a case of palpably 'unfaithful' power. We are due another visit to Project Blitz.

Unfaithful power – Project Blitz

Project Blitz is another manifestation of the constantly reproducing movement known as the American 'religious right'. Launched in 2015 by a coalition of powerful evangelical organizations,[10] it promotes the introduction of model 'Christian' bills in state legislatures across the USA, intended both to protect religious freedom and to shore up the 'Judeo-Christian' foundations of the nation.[11] In 2017, the project distributed copies of its action programme to 750 sympathetic state legislators, announcing in 2018 that 70 such bills had by then been introduced.[12] Some bills seek to promote 'our country's religious heritage' and include measures like requiring the display of the USA's national motto 'In God We Trust' in public buildings, especially schools and colleges. Others are 'proclamations or resolutions' publicly marking the nation's religious heritage, such as a Religious Freedom Day or a Christian Heritage Week (35). The most controversial type of bill is 'religious liberty protection legislation', intended to safeguard 'the ability of citizens to speak and act upon their religious convictions' (6).

Contrary to the charge of several critics, Project Blitz does not seek a 'theocracy' – the conferral of legislative power on clergy or churches.[13] It does not (yet) seek a Christian confession in federal or state constitutions, otherwise to accord political or civil privileges to Christian churches or organizations, or to abridge non-Christian citizens' rights to conscientious freedom. It certainly promotes a maximalist reading of the First Amendment right to the 'free exercise of religion', for example by making capacious demands for individual 'exemptions' and associational 'autonomy' for religious believers (11, 106, 126). Such measures would certainly tilt the balance decisively in favour of religious liberty claimants and against defenders of generally applicable equality laws. But they differ in degree, not in kind, from those sought by plaintiffs in UK cases such as *Ladele, Catholic Care* and *JFS*.[14]

At times the project's action programme invokes the language of defending 'pluralism', respecting 'diversity' and promoting 'civic peace'.[15] But its 'religious freedom' proposals also include model 'public policy resolutions' on sex and gender intended as strategic directives to guide state legislation. However, these plainly do not protect religious liberty for believers but rather seek to change public policy, and civil rights, for everyone. Indeed, their goal is to 'define public policies of the state in favor of biblical values concerning marriage and sexuality' (6). This is not, on my understanding of democratic pluralism, constitutionally illegitimate. Nor does the wording of the proposed bills breach the principle of justificatory secularism: the document advises advocates not to invoke 'biblical values' but present the bills as 'reasonable and rational in light of the available empirical evidence' (37). I estimate that they would put laws on sex and gender in most liberal democracies back by 15 to 20 years – a disturbing prospect to many, but not yet a lurch towards *The Handmaid's Tale*. Such stances would not eliminate pluralism but only attempt to redefine its proper limits: limits that any version of constitutional democracy (including liberal ones) must draw, however committed they are to upholding convictional diversity generally.

However, when we read the specific ambitions of Project Blitz against the much more ambitious strategies of the organizations sponsoring it, a troubling picture emerges. In spite of its lip-service to pluralism, the movement's vision and methods are in fact profoundly anti-pluralistic. Project Blitz is part of a wider 'Christian nationalist' movement that is motivated by a hegemonic vision of America as a 'Judeo-Christian nation'. This goes well beyond the modest aspirations of British defenders of that idea noted in Chapter 3. One of the intellectual feeders of the movement is the theology of 'dominion', according to which God desires Christians to rule the commanding heights of the nation.[16] While many Christian nationalists do not share that specific theology, most would hold that America will not be healed from its present corruptions and restored to its true destiny unless those supporting 'Judeo-Christian' values assume positions of dominance across the major institutions of society.[17] The fact that Christian nationalists have been among the most enthusiastic cheerleaders for Donald Trump indicates a readiness to see fundamental norms of constitutional democracy cast aside for the greater good of an advance of supposed public 'righteousness' (crucially, an overturning of *Roe v Wade*, which created the right to abortion). It is one thing for a faith-based group to exercise 'faithful power' by projecting its own vision of 'public righteousness' into democratic forums (in this case, as a push-back against what it sees as the disproportionate influence of a hostile 'secular elite'). It is entirely another to seek to replace one dominant and exclusivist elite with just another. This is to engage in a zero-sum game of competitive hegemony rather than to seek to enable a truly representative democratic pluralism. As Katherine Stewart puts it, the movement 'does not seek to add another voice to America's pluralistic democracy but to replace our foundational democratic principles and institutions with a state grounded on a particular version of Christianity'.[18]

Christian nationalists profess a desire to restore the religious inspirations behind American democracy but offer no substantive theological defence of democracy itself, nor show any interest in making democratic institutions or procedures work better for everyone. On the contrary, in their use of democratic processes they breach two fundamental political virtues implicit in my account of Christian democratic pluralism. The first is *transparency*. While Project Blitz eagerly disseminates its message via its vast network of supporting churches, it makes no attempt to engage in any wider public explanation of its aims and goals. The project was launched without any public announcement of its intentions or methods, forcing state legislators with objections to the bills immediately on to the back foot. It has successfully recruited a mass of volunteers via local churches – supplying them with 'voters' guides', moving them around on 'values buses' and organizing them into 'cultural impact teams'. These familiar mobilization tactics are not illegitimate, even if they seem alien to British religious practice (though, ironically, not secular practice). But the project also privately utilizes deeply undemocratic techniques, such as 'high-tech data mining operations', in order to identify and manipulate its target voters.[19]

The second democratic virtue it breaches is *anti-sectionalism*. Participating in those aspects of the American system that demand a manipulative form of interest-group lobbying is already corrosive of a politics of the common good. Energetic lobbying for specific interests is, of course, a perfectly legitimate democratic activity, so long as it is practised by methods, and justified by arguments, that seek to persuade and are open to scrutiny. But much Christian nationalist lobbying is overwhelmingly funded by a network of mostly Christian corporate dynasties, giving advocates a capacity to mobilize, organize and manipulate political agendas far beyond the dreams of most campaigning groups, especially those representing the voiceless and marginalized – democracy's 'politically poor'. Frederick Clarkson claims that the project utilizes 'a sophisticated level of coordination and strategizing that echoes the American Legislative Exchange Council (ALEC), which infamously networks pro-business state legislators, drafts sample legislation, and shares legislative ideas and strategies'.[20] While the movement's leaders denounce 'identity politics' as corrosive of American values, from the outside they look like just another example of a (mostly white, self-serving, conservative) Christian identity politics. Their goal is not to renew democracy and empower citizens generally – so that no elite could again seize control – but rather to (re)capture the levers of power themselves: to replace a 'corrupt, godless' elite with a 'righteous' one. Their interest is not in enabling 'the people' in all its extant diversity to participate in a common search for public justice, but in exploiting existing procedures to the very limits of the law so that their vision of a Christian nation will secure ever greater public sway.

Project Blitz is not theocratic, but it is part of a concerted, long-term Christian nationalist campaign to inaugurate a new religious 'establishment' that would effectively declare those not endorsing their highly contestable reading of a 'Judeo-Christian' vision second-class citizens and render them vulnerable to the latest enthusiasms of a manipulative religious majoritarianism. It is an abuse of faithful power.

Christian Democracy

British observers of public religion have frequently been exercised – to the point of morbid fascination – by the latest machinations of the American religious right. But they have typically neglected a remarkable but largely unsung (in the UK) example of faithful power on their own doorstep: European Christian Democracy. Christian Democracy took shape in a number of 'confessional' political parties in several European states, first emerging in the late nineteenth century. Many repeatedly entered governments, often as coalition partners alongside secular or other religious parties. Arguably it is the most influential example of the democratic deployment of faithful power through the state in the modern world.[21] It was a leading player in the movement towards European integration.

Post-war Christian Democracy was not an artifice of religious elites. It was birthed from a dense network of faith-based associations and other initiatives located in civil society – schools, youth and women's movements, charitable bodies, cooperatives, trades unions, employers' associations, newspapers, journals and summer schools. These gathered momentum in the late nineteenth and early twentieth centuries in response to the social disruptions and economic exploitation of capitalist industrialization. On the Catholic side they came to be known collectively as 'social Catholicism'.[22] There were Protestant parallels – most impressively, the 'neo-Calvinist' movement in the Netherlands, which spawned dozens of such civil society bodies and played a vital role in the emergence of democratic pluralism in that nation.[23]

Such associations prepared the ground for the formation of confessional parties that aspired to enter government (the Catholic ones becoming known as 'political Catholicism').[24] Two such parties, the German Centre Party and the Austrian Christian Social party, performed tolerably well in representing Catholic interests for a time, but came to a catastrophic end by failing consistently to resist fascistic regimes in the 1930s. By the time of the post-war period, however, the Christian Democratic parties that re-emerged had renounced any lingering authoritarian sympathies and were consistently committed to the promotion of democracy, human rights and religious liberty. Indeed, in some countries – such as West Germany, Austria, Belgium, the Netherlands – they led the process whereby norms of constitutional democracy were restored in the aftermath of fascism, war and occupation.[25]

An important initial impetus for such parties in the late nineteenth century was resistance to the 'exclusivist secularism' of anti-clerical liberal and socialist parties, seen, for example, in education. The absence of anti-clerical parties in Britain – or to put it more positively, the presence of significant religious inspirations in all three main parties – is a key reason why Christian Democratic parties did not emerge here. Christian Democratic parties continued to be especially solicitous of the interests, and of course the electoral support, of the churches – just as, for example, social democratic parties were of those of the trades unions. But in most countries after 1945, Christian Democratic parties had moved well beyond merely defensive and self-interested stances and embraced wide-ranging, constructive visions of the common good. These included not only principles of constitutional democracy but also interventionist ('social market') economic policies, generously funded welfare systems, internationalist (notably anti-communist) foreign policies and, later, gender equality, global development and environmental responsibility. They protected 'faithful conscience' and promoted pluralistic models of 'faithful association' in the public realm. Public funding was in many cases granted to faith-based schools, welfare organizations, hospitals and so forth. Public recognition was in some cases also given to faith-based trades unions, employers' associations and broadcasting outlets. These were regarded as legitimate 'social partners' in consultative and regulatory bodies in various areas of public policy. Some Christian Democratic parties deviated from full equal treatment, at times invoking 'Christian nation' language or defending a limited public priority for Christianity (Catholicism in Italy, for example). But these tended to peter out over time as Christians lost electoral ground.

By the 1980s – due to pressures of internal secularization and external competition – many Christian Democratic parties were drifting away from their distinctive Christian social visions and increasingly resembled conventional centre-right conservative parties.[26] Over the decades they also found themselves displaying the familiar vulnerabilities afflicting most democratic parties – pragmatic power-seeking, internal division and occasional scandal. But in the three or four decades after 1945, they stood as credible attempts to exercise faithful power for the common good. In the case of the Catholic parties, their vision and policies were directly informed by the developing body of Catholic social teaching represented in papal social encyclicals and the extensive work of Catholic political thinkers such as Jacques Maritain. Whatever we make of the specific policies or methods of post-war European Christian Democracy, it is undoubtedly a legitimate example of the democratic deployment of faithful power. Collectively, the movement made a decisive, faith-inspired contribution to the consolidation of constitutional democracy in post-war Europe.[27]

Faithful power in Britain

'Faithful power' – the democratic steering of state power towards object-ives shaped by faith – is, in fact, already amply at work in Britain, albeit much less influentially and visibly than in European Christian Democracy. It displays a diversity, creativity and scope that cannot remotely be sum-marized here. What follows are merely some indicative examples of constructive democratic engagement from Muslims and Christians. While some of the Christian examples may be familiar to readers, I expect most of the Muslim ones are not. I begin with them.

An emerging 'Muslim civil society'

'Every Muslim is commanded by God Almighty to partake in society and struggle against [munkar: injustice, inequality, poverty, immorality, indecency, manipulation, exploitation, hoarding, criminality, oppression, all forms of abuse, domestic violence, neglect] and to help free people from these evils.'[28] Such is one of the animating visions of a wide-ranging report, Our Shared British Future: Muslim Integration in the UK, pub-lished in 2018 by the Muslim Council of Britain. The report documents extensive Muslim involvement in numerous areas of social, economic, cultural, educational and environmental life.[29] It marks the substantial advance over the last 30 years by British Muslim communities as they explore how to make constructive contributions to the common good – notwithstanding discrimination, rising Islamophobia and persisting barriers to participation.[30] Muslims are, for example, exceptionally generous donors: one study found that Muslims, fulfilling the duty of *zakat*, give twice as much to charity as the average Briton and more than most Christians.[31] Muslims readily collaborate on many social action endeavours with other religious or secular social organizations, for example via the ongoing Near Neighbours national programme noted in the last chapter, or through local 'emergency response' initiatives, such as the response of the Penny Appeal (based in Wakefield) to the 2016 Carlisle floodings, or the Al Manaar Muslim Cultural Heritage Centre's response to the Grenfell Fire.[32]

Muslims are also increasingly engaged in political activities, deploying faithful power in many ways at multiple levels.[33] As with other religious citizens, much of this occurs 'anonymously' via 'secular' campaigning or other civil society groups, NGOs or political parties, and so cannot be easily quantified. Muslim turnout at elections is at least as high as in the general population. A 2016 survey found that 93 per cent of Muslims reported feeling that they belonged to Britain, over half saying they felt this 'very strongly.'[34] By 2017 there were 300 Muslim councillors and 15 MPs across many political parties. Philip Lewis and Sadek Hamid suggest that we can now speak of 'the normalisation of [Muslim political participation] across the full range of positions and parties, encompassing cabinet ministers and lord mayors'.[35] Muslim concerns are increasingly represented in parliament, and in 2017 an All-Party Parliamentary Group on British Muslims was established.[36]

A burgeoning network of Muslim civil society associations has also been emerging, addressing not only 'Muslim issues' but others too. Much of this work is not intended to engage directly with the state. But some of it involves faithful power in the sense I have defined it – consciously deploying the resources of faith to change public policy and law, albeit not necessarily towards what practitioners would label distinctively 'Islamic' stances. Today, many such bodies are explicitly committed to the principal features of 'democratic pluralism' as I have outlined it.[37] They are steadily building participatory capacity among Muslims while promoting a wide diversity of social and political goals, some widely supported, others more contested.

Sometimes this activity is mosque-based, as in the extensive (and sometimes controversial) civic engagements of the East London Mosque, which, for example, operates the Nafas Drugs Project and the Muslim Women's Collective and is a founder member of TELCO (The East London Communities Organisation, a member of Citizens UK).[38]

Increasingly, however, such civil society activity takes place in independent associations such as MWNUK (which has over 700 members), and a continually expanding network of smaller entities.[39] The largest and most influential, the Muslim Council of Britain (MCB), which represents 500 mosques and Islamic organizations, has proved a powerful if also controversial voice for a range of Muslim political concerns since its foundation in 1997.[40] From 2000 it began issuing pre-election statements identifying Muslim concerns and urging Muslims to vote. Earlier, a manifesto, *For a Fair and Caring Society*, had been issued ahead of the 1997 election by the UK Action Committee on Islamic Affairs (UKACIA), which not only highlighted Muslim interests but 'showed that Muslims had a point of view on issues to do with the common good'.[41] This is confirmed in *Our Shared British Future* and in MCB's 70-page *British Muslim Perspectives at the 2019 General Election*.[42]

While the leadership of MCB was originally overwhelmingly conservative-leaning and male (this is changing), much of the leadership of the newer associations represents a new generation of younger and female Muslims keen (as MCB also now is) to move beyond past insular ethnic concerns or doctrinal sectarianisms and to embody a 'British Islam'. Such an Islam seeks to deploy the resources of reformist streams of Islamic ethics and politics towards constructive engagement in a pluralist democracy. Many such bodies wish to do so, yet without merely echoing standard secular languages.[43] MWNUK, for example, seeks to 'achieve an equal and just society through Islamic feminism', offering a wide range of welfare, advice and support services for Muslim women and campaigning on policy issues within the Muslim community and beyond.[44] For example, in 2016 it filed a complaint with the Charity Commission calling for an investigation of why none of Birmingham Central Mosque's 39 trustees were women, and later wrote to prime minister David Cameron and Labour leader Jeremy Corbyn calling on them to address the practice (noted above) whereby male clan leaders, in cooperation with local parties keen for their bloc votes (especially Labour), were preventing Muslim women from becoming candidates.[45]

Some Muslim associations have made significant public interventions. Just Peace and the Muslim Association of Britain (MAB) played important roles in mobilizing Muslims against British involvement in the Iraq war in 2003. Fourteen years earlier, a 70,000-strong Muslim demonstration had taken place in London against Salman Rushdie's *The Satanic Verses*, where the British flag was burned – an event described as a 'PR disaster' for British Muslims.[46] But as Lewis and Hamid put it, the participation of tens of thousands of Muslims in the Stop the War Coalition's demonstration in 2003 was an example of 'a new generation of British

Muslims catalysing an alliance across sectarian and ethnic differences ... on a common anti-war platform, involving a huge array of organisations and activists'.[47]

Few Muslims seem interested in the idea of an Islamic party. The Islamic Party of Britain, founded in 1989 in the aftermath of the Rushdie affair, contested seats until 2003 but secured minimal votes.[48] The People's Justice Party (PJP), spurred by concerns over Kashmir and supported by many Muslims, won council seats in Birmingham between 1998 and 2006. The left-wing Respect Party, launched in 2003 in the wake of the Stop the War Coalition, attracted a preponderance of Muslims for a while, especially from women and young people; and some candidates claimed support from Muslim scholars. It was led until 2012 by the Muslim Salma Yaqoob, who co-founded it with George Monbiot. Later George Galloway became a Respect MP in London and Bradford. The party successfully challenged Muslim clan politics in Birmingham and Bradford. Its fortunes declined after the resignation of Yaqoob in 2014.[49] Neither PJP nor Respect was officially Islamic. They do, however, reveal a potential for Muslim electoral mobilization outside the main parties. Such potential is implicitly confirmed in the detailed findings of an independent project, YouElect, launched in 2009 by Muslim activists. This yielded extensive electoral data of use to Muslim voters and offered information on where candidates stood on a broad suite of policy issues.[50] The goal was not to prepare the ground for a new party. Among its published findings, however, was evidence that Muslim voters, sometimes bringing distinctive concerns, could possibly prove decisive in several marginal constituencies.

Since the 1990s, British governments have steadily increased their engagement with Muslim organizations across multiple forums and on a wide range of issues.[51] Yet they have struggled to respond constructively and consistently to the new Muslim activism, arguably hampering the development of effective 'Muslim faithful power'. Pursuant to their larger commitments to 'multiculturalism' and the 'mainstreaming' of 'faith' (noted in the previous chapter), Labour governments after 1997 warmly embraced the MCB and other selected bodies. They responded positively to Muslim concerns around discrimination, a notable outcome of which was the Racial and Religious Hatred Act 2006, and equal treatment, such as funding for Muslim schools. They also sought, with mixed success, to enlist Muslim communities behind policies of 'inclusion' and 'cohesion'.[52]

The trauma of the 7/7 London bombings led to a chilling of relations between the Labour government and those Muslim bodies, including MCB, judged not to be taking a robust enough stand against Islamist extremism. Labour's subsequent counter-radicalization Prevent agenda (Preventing Extremism Together) seriously complicated relations with Muslim communities and evoked acrimonious debates over the 'securitization' of government relations with Muslims and the blurring of 'security' and 'cohesion' policies. The outcome was deep divisions within and outside the Muslim community.[53] These were not allayed by a significant refocusing of Prevent under the coalition government after 2010, pursuant to David Cameron's shift from 'state multiculturalism' to 'muscular liberalism', leading to a new and controversial duty on public employees to report 'at risk' Muslims to counter-terrorism authorities. Assessments of Prevent differ widely. Lewis and Hamid – robust critics of insular traditionalism and aggressive Islamism – conclude that it was 'fundamentally flawed in its conceptualisation and undermined in its delivery'.[54] Others report that, for all its successive failings, it has nevertheless spawned modest successes on the ground in spite of confusion at the national level (with local authorities and groups adapting Prevent funding for their own purposes). They claim that it has, intentionally or not, contributed to the strengthening of a 'Muslim civil society'.

The perception continues, however, that governments lack a sufficiently consistent and nuanced policy in its engagement with Muslim organizations – witness the unresolved issue of how to distinguish between so-called 'moderate' Islam and 'extremism'. After 2007 there was a deliberate policy to treat MCB as merely one of many groups and to embrace a 'democratic constellation' of Muslim associations in order to engage with broader sections of an increasingly diverse Muslim community.[55] This began to address the charge that governments were consulting with too narrow a range of favoured 'establishment' Muslim bodies (the 'Take me to your leader' or 'Here is your leader' approaches). It also led MCB to seek out a broader range of Muslim and other partners.[56] But Labour never settled on stable terms of engagement with Muslim civic and political activists.

Pursuant to its Big Society agenda, the 2010 coalition government retreated from the corporatist model adopted by Labour (one that favoured large established bodies) and shifted its focus to local multifaith initiatives. Confusingly for some, this took place within a 'Christian heritage' model in which the Church of England would, however, function as a kind of broker among faith communities, such as via Near Neighbours. The government appointed Sayeeda Warsi to head a Faith Engagement team in the Department for Communities and Local Government, who, among other initiatives, spearheaded work to combat Islamophobia.[57] Warsi later took distance from the government's approach, not least because of the growing perception that the Conservative party itself, having lambasted Labour for its indulgence of anti-Semitism, was failing to address Islamophobia in its own ranks.

Four conclusions on 'Muslim faithful power' are suggested by this brief (and admittedly selective) review. First, it is clear that a vigorous 'Muslim civil society' is indeed emerging, from which an impressive array of contributions to diverse projects of justice and the common good in British society are being made. These include initiatives as diverse as the Brixton-based STREET initiative (Strategy to Research, Educate and Empower Teenagers), Tell MAMA, the national counter-extremism think tank Quilliam (founded by two ex-Hizb ut-Tahrir activists) and the Mosques and Imams National Advisory Board (MINAB). Some are also engaged in legitimate attempts to deploy the resources of faith to shape law and public policy. Here it is vital to discriminate carefully between such democratic uses of Muslim faithful power and a minority of conservative Muslims who, for example, seek to exercise undue power over what are open public spaces. This seems one valid charge against some of those involved in the 'Trojan Horse' affair in some Birmingham schools, who appear to have attempted to run some public academies as if they were Muslim faith schools.[58] It is even more important to distinguish these peaceful strands of Muslim activism sharply from the persisting fringe of radical Islamist extremists willing to use violent power to attack the British state and subvert democracy. Commentators who fail to make such elementary distinctions – they are routinely flouted in many media outlets – are only fuelling the twisted narratives of exclusion perpetrated from those extremes.

Second, the new Muslim civil society is itself highly diverse, even as it seeks to explore a distinctive form of British Islam. It ranges from initiatives with traditionalist roots, to progressive reformist movements, to post-Islamist organizations, to entities that align themselves more thoroughly with 'secular' objectives. As noted, many Muslim activists do not present their stances as 'Islamic' at all, even when they may, in fact, be inspired by their faith. The same is true for Christians or people of other faiths (religious and secular). Nor should we expect common fronts on specific policy issues, or unified representative organs, from the Muslim community any more than we do from other faith communities.

Third, those outside the Muslim community need to be more discerning of distinctive faith-inspired insights from their Muslim fellow citizens. They need to grant them the same respectful, if critical, public hearing offered to other contributions to public debate and to be receptive enough to embrace them where they can. For example, a capitalist economy as badly distorted as ours through an egregious dependency on astronomical levels of debt might have things to learn from Islamic reflections on the moral hazards of usury. Given the massively disproportionate media obsessions with issues of segregation, security and extremism (which remain serious concerns), it is vital that the contributions of such Muslim faithful power – and its complete legitimacy – be responsibly communicated to the public. There are also further possibilities of cooperative democratic alliances between Islamic and other faith-based (and secular) civil society groups yet to be explored.[59]

Fourth, government engagement with Muslim organizations needs to be marked by greater respect, intelligence and consistency. Attempts by central governments to manage Muslim faithful power from the top down – pursuant to their own often inchoate and shifting objectives – do not show adequate appreciation for Muslim agency and equality.[60] This risks undermining the work of the more creative Muslim contributors to civil society and democracy and reinforcing the apocalyptic narratives of the fringes. But governments will be able to show such respect only if they work harder to listen attentively to those contributors. This will require becoming more religiously intelligent, renouncing stereotypes and tendentious assumptions about 'what Muslims think' – or who counts as 'moderate' – and properly taking the measure of Muslim creativity and diversity.

Christianity: privilege, plurality and 'hospitality'

The sector of Christian 'faithful power' in Britain is obviously vastly greater and more influential than that of Islam. Christianity has moulded the nations of the UK over centuries; England's national church still retains its established position; and many other denominations and inter- or non-denominational bodies are active in many areas of civil society and politics in ways too complex to map. In addition, Christians routinely participate in many public forums 'anonymously' through a multitude of secular organizations: this is their largest, if least visible, contribution to democracy.

The deep and abiding legacy of Anglican establishment has bequeathed significant elements of public privilege to the Church of England and, in its train, other Christian churches. This lends Christian churches obvious advantages in deploying faithful power as compared to other faiths. At the constitutional level, the advantages enjoyed by the Church of England include its ceremonial role in the coronation service or at local level in Remembrance or other civic events, 'Protestant Succession' to the monarchy, or daily prayers in parliament. Strictly speaking these are departures from 'jurisdictional secularism', albeit not particularly consequential ones.

More consequential is the automatic right of 26 diocesan bishops to sit in the House of Lords, granting them, controversially, a privileged voice (and vote) in the national legislative process. Although the number of occasions on which their votes prove decisive is small, sometimes they exercise considerable persuasive influence in debates as varied as bio-ethics, poverty and welfare, homelessness, prison reform, immigration or global justice.[61] Of even greater significance is the historically embedded stake of Christianity in the public sector noted in the last chapter as well as in higher education or chaplaincy. This presence is widely, if not uncritically, appreciated on the ground by many beneficiaries of such services. But my model of democratic pluralism would imply a more equitable public standing for other faiths in these sectors, especially where there is evidence of an unwarranted and correctable 'majority bias'. This is already occurring, of course, as seen in the transition from dominantly Christian chaplaincies towards multifaith chaplaincy services. More pertinent for the argument of this chapter, however, is the deployment of the political resources of Christian faith in civil society and other democratic platforms. I will illustrate this with examples from denominational bodies, civil society associations, and initiatives at the level of state institutions.

Denominational and ecumenical bodies

The Church of England and other Christian denominations have long sought to contribute to public debate on a wide range of political issues.[62] They have done so either through statements of individual leaders (such as those made by a handful of Anglican bishops during the Brexit process) or through public advocacy agencies such as the Roman Catholic Church's Bishops' Conferences, the Church of England's Mission and Public Affairs Council and its House of Bishops, the Joint Public Issues Team (JPIT), which represents three independent churches and the Church of Scotland, or ecumenical bodies such as Churches Together in Britain and Ireland (whose Churches' Refugee Network supported the Lift the Ban campaign demanding a right to work for asylum seekers). They also seek to utilize whatever opportunities they possess for access to government or parliament on matters of immediate concern.

From time to time, churches also offer more substantial interventions. Sometimes these might address broad visions of public theology, such as *The Common Good and the Catholic Church's Social Teaching*, published in 1996 by the Roman Catholic Bishops of England and Wales; *Who Is My Neighbour?*, a pastoral letter issued by Church of England bishops ahead of the 2015 general election;[63] or *Black Church Political Mobilisation – a Manifesto for Action*, the first ever Black political manifesto, issued by the National Church Leaders Forum before the 2015 election.[64] At other times, such statements (within legal limits on charities' political activities) might focus on more specific policy questions, such as *Faith in the City*, produced by the Church of England in 1985, on urban deprivation; JPIT's *Universal Credit: Increasing Hunger by Design* (2018);[65] the Methodist Church's *Gambling Position Paper* (2013);[66] or Scottish churches' contributions to campaigns on homelessness and social care from the 1980s to the 2000s[67] and to the 2014 independence referendum.[68]

Civil society associations

The foregoing are cases of official interventions by ecclesial bodies. They tend to receive the most attention because of the public prominence of their leaders and because of a widely held assumption, not only among the churches, that 'the Church should speak out on ...' (the Church meaning ecclesial institutions). But at least as significant, however, are uses of faithful power by scores of independent Christian civil society associations, such as charitable, educational, professional or campaigning bodies or think tanks. Alongside or as part of their core work, some of these aspire to inject Christian thinking into wider public debates and some also campaign to change law or public policy. A few examples can illustrate the diversity of the landscape.

Theos – the only independent, explicitly Christian, broad-based think tank in England – does not campaign but offers research and commentary on a wide range of public issues, some of which have a bearing on the broad direction of public policy in areas such as economics, welfare, justice and legal reform.[69] Similar entities include the St Paul's Institute at St Paul's Cathedral, which has a specific brief for economic, business and finance issues,[70] the Westminster Abbey Institute, which works especially on issues of public leadership,[71] or non-denominational bodies like the Jubilee Centre[72] or Ekklesia.[73]

Here it is also worth noting the existence of think tanks that while not religious are hospitable to religiously influenced ideas. ResPublica is a leading example.[74] Its founder and director, 'Red Tory' scholar Phillip Blond, was an early member of the theological movement known as Radical Orthodoxy, co-founded by 'Blue Labour' theologian John Milbank (who chairs ResPublica's trustees). ResPublica claims to have been influential in the early years of the coalition government after 2010, and to have shaped the policy stances of both main parties on a number of issues. Blue Labour, of whom (Lord) Maurice Glasman is the leading representative, draws eclectically on Catholic social teaching, British Christian socialism, community organizing, cooperativism, the Italian 'Civil Economy' school and others.[75] Blue Labour leaders have had the ear of prominent Labour figures from time to time but the movement has not yet registered a lasting impact on party policy. Red Toryism and Blue Labour are both reviving themes that were formative in European Christian Democracy.[76]

Other examples of think tanks receptive to Christian ideas include the Centre for Social Justice, a centre-right think tank established by former Tory leader Iain Duncan Smith, founded to promote a form of 'compassionate conservatism' that in part reflects Christian influence and whose reports have shaped Conservative party policy.[77] The Relationships Foundation engages in research, education and policy thinking aimed at improving the 'relational' dimensions of many areas of social and economic life. It grew out of the work of the Cambridge-based Jubilee Centre; while it operates without a religious basis, it displays the influence of an approach formed by the Centre.[78] While these entities embrace a wide diversity of people and perspectives, they are noteworthy by virtue of being distinctly more receptive to ideas with a religious provenance than most other British think tanks (Demos being one exception).[79] Not surprisingly, they are much more influential on public policy than any officially Christian parallel.

Another source of Christian influence within civil society is Christian development or environmental bodies, some of which have acquired the capacity to exercise a form of faithful power. Alongside its development work, Christian Aid publishes reports and statements on many global and national social justice issues, such as the impressive *Tax For The Common Good: A Study of Tax and Morality*.[80] Several large UK Christian aid agencies lay behind the globally influential Jubilee 2000 campaign to urge governments – with some success – to cancel the debts of the most highly indebted developing countries (and, later, lent their support to Make Poverty History). Jubilee 2000 publicly justified its goals by appeal to the Bible (such as the 'jubilee laws' of Leviticus 25). In the environmental field, while an organization like A Rocha concentrates on conservation and education, other groups seek to change policy – such as the climate change campaigning organization Operation Noah and the direct action network Christian Climate Action (part of Extinction Rebellion). Numerous Christian and other faith groups also participate in the Climate Coalition.

Another cluster of Christian civil society groups are active across a range of more traditional ethical concerns. Christian Concern (and its associated Christian Legal Centre) and The Christian Institute educate, lobby and litigate primarily on religious freedom (discussed in Chapter 6), family, sexual and bioethical issues. They speak from a conservative evangelical perspective, occasionally invoking 'Christian nation' language. Some, notably Christian Concern, have proved able to generate a high media profile, especially around contentious legal cases. Critics have charged that such groups are amounting to something comparable to the American religious right. A Theos investigation in 2013 did note 'evidence of greater coordination among Christian groups with a strong socially conservative commitment ... about which they are vocal and often willing to resort to legal action'.[81] But it concluded that such groups do not amount to anything resembling a British religious right. Such groups, it reported, lack the scale, resources and access to political power of movements like Project Blitz. They also do not display the ideological partisanship of religious right groups, although they have been criticized as manifesting a form of 'evangelical identity politics'.[82] The majority of British evangelical supporters of such groups would be deemed in US terms to be economically centrist or left-leaning, and the range of issues the groups take up does not map closely on to those motivating American religious right concerns. Thus, the evangelical organization CARE campaigns on issues relating to 'Life' and 'Family' but, under its 'Justice' head, also on issues of sexual exploitation and human trafficking.[83]

It cannot be said that the political influence of churches or Christian civil society groups is all that substantial in comparison to most secular organizations. Generally they lack the scale of resources, relative ease of access and media interest enjoyed by secular parallels. Their diverse interventions are often ad hoc and piecemeal rather than pursuant to concerted, coherent public theologies with wide public traction. One possible exception is the impact of *Faith in the City* on debates around urban regeneration policy in the 1980s and 1990s (even though its theological foundation was slender). The impact of such contributions will depend on the perceived degree of support they represent in their faith communities (to which vote-hungry politicians are attentive) and the expertise, time, communicative dexterity and political 'nous' marshalled behind them, which can be variable. At times, such interventions do nudge policy or modify law. Evidently, the more they were able to cooperate with each other, and, no less important, with those from other faiths, the greater their potential influence. Here there may be significant untapped possibilities for the deployment of faithful power.

Under the 'civil society' head must also be included the considerable contribution of Christians to 'broad-based community organizing'

(BBCO), of which the chief expression in the UK is Citizens UK, claiming over 450 member organizations.[84] Theologian Luke Bretherton has extensively documented its work.[85] BBCO organizations are not religious bodies, nor do they campaign on 'religious interest' issues. But as the role of East London Mosque in TELCO shows, they are positively welcoming of the contributions of faith groups. Churches and Christian bodies have been deeply involved in the British movement since its inception. Community organizing is a form of relational, place-based participatory politics located in civil society. Committed to resisting both predatory markets and bureaucratic states, its stated goal is to empower people to discern for themselves, and to campaign for, limited and shared 'common goods' that will address specific injustices they face.[86] It does not prescribe issues in advance but allows participants to identify their own campaigning agendas through a process of in-depth 'listening' and 'conversation'.[87] It employs professional staff to lead its effort and to train its participants in a suite of distinctive organizational skills. Some campaigns are directed at other institutions in civil society or at business organizations and others at political institutions. Among Citizens UK's notable achievements is the Living Wage Campaign, which has persuaded over 2,000 private and public employers to commit to paying a 'living wage' (higher than the statutory minimum wage).[88]

Championing associational and convictional pluralism, community organizing works with a wide range of secular and religious affiliates while remaining independent of political parties and mainstream sectoral groups. It claims to eschew both interest-group politics and identity politics, seeking to elicit local expressions of solidarity that transcend what it regards as these narrow constituencies. It depends crucially on permanent, civically minded local associations, like churches or mosques, as sources of energy and resilience. Equally, it seeks to honour and utilize the plural faith convictions, traditions and even sacred texts of affiliates, encouraging participants to bring these to the fore during the process of discerning common projects.[89] These are seen not as eccentricities to be tolerated but as powerful civic resources to be harnessed for common purposes.[90] It thus embodies a highly distinctive form of 'confessional candour' in civil society, while expecting of each partner a stance of 'hospitality' towards others.[91]

Bretherton offers an appreciative theological reading of the ethos and methods of BBCO.[92] He presents it as a form of civic action particularly suited to the age of the 'secular' – understood not as an age dominated by 'secularism' but as one in which the full realization of 'the' common good remains beyond our grasp. In such an age it yet remains possible to identify and pursue specific common goods that can unite people across their differences, empower them for common action and enhance their dignity. The 'secular' offers a public space open to all faiths and dominated by none, and community organizing situates itself in that space. It thus embodies a distinctive form of 'faithful secularity' in which religious citizens and associations contribute to the democratic formation of political life alongside others on the basis of parity, not privilege.

Community organizing is an exemplary practical enactment of what I am calling democratic pluralism open to faithful power. It is, of course, only one such instance. However broad-based it is, it cannot and does not claim to replace the many other forms of civic and political action required if people's diverse faith-based convictions are to be precisely voiced in the ways they wish them to be. For example, BBCO cannot fulfil the tasks performed by more conventional bodies such as political parties or sectoral entities like trades unions, professional associations and employers' organizations, or single-issue campaigning groups like Friends of the Earth or the Howard League for Penal Reform. Organizations like these will continue to be indispensable channels for the expression of people's convictions about justice and the common good. Equally, there will be a continuing need for single-faith civil society associations as diverse as MWNUK and CARE.

Faith-based organizations operating in civil society (Christian or otherwise) can, at their best, perform the particular function of speaking creatively into the public sphere, alongside a plurality of other groups, in order to challenge prevailing assumptions and to propose alternatives inspired by a different vision. As José Casanova puts it, they can aspire to help in 'renormativizing' the public sphere, without seeking to wield state power themselves.[93]

Faithful power in state institutions

Some Christians sit much closer to the exercise of political power, even if not wielding it as Christians. At the level of national politics, there is actually a considerable organized Christian presence in the UK, although its influence seems modest. Christians in Government UK is one of the least well known, not surprisingly since it is an association of Christian civil servants who will want to avoid public prominence. Its aims are 'supporting our members to serve Ministers and the public, and to bring the blessing of God to the heart of Government for the benefit of all'. It operates as a non-partisan support group for Christians and does not address policy issues, although it is formally recognized by the Cabinet Office to represent civil servants.[94]

The three largest national British parties contain Christian affiliates: Christians on the Left (formerly Christian Socialist Movement), Conservative Christian Fellowship and Liberal Democrat Christian Forum.[95] Each rightly claims that their party's traditions have been significantly formed by Christian influences and each seeks not only to honour that memory but to develop it creatively in shaping the ethos of the party today.[96] An umbrella body, Christians in Politics, seeks to build partnerships among such groups and, more generally, to mobilize Christians for political involvement at all levels.[97] The primary purposes of these groupings are to facilitate fellowship and offer theological resources to inform participation in politics. They rarely, if ever, attempt to frame policy stances or directly shape party or government policy. Nor, when working together, do they seek to explore common Christian policy stances. They perform valuable social and pastoral functions, albeit only at the fringes of faithful power. In partial contrast, Christians in Parliament not only offers pastoral support for Christians working in the Palace of Westminster but also, as an All-Party Parliamentary Group, issues 'briefings' on selected areas of policy (recently, on automation, British values and mental health) and 'reports' (so far, mostly on religious freedom).[98] Unsurprisingly, while valuable, these are also non-partisan statements that do not challenge any particular party's policy.

This latter type of work, however, does raise the interesting question whether groups like this (not only in Westminster), or the single-party Christian groups listed above, might at some point take the risk of adopting policy positions that articulate a more explicitly Christian stance, perhaps even at variance with party policies. The barriers to such a development are substantial. The prospects of getting cross-party theological consensus on any policy position are already limited and the powerful constraints of party discipline further inhibit its emergence. But continuing turbulence in the traditional party system – coupled with the introduction of proportional representation – might open up new possibilities for an independent Christian political voice (or more than one) to emerge in such settings.

Such a prospect seems very unlikely to lead to the arrival of a new Christian political party. In fact, two small Christian parties already exist.[99] The Christian People's Alliance (CPA) was launched in 1999 by former participants in the Movement for Christian Democracy (MCD) and claims to be of Christian Democratic inspiration (as MCD indeed was).[100] In its early days, CPA succeeded in winning a few seats in local elections. Within a short space of time, however, its public stances began to be dominated by an increasingly aggressive anti-secularist and anti-Islamic tone, narrowing its potential appeal. The Christian Party, formed in 2004, espouses an eclectic mix of socially conservative and economically progressive positions. It holds a few council seats and fielded 30 parliamentary candidates in 2019 in an electoral alliance with CPA. Both parties remain relatively unknown, even to the Christian public, but given that CPA secured 250,000 votes in the 2009 European Parliament elections there may well be a larger electoral base for such parties that could come to the fore if proportional representation were introduced.[101]

Among many British Christians there remains a profound (if not always well-informed) suspicion of religious parties. There would need to be some fairly dramatic political upheavals for that suspicion to be overcome. A large number of Christians across the political spectrum would have to reach the conclusion – as did many Catholic Christians in late nineteenth-century Europe – that existing parties had become so inhospitable to their concerns as to warrant the need for a new conduit of political engagement. This would also presuppose a fundamental element that remains absent in the UK: the presence of a coherent faith-based political vision and programme around which a large enough swathe of Christians could rally. The political stances of most Christians continue, however, to be dispersed across the ideological spectrum and, in any case, often seem only weakly related to their theology, making this an unlikely prospect.[102] Christians seem likely to remain dispersed right across the political spectrum. It is, perhaps, remarkable how British Christians remain content with the limited menu of party options available to them. This is in spite of the fact that significant numbers of them have declared themselves opposed in principle to flagship policies of all the main national parties – Thatcherite economic policies in the 1980s, Labour's promotion of equality legislation in the 2000s, Conservative policies on universal credit and the coalition's adoption of same-sex marriage in the 2010s. These party positions, while regarded as theologically objectionable to significant numbers of Christians, have proved unable to persuade more than a handful to break ranks with the current party system. The diverse groups of disaffected Christians among party followings have never coalesced into a single movement. Insofar as Christians aspire to apply faithful power directly on the state, then, they will likely continue to do so either from the platform of existing secular political organizations, or at a distance, via Christian organizations located in civil society. This still amounts to a tangible, if inchoate, influence.[103] As was the case with Muslims, the dispersal of Christian political influence will limit and partly conceal its impact. But since, as I have argued, the goal of democratic activity is not merely for people to put their convictions on display (as I expressed it in the Introduction) but rather to contribute to justice and the common good, this does not necessarily make their use of power any less 'faithful' than where it might be more concerted or publicly visible.

Conclusion: faithful power in service of the common good

I conclude with three suggestions about the deployment of 'faithful power' in the UK.

First, in pursuing faith-motivated political objectives, practitioners may, in principle, avail themselves of any legitimate avenue of democratic influence available to all citizens and associations. As equal members of the political community – of 'the people' – they enjoy the same civil and political rights as any others. Equally, they stand under the same demo-cratic obligation as others to participate as far as they are able in the practices of good citizenship as they best understand it. Many may pur-sue such goals from the platform of 'civil society'. But those who operate closer to the heart of the political system, such as through party or parlia-mentary groupings or even religious parties, are also using faithful power legitimately. In responsibly exercising their democratic rights, far from breaching any norms of constitutional democracy, practitioners of faith-ful power will consolidate them. Faith-based democratic initiatives need not only 'speak truth to power'. They may also – with all due humility and vigilance – 'put power to the service of truth'.

Second, when and how – indeed whether – to seek to deploy such democratic rights is a contextual question demanding careful communal discernment within and outside communities of faith. It will not always be prudent, or conducive to the public good, to invoke all one's rights, seek a seat at every available table, litigate every curtailment of religious freedom or attempt to win every winnable battle. For example, even given a large, literate and well-mobilized community of religious citizens, numerous strategic and tactical questions arise as to how its democratic power should be wielded. As the fate of Lutfur Rahman demonstrates on a small canvas and Project Blitz does on a larger one, not every oppor-tunity for political influence will be judged spiritually commendable (or even legal). Faithful power must be informed by a theologically coherent vision of the common good and guided by an unwavering commitment to civic respect.

Third, practitioners of faithful power should fully embrace jurisdic-tional secularism and not seek, or retain, special political faith-based advantages. This is a constitutional baseline for any project of 'faith in democracy'. Relatively minor departures from it – notably Anglican establishment in England – may be tolerable (or, for some, desirable). But insofar as the Church of England, and to a lesser extent other Christian churches, continue to enjoy the comparative advantages of what Cécile Laborde calls 'majority bias', they ought to take the lead in promoting public parity for other faiths (religious and secular). The Church of England regards itself, and is regarded by some others, as employing its privileged standing generously in order to offer 'hospitality' to others in the public square. But practising such hospitality (not all, not even all Anglicans, perceive it as such) can go along with a steady determination to relinquish unwarranted constitutional privilege, and work where appropriate to 'level up' the standing of all faiths who desire it. The image should be not one of other faiths hanging on to the coat-tails of Anglican advantage but of all faith communities standing shoulder to shoulder to maintain a voice for faith in the forums of democracy, for the common good.

Notes

(Websites accessed 16/10/20)

1 Muslim Women's Network UK, 'Media Statement. MWNUK Urges British Values in Response to Refugee Crisis', *Muslim Women's Network UK* (4 September 2015), www.mwnuk.co.uk//go_files/resources/847052-Refugee%20Crisis.pdf.

2 *Erlam & Ors v Rahman & Anor* [2015] EWHC 1215 (QB), para. 529.

3 Giles Fraser, 'The Lutfur Rahman Verdict and the Spectre of "Undue Spiritual Influence"', *The Guardian* (29 April 2015), www.theguardian.com/commentisfree/2015/apr/29/lutfur-rahman-tower-hamlets-mayor-verdict-undue-spiritual-influence.

4 *Biraderi* are made up of 'related family groupings linked by ancestral ties'. *The Missing Muslims: Unlocking British Muslim Potential for the Benefit of All*, Report by the Citizens Commission on Islam, Participation and Public Life (London: Citizens UK, 2017), 46–7.

5 Parveen Akhtar, 'The Paradox of Patronage Politics: Biraderi, Representation and Political Participation among British Pakistanis', in Timothy Peace, ed., *Muslims and Political Participation in Britain* (Abingdon: Routledge, 2015), 15–31.

6 *Missing Muslims*, 47. This report recommends a voluntary code of conduct for political parties to diminish the impact of clan politics (49).

7 Whether the idea of 'undue spiritual influence' as a legal notion is valid any longer is another question. See David Pocklington, '"Undue spiritual influence" – Where Next?', *Law and Religion UK* (30 August 2016), www.lawandreligionuk.com/2016/08/30/undue-spiritual-influence-where-next/.

8 In this chapter I use the term 'power' broadly to include what is often called 'influence'.

9 Jonathan Bartley argues in *Faith and Politics After Christendom: The Church as a Movement for Anarchy* (Milton Keynes: Paternoster, 2006) that the Church should be motivated by 'a suspicion of top-down notions of political engagement and a confidence in the subversive and creative potential of prophetic truth-telling

and grass-roots action' (10). That is part of what I mean by 'faithful power' but I don't think it implies that the Church's posture should always be 'marginal and contrary' vis-à-vis the state, as Bartley proposes (9).

10 The Congressional Prayer Caucus Foundation (CPCF), Wallbuilders Pro-Family Legislators Conference and the National Legal Foundation.

11 Sensitive to the charge of bias, in 2019 the project changed its name to Freedom for All, but this seems to have been for presentational rather than substantive reasons.

12 The 2018 version stretched to 148 pages: *Report and Analysis on Religious Freedom Measures Impacting Prayer and Faith in America: 2018–2019 Version* (Chesapeake, VA: Congressional Prayer Caucus Foundation, 2018). In this section page references in the text and notes refer to this document. See www.cpcfoundation.com (as of December 2020, site unavailable in the UK under EU GDPR regulations).

13 Katherine Stewart describes the project's method as 'turning the states into laboratories of theocracy'. *The Power Worshippers: Inside the Dangerous Rise of Religious Nationalism* (New York: Bloomsbury, 2019), 53.

14 Its model Child Protection Act (88–97) seeks to secure what would have been the desired outcome for Catholic Care, the Catholic adoption agency discussed in Chapter 7 (94).

15 See *Report and Analysis*, page 86, notes 26–28, 30.

16 See C. Peter Wagner, *Dominion! How Kingdom Action Can Change the World* (Ada, MI: Chosen, 2008), which espouses the idea of the '7 Mountain Mandate' – the mountains being the leading spheres of society. This idea is indebted to the 'Theonomist' theology of Rousas John Rushdoony, on which see Gary Scott Smith, ed., *God and Politics: Four Views on the Reformation of Civil Government* (Phillipsburg, NJ: Presbyterian & Reformed Publishing Co., 1989).

17 See www.nytimes.com/2018/05/26/opinion/project-blitz-christian-nationalists.html.

18 Stewart, *Power Worshippers*, 3.

19 Stewart, *Power Worshippers*, 7–9, 21–2; chapter 8.

20 Frederick Clarkson, '"Project Blitz" seeks to do for Christian Nationalism what ALEC does for Big Business', *Religion Despatches* (27 April 2018), https://religiondispatches.org/project-blitz-seeks-to-do-for-christian-nationalism-what-alec-does-for-big-business/.

21 There were also British initiatives inspired by Christian Democracy in the mid-twentieth century. See Joan Keating, 'The British Experience: Christian Democrats without a Party', in David Hanley, ed., *Christian Democracy in Europe: A Comparative Perspective* (London: Pinter, 1994), 168–81; Tom Buchanan, 'Great Britain', in Tom Buchanan and Martin Conway, eds, *Political Catholicism in Europe 1918–1965* (Oxford: Oxford University Press, 1996), 248–74.

22 Alec R. Vidler, *A Century of Social Catholicism 1820–1920* (London: SPCK, 1964); Michael Fogarty, *Christian Democracy in Western Europe 1820–1953* (London: Routledge & Kegan Paul, 1957).

23 James W. Skillen and Stanley Carlson-Thies, 'Religion and Political Development in Nineteenth-Century Holland', *Publius* 12.3 (1982), 43–64; James W. Skillen, 'From Covenant of Grace to Equitable Public Pluralism: The Dutch Calvinist Contribution', *Calvin Theological Journal* 31 (1996), 67–96.

24 Buchanan and Conway, eds, *Political Catholicism*.

25 See Thomas Kselman and Joseph A. Buttigieg, eds, *European Christian Democracy* (Notre Dame, IN: University of Notre Dame Press, 2003); Emiel Lamberts, ed., *Christian Democracy in the European Union 1945/1995* (Leuven: Leuven University Press, 1997).

26 The original vision is still visible in the outputs of some party research institutes: the Dutch Wetenschappelijk Instituut – CDA; the Belgian study centre Ceder; the German Konrad-Adenauer-Stiftung; the European People's Party's Martens Centre for European Studies.

27 See Bryan McGraw, *Faith in Politics: Religion and Liberal Democracy* (Cambridge: Cambridge University Press, 2010). For a parallel argument that American churches have often contributed to the formation of democratic citizens, see Paul J. Weithman, *Religion and the Obligations of Citizenship* (Cambridge: Cambridge University Press, 2002).

28 Shaykh Fazl e Mohammed, 'Speak out against Injustice Everywhere', in *Our Shared British Future: Muslim Integration in the UK* (London: Muslim Council of Britain, 2018), 123.

29 See also *Missing Muslims*. On the substantial Muslim charitable sector, see All-Party Parliamentary Group on British Muslims, *Faith and the Fourth Emergency Service: British Muslim Charitable Contributions to the UK* (2017), https://static1. squarespace.com/static/599c3d2febbd1a90cffdd8a9/t/5ae09b288a922d758d2cd4 14/1524669250245/+Faith+as+the+Fourth+Emergency+Service+V3+Print.pdf.

30 As Philip Lewis and Sadek Hamid put it, the Muslim community faces a 'combination of state counter policies, imbalanced media reporting, discrimination and increase in anti-Muslim hate crimes and general hostile societal climate which stigmatizes Muslims, [providing] jihadist recruiters with evidence that there is a "War against Islam" and that Muslims are not welcome in the UK' (*British Muslims: New Directions in Islamic Thought, Creativity and Activism* (Edinburgh: Edinburgh University Press, 2018, 168).

31 See www.thirdsector.co.uk/muslim-donors-give-average-religious-groups-uk/ fundraising/article/1192969.

32 Aamer Naeem, 'How Muslims Come to Aid Fellow Britons in Need', in *Our Shared British Future*. On Al Manaar's response, see Amy Plender, *Al Manaar Muslim Cultural Heritage Centre, Grenfell, and Mosques in Britain Today* (London: Theos, 2019). See also Amy Plender, *After Grenfell: The Faith Groups' Response* (London: Theos, 2018).

33 See Peace, ed., *Muslims and Political Participation*; Therese O'Toole et al., *Taking Part: Muslim Participation in Contemporary Governance* (Bristol: Centre for the Study of Ethnicity and Citizenship, University of Bristol, 2013); DCLG, *Contextualising Islam in Britain* (London: DCLG, 2009).

34 *British Muslim Perspectives at the 2019 General Election* (London: MCB, 2019), https://mcb.org.uk/wp-content/uploads/2019/11/MCB-2019-General-Elec tion-Policy-Platform.pdf. See *Missing Muslims*, 44.

35 Lewis and Hamid, *British Muslims*, 106.

36 This built on the work of the earlier APPG on Islamophobia.

37 Robin Wright observes that 'Islam is not lacking in tenets and practices that are compatible with pluralism. Among these are the traditions of *ijtihad* (interpretation), *ijma* (consensus), and *shura* (consultation).' 'Two Visions of Reformation', in Larry Diamond, Marc F. Plattner and Philip J. Costopoulos, eds, *World Religions and Democracy* (Baltimore, MA: Johns Hopkins University Press, 2005), 181.

38 Lewis and Hamid, *British Muslims*, 110–11.

39 For example, New Horizons, The Muslim Institute, The Cordoba Foundation.

40 See Ekaternia Braginskaia, 'The Muslim Council of Britain and its Engage-ment with the British Political Establishment', in Peace, ed., *Muslims and Political Participation*, 196–214.

41 Jamil Sherif, Anas Altikriti and Ismail Patel, 'Muslim Electoral Participation in British General Elections', in Peace, ed., *Muslims and Political Participation*, 40. See also *Mend Muslim Manifesto 2015* (London: Muslim Engagement and Development, 2015).

42 See https://mcb.org.uk/wp-content/uploads/2019/11/MCB-2019-General-Elec tion-Policy-Platform.pdf. MCB also runs a 'Muslims Vote' project, https://mcb.org. uk/project/muslimsvote/.

43 See Lewis and Hamid, *British Muslims*, chapter 3. 'Reformist' does not neces-sarily mean anti-traditional. See, for example, Abdullah Sahin, 'Islam, Secularity and the Culture of Critical Openness: A Muslim Theological Reflection', in Yahya Birt, Dilwar Hussain and Atuallah Siddiqui, eds, *British Secularism and Religion: Islam, Society and the State* (Markfield: Kube Publishing, 2011), 3–24.

44 See www.mwnuk.co.uk/; also Lewis and Hamid, *British Muslims*, 119–23.

45 See www.mwnuk.co.uk//go_files/resources/169296-PM%20Letter%20(Muslim %20Women%20Empowerment).pdf; also www.mwnuk.co.uk//go_files/resources/ 422693-Labour%20Party%20Complaint%20Letter.pdf.

46 Timothy Peace, 'British Muslims and the Anti-war Movement', in Peace, ed., *Muslims and Political Participation*, 126.

47 Lewis and Hamid, *British Muslims*, 105.

48 See www.islamicparty.com.

49 Timothy Peace, 'Introduction', in Peace, ed., *Muslims and Political Partici-pation*, 5.

50 Sherif et al., 'Muslim Electoral Participation in British General Elections', 42–7.

51 Lewis and Hamid, *British Muslims*, 107. See O'Toole et al., *Taking Part*, 22.

52 See Commission on Integration and Cohesion (London: DCLG, 2007).

53 Khadijah Elshayyal, 'From Crisis to Opportunity – 9/11 and the Progress of British Muslim Political Engagement', in Peace, ed., *Muslims and Political Partici-pation*, 174–91.

54 Lewis and Hamid, *British Muslims*, 156.

55 O'Toole et al., *Taking Part*, 28.

56 O'Toole et al., *Taking Part*, 12.

57 Braginskaia, 'The Muslim Council of Britain', 203–9. Mounting allegations of Islamophobia within the Conservative Party emerged after 2016. The Conserva-tive Muslim Forum campaigns on this and other issues.

58 The affair occasioned an official government report, and a torrent of mis-leading and tendentious commentary from the media and politicians, but did bring to light unacceptable practices within a few of the inspected schools, and offensive views held by a small number of the Muslim staff and governors involved. See Samira Shackle, 'Trojan Horse: The Real Story behind the Fake Islamic Plot to take over Schools', *The Guardian* (1 September 2017), www.theguardian.com/ world/2017/sep/01/trojan-horse-the-real-story-behind-the-fake-islamic-plot-to-take-over-schools.

59 For a proposal for an 'alliance sacrée' among 'orthodox' believers, see

Abdal Hakim Murad [Tim Winter], 'Can Liberalism Tolerate Islam?, *ABC Religion & Ethics* (20 April 2012), www.abc.net.au/religion/can-liberalism-tolerate-islam/10100608. Others might envisage coalitions of different complexions.

60 For example, Near Neighbours has attracted both positive and negative views from Muslims, some complaining that the use of Anglican parishes as channels of activity has little meaning for Muslims (O'Toole et al., *Taking Part*, 48–9).

61 See Martin H. M. Steven, *Christianity and Party Politics: Keeping the Faith* (Abingdon: Routledge, 2011), chapter 4.

62 On the Church of England, see George Moyser, ed., *Church and Politics Today: The Role of the Church of England in Contemporary Politics* (Edinburgh: T & T Clark, 1985); Eve Poole, *The Church on Capitalism: Theology and the Market* (Basingstoke: Palgrave Macmillan, 2010).

63 See also the ecumenical pre-election statement, 2020 *Vision of the Good Society* (London: Churches Together in Britain and Ireland, 2015).

64 National Church Leaders Forum, *Black Church Political Mobilisation – A Manifesto for Action* (London: National Church Leaders Forum, 2015), https://nclf.org.uk/wp-content/uploads/2015/10/Black-Church-Political-Mobilisation-FINAL-WEB-Apr15.pdf.

65 See www.jointpublicissues.org.uk/wp-content/uploads/2019/04/Universal-Credit-Increasing-Hunger-by-Design.pdf.

66 See www.cfbmethodistchurch.org.uk/ethics/position-papers/cfb-gambling-position-paper.html.

67 Steven, *Christianity and Party Politics*, 94–101. For example, they did so via Scottish Churches Housing Action.

68 Church and Society Council, *Our Vision: Imagining Scotland's Future* (Edinburgh: Church of Scotland, 2014); SEC Doctrine Commission, *The Church and Scottish Identity*, Grosvenor Essay No. 10 (Edinburgh: General Synod Office, 2014). Representatives of the Church of Scotland and the Roman Catholic Church had earlier contributed to the Scottish Constitutional Convention founded in 1989, which culminated in devolution. See Steven, *Christianity and Party Politics*, 92–4. Steven also explores the continuing impact of 'the Presbyterian conscience' in Scottish politics (chapter 5).

69 For example, Simon Perfect, *Bridging the Gap: Economic Inequality and Church Response in the UK* (London: Theos, 2020); Nathan Mladin and Barbara Ridpath, *'Forgive Us Our Debts': Lending and Borrowing as if Relationships Matter* (London: Theos and St Paul's Institute, 2019); Nick Spencer, ed., *The Future of Welfare: A Theos Collection* (London: Theos, 2014); Nick Spencer, ed., *Religion and Law* (London: Theos, 2012).

70 See www.stpaulsinstitute.org.uk/.

71 See www.westminster-abbey.org/institute.

72 See www.jubilee-centre.org/.

73 See www.ekklesia.co.uk/.

74 See www.respublica.org.uk/; also Phillip Blond, *Red Tory: How Left and Right Have Broken Britain and How We Can Fix It* (London: Faber & Faber, 2010).

75 On Blue Labour, see Ian Geary and Adrian Pabst, eds, *Blue Labour: Forging a New Politics* (London: I. B. Tauris, 2015).

76 See Nicholas Townsend, 'Blue Labour + Red Tory = Christian Democracy?', *Ethics in Brief* (Cambridge: KLICE, 2015).

77 See www.centreforsocialjustice.org.uk/.

78 See https://relationshipsfoundation.org/. On the theological influences behind it, see Michael Schluter and John Ashcroft, eds, *A Jubilee Manifesto: A Framework, Agenda and Strategy for Christian Social Reform* (Leicester: Inter-Varsity Press, 2005).

79 See Jonathan Birdwell, ed., *The Faith Collection* (London: Demos, 2013).

80 By Esther Reed (London: Christian Aid, 2014), www.christianaid.org.uk/resources/about-us/tax-common-good-study-tax-and-morality-0.

81 Andy Walton with Andrea Hatcher and Nick Spencer, *Is There a 'Religious Right' Emerging in Britain?* (London: Theos, 2013), 8.

82 Elaine Graham, *Between a Rock and a Hard Place: Public Theology in a Post-Secular Age* (London: SCM Press, 2013), chapter 5.

83 See https://care.org.uk/cause/human-trafficking/our-work-on-human-trafficking.

84 See www.citizensuk.org/.

85 Luke Bretherton, *Christianity and Contemporary Politics: The Conditions and Possibilities of Faithful Witness* (Chichester: Wiley-Blackwell, 2010), chapter 2; *Resurrecting Democracy: Faith, Citizenship, and the Politics of a Common Life* (Cambridge: Cambridge University Press, 2015).

86 Bretherton, *Christianity and Contemporary Politics*, 106.

87 Bretherton, *Christianity and Contemporary Politics*, 102.

88 See www.citizensuk.org/the_living_wage_campaign_rix_u-igroucqykv7quhtq.

89 David Barclay, *Making Multiculturalism Work: Enabling Practical Action Across Deep Difference* (London: Theos, 2013).

90 Bretherton, *Resurrecting Democracy*, 8; *Christ and the Common Life: Political Theology and the Case for Democracy* (Grand Rapids, MI: Eerdmans, 2019), chapter 8.

91 See Bretherton, *Resurrecting Democracy*, 82–94.

92 See also Austen Ivereigh, *Faithful Citizens: A Practical Guide to Catholic Social Teaching and Community Organising* (London: Darton, Longman & Todd, 2010).

93 José Casanova, *Public Religions in the Modern World* (Chicago, IL: University of Chicago Press, 1994), 57–8.

94 See https://christiansingovernment.org.uk/.

95 See Steven, *Christianity and Party Politics*, 53–60.

96 See the series produced by the Bible Society and KLICE in cooperation with the groups just mentioned: Stephen Backhouse, *Experiments in Living: Christianity and the Liberal Democrat Party* (Swindon: Bible Society, 2010); Paul Bickley, *Building Jerusalem: Christianity and the Labour Party* (Swindon: Bible Society, 2010); Joshua Hordern, *One Nation but Two Cities: Christianity and the Conservative Party* (Swindon: Bible Society, 2010).

97 See www.christiansinpolitics.org.uk/. The Green Party and the SNP also claim to reflect Christian influences. In 2015, UKIP produced a controversial 'Christian Manifesto' claiming it was the only major party committed to cherishing Britain's 'Judeo-Christian heritage'.

98 See www.christiansinparliament.org.uk/resources/.

99 See Walton et al., *Is There a 'Religious Right'*, chapter 3.

100 It is a member of the European Christian Political Movement, which has Christian Democratic influences. See https://cpaparty.net/values/#.

101 This possibility is encouraged by the long-term shift in voting behaviour, noted by Steven, away from traditional class allegiances towards 'issue voting', 'valance voting' and the growth of 'conscience-based issues': 'If the British voter is much less likely to identify with a party as a consequence of social factors ... the scope for a more "faith-based" form of religious voting is concurrently much greater' (*Christianity and Party Politics*, 36). The new 'Remainer v Leaver' cleavage might complicate that.

102 See Ben Clements and Nick Spencer, *Voting and Values in Britain: Does Religion Count?* (London: Theos, 2014).

103 As Stevens concludes in *Christianity and Party Politics*: 'the Christian Church continues to have power in Britain because it continues to affect public opinion, which in turn affects public policy' (14). Accordingly, parties sometimes seek to accommodate Christian preferences in their policy stances; and, while churches rarely officially align with a single party, the religious vote, even the traditional 'denominational cleavage', are still factors in British politics (chapter 8). He even speaks of an 'alpha vote' (39).

Conclusion
Restoring Faith in Democracy

Today we ... are again fighting the battles of the sixteenth century – over revelation and reason, dogmatic purity and toleration, inspiration and consent, divine duty and common decency. We are disturbed and confused. We find it incomprehensible that theological ideas still inflame the minds of men, stirring up messianic passions that leave societies in ruins. We assumed that this was no longer possible, that human beings had learned to separate religious questions from political ones, that fanaticism was dead. We were wrong.[1]

So Mark Lilla opens his account of the unexpected and, to him, unwelcome return of religion to the political realm. In this book I have tried to make the presence of religious influence in democratic societies less 'incomprehensible' and to show that while certain kinds of religion continue dangerously to 'inflame' some minds, other kinds can furnish powerful resources for the renewal of democracy as an arena for advancing justice and the common good. Religion can not only 'stir up messianic passions', it can also inculcate reason, toleration, consent and decency. It is doing so now in Britain. In this Conclusion, I offer a brief summary of my argument and some final reflections on its implications for democracy in twenty-first-century Britain.

In Part 1, I argued that we will not be able to grasp the proper place of faith in democracy unless we proceed from a clear account of the very *point* of democracy – something liberal democracies have increasingly lost sight of, allowing undemocratic forces and movements (religious and secular) to seize upon its weaknesses for their own increasingly partisan and destructive ends. To explain the 'point' of democracy, I drew on diverse strands in Christian political thought to propose accounts of 'the political community' and 'constitutional democracy'. I argued that, for all their palpable shortcomings, our political communities exist to unite state and people in a common struggle for society-wide justice. That is their *raison d'être* – the unique contribution they make, alongside many other social institutions, to the common good of society. 'Public justice' is the particular name I gave to that purpose, while recognizing that others will name it differently.

I proposed that we should regard political communities as consisting of both the institutions of state and 'the people'. The people must be recognized as an active, critical participant in the struggle for public justice. Christianity is thus emphatically 'populist' in the sense that it champions the indispensable agency of the people in the discernment and implementation of the political community's defining purpose. This is why Christian political thought robustly affirms democracy. It does so, I showed, as an expression of consent to that purpose, a means of participation in it and as a defence against violations of it. The point of democracy, then, is not the venting of the mere 'will' of the people as if that had any value in itself, nor the manifestation of 'popular sovereignty', but the facilitation of a vigorous, participatory search by people and state for public justice. The structures of a just constitutional democracy – such as the diffusion and limiting of powers, civil and political rights, or a fair electoral system – should be designed so as to enable that search.

In Part 2, I examined the 'rights and wrongs' of secularism. Here I set out the basic features of my model of Christian democratic pluralism. This involved distinguishing carefully between the confusing array of terms often invoked in faith and democracy debates – 'the secular', 'secularization', 'secularism', the 'post-secular' and 'political secularism'. The undergrowth thus cleared, my chief goal was to defend one variant of political secularism: 'jurisdictional secularism'. This mandates a state that is impartial among all faiths extant in its territory and guarantees extensive conscientious freedom for all.

Jurisdictional pluralism is an indispensable dimension of constitutional democracy. A just constitutional democracy will consist of many things, but an indispensable one is the protection and support of wide public spaces for the free articulation of faith-based political convictions and (within the law) the practical consequences that flow from them. Public justice requires that the convictional diversity of 'the people' is permitted to come to full and equal expression in the forums of democracy. Advocates of public faith should not seek a position of political privilege within democracy, but nor should they adopt a stance of pliant conformity to whatever happens to be the favoured democratic consensus. Rather, they should enter the democratic arena with full confidence as equal citizens, embodying a 'confident pluralism'.[2] Such a pluralism resists the idea of a 'Christian nation' that would confer official privilege on just one faith, but creates capacious opportunities for appeals to faith-based convictions in democratic debates about law and policy. It resists those who seek to shut religious reasons out of such debates by imposing on citizens a 'doctrine of restraint' (the wrong kind of 'justificatory secularism'). Well-formulated religiously informed reasoning can be a legitimate partner in democratic deliberation both because religious citizens enjoy identical political rights to others and because such reasoning can, after all, be 'public' in the correct sense of that term, even if not 'secular' in motive or content.

Part 3 elaborated what Christian democratic pluralism might look like in four major areas of democratic life: speech, conscience, association and power. 'Faithful speech' is political reasoning that is grounded in faith-based convictions (whether or not these are made explicit) but disciplines itself to address the specific agenda of the political community ('public justice'). I argued that such speech may be freely invoked in the 'representative sphere' of the polity, namely civil society and the deliberative phases of legislation and policymaking. This would likely issue in a more 'argumentative', even 'agonistic', style of democratic debate in which participants would, without censure or condescension from others, be permitted to disclose their deepest political convictions if they found it necessary to do so. All participants in such debate would thus need to learn how better to listen respectfully to the forms of political reasoning others actually choose to deploy, even if such forms are unfamiliar or unsettling. I also argued, however, that state officials should refrain from invoking faithful speech (religious or secular) at moments when they justify laws and public policies to the public. At that point, they speak on behalf of the whole political community, rather than as representatives of only one part of it, and must confine themselves to the 'public justice' reasons for state decisions. This is a consequence of the state's commitment to impartiality among plural faiths. It is one of the things that is 'right with secularism'.

Christian democratic pluralism also calls for ample space for the conscientious participation of citizens in the public realm. It implies extensive latitude for the public 'manifestation' of both 'faithful conscience' on the part of individual citizens and 'faithful association' on the part of faith-based associations. I showed how, while there is already ample space for faith in the public realm in Britain, and while recent governments have enthusiastically sought to embrace it, there remain troubling legal and political trends, such as a state-imposed 'logic of congruence' and the inadvertent and unnecessarily constraining of the public manifestation of faith by expanding equality law. Such trends need to be resisted. That said, Christian democratic pluralism recognizes that latitude for such manifestation is not limitless. The wider demands of public justice –

including certain demands of equal treatment – inevitably set constraints on the acceptable public behaviour of individuals and associations, religious or otherwise. Christian democratic pluralism does not advocate a free-for-all that could place vulnerable citizens in jeopardy, but a balanced adjudication of conscientious freedom, associational autonomy, equal treatment and the wider public good.

Finally, Christian democratic pluralism allows for the possibility of 'faithful power' – the democratic deployment of the resources of faith towards projects pursuant to public justice. I presented cases of how faithful power can go badly wrong. Project Blitz deploys power through democratically dubious means and for veiled and sectional ends. But I described and defended forms of faithful power that are both legitimate within a constitutional democracy and in many cases conducive to its consolidation. Christian Democracy is a highly successful European instance, one from which British observers should learn more, even in the absence of a tradition of religious political parties. I also presented an array of examples of constructive faithful power deployed by Muslims and Christians in Britain today. These operate both at the level of civil society (including denominational, charitable, educational and campaigning groups) and – if mostly for Christians – in closer proximity to state institutions. I indicated the very different platforms from which various Muslim and Christian initiatives exercise faithful power and noted the wide diversity of their standpoints, organizational forms and public receptions. Such manifestations of faithful power are likely to continue to be dispersed and relatively uncoordinated, even as they make valuable contributions to the 'renormativization' of public discourse. But latent prospects for more concerted action might yet come to the fore.

The book has been motivated by a desire for a better debate about the place of faith in democracy in Britain – about how our deep, but often occluded and confused, convictions about fundamental human purposes shape our engagements as citizens in our political communities. I have attempted to untangle questions in the debate that are often conflated, misconstrued or overlooked, sometimes generating intense heat but little light. Readers will judge how far I have succeeded in that goal. The book also hopes to elicit fresh responses from those of other persuasions, religious and secular, on how more intelligently we might 'frame' faith in democracy, amid conditions of deepening diversity in Britain. Some may think I have framed – or perhaps 'stacked' – the debate in a way that serves my own purposes. I invite them to propose better framings that avoid such bias (or, at least, *my* bias). While we will never acquire a fully shared framing, we can at least try to get beyond a situation where, for example, vocal representatives of both Christianity and secularism equally charge that they are the marginalized minorities discriminated against in a system dominated by the other. Moreover, however we assess the current relative power balance between these two historical hegemons (Christianity and secularism), we must also work hard to extend the terms of the debate more fully to include minority faith communities, and not only Islam. Other faiths – such as Hinduism, the next largest minority faith after Islam but one with no less formative historical links to Britain – must be granted parity of esteem in the debate about the place of faith in democracy. We might sometimes expect from such quarters unsettling but perhaps highly pertinent challenges to the very 'framings' of the debate offered by Christians, secularists or Muslims, each of whom currently holds more discursive power than other minority faiths. The broader the dialogue on the place of faith in democracy, the more likely it is to approach a consensus – or, at least, a better and more respectful disagreement.

To conclude, I offer brief remarks on how Christian democratic pluralism, working in partnership with other visions, could help mitigate the deep and pervasive loss of trust in the health of British democracy itself. The focus of this book has been the *place of faith* in democracy, but it also offers glimpses on how we might restore *trust in* democracy generally. This loss of trust has specific British pathologies but it is a global phenomenon. A study from the Centre for the Future of Democracy, *Global Satisfaction with Democracy 2020*, reports that democracy worldwide is in 'a state of deep malaise':

> In the West, growing political polarisation, economic frustration, and the rise of populist parties, have eroded the promise of democratic institutions to offer governance that is not only popularly supported, but also stable and effective. Meanwhile, in developing democracies the euphoria of the transition years has faded, leaving endemic challenges of corruption, intergroup conflict, and urban violence that undermine democracy's appeal.[3]

Some concluding thoughts, then, on how restoring faith in democracy might address three significant deficits British democracy currently faces: deficits of representation, of legitimacy and of solidarity.

First, the four manifestations of public faith I have discussed already point to ways in which the British political system could become more *representative*. Facilitating faithful speech would encourage a style of public discourse more receptive to the expression of citizens' deepest motivations. This could increase both the number of participants who feel empowered to contribute to political debates and the honesty and depth of those contributions.[4] Respecting faithful conscience would better protect the ability of some individuals to participate in public life with greater integrity. A framework guided by the principle of the 'reasonable accommodation' of conscientious plurality would enable a better integration of personal conviction and public role. Safeguarding the possibility of faithful association could better empower faith-based organizations to offer distinctive contributions to the common good via public services, thereby also helping towards a much-needed renewal of civil society. Acknowledging the legitimacy of faithful power might elicit a wider range of constructive faith-based contributors to the shaping of public policy. The 'rough ride' that might follow could, however, help 'tone up the muscles' of democracy – muscles that are currently atrophying due to neglect.

Second, a democracy that works hard to enable contributions like these from the plural faiths represented among its people will already have taken steps towards shoring up the *legitimacy* of the polity. A truly representative democracy will demonstrate that the political community is worthy of a diverse people's trust because it is solicitous of – even as it interrogates – what its plural citizens regard as the highest human goods. The legitimacy of the public policy 'outputs' of the democratic process will be broadened and deepened to the degree that the deliberative 'inputs' into that process are reflective of (even if not submissive to) the people's deepest aspirations. The necessary constraints a state will have to place on the expression of such commitments in public will then be seen as the outcome of a democratic dialogue in which as many voices as possible were heard, if not always heeded. This could mitigate the danger that minority communities might come to feel permanently 'out in the cold', fundamentally alienated from the political community itself.

Third, greater openness to the democratic expression of the people's plural faiths could, at its best, help nurture a sense of politics as an expression of *solidarity* – an arena for the pursuit of common goods. It could work against citizens regarding politics as purely instrumental to the pursuit of their own or their identity group's interests, and encourage them to see it also as a civic vocation tasked with advancing justice and the common good. Of course, powerful economic, technological and cultural forces driving liberal democracy continue to reinforce its tendency towards the pursuit of self-interest. These include individualistic consumerism, self-enclosure in a digital world and nativist forms of populism and nationalism that destroy the solidarity of the people as a whole and fragment it into warring tribes. A healthy democracy needs actively to mitigate the forces that undermine citizens' vision of and capacity for civic participation and to replenish those that strengthen them. Robust communities of faith (religious and secular) can at their best help induct their members into essential civic virtues – not least including 'prophetic resistance' – without which no democracy can endure for long.

The ultimate point of restoring trust in democracy, of course, is not just to maintain it as a platform for the articulation of 'faith' but to strengthen it as an arena for the delivery of justice and the common good. That, ultimately, is the deepest rationale for 'faith in democracy'.

Notes

1 Mark Lilla, *The Stillborn God: Religion, Politics, and the Modern West* (New York: Alfred A. Knopf, 2007), 3.

2 John Inazu, *Confident Pluralism: Surviving and Thriving Through Deep Difference* (Chicago, IL: University of Chicago Press, 2016).

3 The Centre for the Future of Democracy, *Global Satisfaction with Democracy 2020* (Cambridge: Bennett Institute for Public Policy, 2020), 3.

4 Hansard Society reported in 2019 that the number of people who feel politically powerless was the highest in its 16 years of reporting. *Audit of Political Engagement 16* (London: Hansard Society, 2019), 22, www.hansardsociety.org.uk/publications/reports/audit-of-political-engagement-16 (accessed 18/12/20).

Index of Names and Subjects